the FEMINIST AVANT-GARDE in AMERICAN POETRY

the FEMINIST AVANT-GARDE in AMERICAN POETRY

ELISABETH A. FROST

University of Iowa Press ψ Iowa City

University of Iowa Press, Iowa City 52242
Printed in the United States of America
Design by Richard Hendel
http://www.uiowa.edu/uiowapress

The publication of this book was generously
supported by the University of Iowa Foundation.

Printed on acid-free paper

Library of Congress
Cataloging-in-Publication Data

Frost, Elisabeth A. (Elisabeth Ann), 1963– .
    The feminist avant-garde in American poetry / by Elisabeth A. Frost.
        p.   cm.
    Includes bibliographical references (p.) and index.
    ISBN 0-87745-836-7 (cloth)
    1. American poetry—20th century—History and criticism. 2. Feminism and
literature—United States—History—20th century. 3. Avant-garde (Aesthetics)—United
States—History—20th century. 4. Women and literature—United States—History—
20th century. 5. American poetry—Women authors—History and criticism. 6. Experi-
mental poetry, American—History and criticism. 7. Feminist poetry—History and criticism.
I. Title

PS310.F45 F76 2003
811'.5099287—dc21   2002035763

05 06 07 08 09 P 5 4 3 2 1

For my family:

MINNIE FROST

LYNNE *and* THOMAS FROST

DAVID FROST *and* MICHELLE RYANG

and, of course, for DEREK

CONTENTS

ACKNOWLEDGMENTS

This book has undergone a lengthy evolution. Perhaps its earliest germ was in discussions with Joseph Conte, to whom I am grateful for introducing me to the poetry of many of the writers who are most important to me today, including Susan Howe and others. I owe the greatest debt to my dissertation committee at UCLA: Lucia Re (especially for providing me with my first grounding in feminist theory and the historical avant-gardes), Valerie Smith (particularly for introducing me to theories of the Black Arts movement), and most especially Cal Bedient and Stephen Yenser. With unflagging support, encouragement, intellectual guidance, and years of generosity, Cal Bedient and Stephen Yenser have stood by me and this project. I cannot thank them enough.

Responding with characteristic warmth to an unknown graduate student's query, Kathleen Fraser welcomed me and my work, introducing me to the history of *HOW(ever)* and providing me with a full archival run of the journal for my research. In the years since, Kathleen has offered me warmth, intelligence, and the great gift of her friendship.

For their encouragement and support at the beginning of this process, and in the years since, I want to thank my friends and comrades David Case, Kevin Finney, Lisa Gordis, Daniel Hayes, Deanne Lundin, Kim Monda, Karl Rosenquist, Eric Selinger (especially for introducing me to the poetry of Mina Loy), Katherine Swiggart, Yuki Terazawa, and Lisa Yu, as well as other friends who provide me with constant support: Kim Cox, Meredith Daly, Carol Ann Johnston, and Elizabeth Youmans.

My thanks to Brenda Silver for first guiding me through the ins and outs of preparing a book proposal, and my eternal gratitude to Lenny Cassuto for serving as adviser extraordinaire with limitless generosity and savvy. I am grateful to my colleagues at Dickinson College, especially Carol Ann Johnston and Sharon O'Brien, for reading and commenting on sections of the manuscript in its early stages. My colleagues at Fordham University have provided much appreciated support and advice, especially Frank Boyle and Lenny Cassuto. A faculty summer fellowship from Fordham University, as well as the Fordham University Ames Fund for Junior Faculty, provided financial support. I am very grateful to my students, especially my graduate students at Fordham, whose readings and responses enrich my thinking and writing.

Thanks to Donna Hollenberg for steering me to the University of Iowa Press, and to the readers at Iowa who provided invaluable commentary and suggestions. Colleagues' readings of part or all of the manuscript were also invaluable: thanks to Kathleen Fraser, Linda Kinnahan, Harryette Mullen, and especially Michael Bibby and Eric Selinger. In addition, Lynn Keller generously commented in detail on the final draft. I know I speak for many when I say that if all acquiring editors were as scrupulous and responsible as Prasenjit Gupta, scholarly publishing would be that much saner. It is with gratitude that I acknowledge Prasenjit's elegant professionalism, his prompt replies to e-mails and telephone calls (including while he was on vacation), and his confidence in this project.

I benefit immensely from a community of women poets and scholars devoted to innovative writing. In particular, my thanks to Aliki Barnstone, Kathleen Crown, Rachel Blau DuPlessis, Kathleen Fraser, Cynthia Hogue, Lynn Keller, Linda Kinnahan, Claudia Rankine, Ann Vickery, and the entire community of the on-line journal *HOW2*. Most of all, I am profoundly grateful to Cynthia Hogue, whose generosity has fostered my own and others' work, and whose friendship is a model of professional nurturing. I thank as well the poets whose work I discuss here, and which continues to provoke and inspire. And special thanks to Kathleen Fraser, Susan Howe, and Harryette Mullen for taking the time to correspond with me and/or be interviewed for this project.

Finally, none of my work would be possible without the emotional and practical sustenance of my family—and my husband, Derek, whose insouciance makes me happy all of the time.

INTRODUCTION

In 1983, Kathleen Fraser published the first issue of *HOW(ever)*, a journal devoted to what coeditor Frances Jaffer described as writing "feminists usually eschew, believing that now is the time for women to write understandable poetry about their own lives." The founders of *HOW(ever)* asserted instead that

> the myths of a culture are embodied in its language, its lexicon, its very syntactical structure. . . . Unhappily, most feminist publications have ignored the experimentalist work which women are writing now and have been writing since early in the century. And unhappily, most publications of "new" writing have had little interest in feminist language issues. . . . We want to publish an exception, however.[1]

As Jaffer's comments imply, the creation of *HOW(ever)* marked a coming of age for feminist avant-garde poets in America. The editors did more than publish innovative feminist texts that, as Jaffer noted, often received little attention elsewhere. They also brought scholars and poets together to recover the neglected work of modernist women, in the process testifying to a vibrant feminist avant-garde tradition.

"And what about the women poets who were writing experimentally?" Fraser asked in that first issue of *HOW(ever)*. This book seeks to respond to that open-ended query by examining the work of modern and contemporary women writers who contest issues of gender, race, history, and sexuality in innovative poetic forms. Espousing varying and idiosyncratic forms of feminist poetics, these writers position themselves in ambivalent relation to the predominantly male avant-garde movements with which they are often associated; further, they distinguish their work from that of feminist poets writing in more traditional forms. The five poets discussed in this study create versions of a linguistically based feminism that locates poetic and other discourses as primary sites of feminist intervention. Most often *not* embracing the idea of a universal or shared female experience, these poets play with words and syntax to reflect the possibility of altering conceptions of rigid gender and racial divisions. Increasingly, I argue, these feminist poets write with a sense of a usable past; as *HOW(ever)* attests, and in contrast to the innovative women writers of the modern period, they recently have sought, and found, a lineage of their own.

Despite scholarly attention to a few now-prominent figures like Gertrude Stein and H.D., criticism of modern and contemporary literature has often ignored experimental poetry by American women.[2] Although scholars such as Marjorie Perloff, Peter Quartermain, and others have provided important readings of recent experimental writing, studies of American women poets have tended to focus on a poetics of personal experience, frequently grounded in identity politics—an approach that, as Jaffer noted, has marginalized avant-gardism in feminist poetics. I trace a complex and multivoiced lineage of American poets who make language the site of feminist politics. Throughout this study, I reveal how previous accounts of poetic avant-gardes in America fail to capture the range of styles and feminist agendas among avant-garde women poets since the modern period. Drawing on the work of Monique Wittig and Judith Butler, among others, I argue that these poets reject the notion of an essential, shared female identity. Whether in Mina Loy's parody of social "breeding" or Harryette Mullen's deconstruction of femininity and race, feminist avant-gardists employ innovative language to subvert binary divisions and to create increasingly hybrid poetries.

The chapters that follow reveal variety in both political agenda and poetic form, from Stein's language play to Sonia Sanchez's militant revolt. Rather than focusing on one writing community (as in Ann Vickery's detailed study of feminist Language poets), I have selected writers who illustrate a broad scope of feminist concerns and of formal or aesthetic strategies. The first two chapters explore intersections between feminist and avant-garde agendas during the period of the so-called "historical" avant-gardes. I argue that feminist avant-garde poets of the modern period position themselves in ambivalent relation to contemporaneous male-dominated avant-garde groups. In readings of texts by Stein and Loy, I focus on experiments with language and gender as feminist responses to a male avant-gardist rhetoric of revolution, and I demonstrate the link each establishes between language and feminist consciousness, particularly their efforts to create poetry that would articulate an antiessentialist politics—one that might topple what Loy called "that rubbish heap of race tradition." If F. T. Marinetti's call to burn down museums and libraries typifies avant-gardist revolt, more recent feminist avant-garde poets tend to experiment with language not so much to "destroy" existing traditions as to articulate an alternative of their own. The two later portions of the book explore this search for heritage in the light of modernist lineage, emphasizing what Fraser has called a "tradition of marginality." A central chapter on Sonia Sanchez and the Black Arts movement takes the study into the late 1960s and brings into dialogue theories of the avant-garde and black feminist consciousness. Defining Black Arts as a quintessentially American neo-avant-garde, I examine tensions between feminism and calls for racial unity, which left Sanchez largely without models for her radical black feminist poetics. By contrast, two final chapters—on Susan Howe and Harryette Mullen—explore the increasing sense in recent years of a plurality of feminist avant-garde "usable pasts." I show the ways in which Howe finds precursors in diverse sources, placing herself in a line of dissident feminist innovators that includes Anne Hutchinson, Emily Dickinson, H.D., and others. Constructing a poetic lineage culled from sources as various as Greek lyric, women blues artists, Steinian language games, and Black Arts radicalism, Mullen forges a hybrid poetics to illustrate the "mongrel" nature of American culture and avant-gardism itself. Seen together, these hybrid texts reveal increasingly self-conscious traditions among feminist poets who share the goal of forging new poetic discourses as the avenues through which gender consciousness might change.

The poets I have chosen all reveal ambivalence toward the rhetoric of contemporaneous avant-garde groups. But what follows is not a historical narrative, nor is my goal to position these writers squarely within such diverse collectives as Futurism, Black Arts, or Language writing. Rather, I reveal their alliances with and divergences from those movements, as well as their often explicit debts to one another. My focus throughout is on *poetics*—the work that results from a desire to create a language for a new feminist consciousness—and the contributions that these texts make to recent debates in feminist theory. Diverse in the views they expound, these poets share a fundamental belief: that language shapes consciousness and that, in its accepted, "correct" forms, language restricts. Yet, in the optimistic paradox that informs all avant-garde ventures, they also believe that language can *change* consciousness; each weds radical politics to formal experiments—the most fundamental gesture of any avant-garde practice. In this respect, these poets share many assumptions with their male peers. What distinguishes their efforts, I argue, is the desire to expand conceptions of what feminism might consist of—in particular, to challenge those assumptions embedded in American culture that dictate the rules of difference.

Feminist avant-garde writing burgeoned with particular intensity in the period of the so-called historical avant-gardes (the 1910s and 1920s), which also brought women unprecedented political advances. Similarly, it has reemerged with renewed vigor since second-wave feminism, a period when avant-garde writing of all sorts has enjoyed a renaissance. Developing extremely varied means of experimentation, collectively the poets I address expose the gendered nature of cultural inheritance and of accepted linguistic practices. But for the most part they offer none of the shared precepts familiar from the manifestos of Futurism, Vorticism, or other self-proclaimed avant-garde movements. In fact, they tend to resist affiliation with existing organizations and agendas. I see this lack of group allegiance as a reflection of their novel explorations of feminist consciousness, and to emphasize that singularity of approach, I focus as much on their individual visions as on their commonalities.

These resistant, difficult texts may seem eccentric exemplars of feminist practice. Yet my fascination with these poets stems in part from my conviction that their strategic uses of language offer alternatives to the predominant models of identity politics on the one hand and "feminine writing" on the other—the two theoretical models that have dominated discussions of feminist poetics in the United States. It is for this reason that I choose "avant-garde" rather than the less vexed but more vague "experimental" or "innovative," or a coinage such as Megan Simpson's recent term, "language-oriented." In fact, because feminist critics rarely employ theories of the avant-garde—even when discussing experimental women's writing—intersections between feminist and avant-garde practices throughout the twentieth century have often gone unexamined.[3] I enter the theoretical dialogue concerning avant-gardism for two reasons: first, to reveal the tensions that arise among women poets who seek to articulate a radical feminist vision in a context or rhetoric established by existing avant-garde groups; and second, to reveal the resulting search for a feminist avant-garde lineage that might establish an alternative history for their poetics.

What qualities make a work of art, feminist or otherwise, avant-garde? I define avant-gardism as any artistic practice that combines radical new forms with radical politics or utopian vision. In popular usage, "avant-garde" can describe any new trend. But such a generalized definition erases meaningful distinctions. Like most critics, I hold that the avant-garde venture unites formal innovation with political engagement: The avant-gardist assumes that a daring new artistic practice has the potential to change the world by inciting a change of consciousness. In my view, radical political belief precedes and *necessitates* formal invention on the part of the avant-garde artist: More than an aesthetic choice, experimentation bears the full weight of urgent social conviction. For others, what epitomizes the avant-garde is the word that so often comes next: "movement." In Robert von Hallberg's view, for example, an avant-garde is a "public confederation" of artists united by their defiance of "the established conventions of a contemporary art community" and by their commitment to "an explicit view of the relation between art and society" (von Hallberg, "Avant-Gardes" 83).

It is undeniable that avant-gardism generates discursive claims, exhortations, the manifestos of a select group of founders. We think of Italian Futurism as having been "born" on February 20, 1909, with Marinetti's "Founding and Manifesto of Futurism," published in the Paris *Figaro.* Surrealism came to being in 1924 with André Breton's "First Surrealist Manifesto." Pronouncements of Ezra Pound's Imagism and Vorticism appeared in 1912 and 1914, the latter resembling Marinetti's manifestos in form and content.[4] These public gestures clearly signal a movement. That kind of coherence has been lacking among feminist avant-garde writers, who have rarely banded together to make proclamations, manifestos, or programs.[5] Many resist the very notion of affiliation. Stein, for example, hardly banded together with other artists—male or female—along political lines. Loy articulated her most radical (and far-reaching) ideas very much alone, in idiosyncratic, even unpublished, documents like the eclectic "Psycho-Democracy." More recently, work by poets like Susan Howe and Sonia Sanchez often defies the labels applied to it—an issue Mullen takes on by challenging just such parochial categorizations. Certainly some of these poets participate in particular avant-garde movements—Loy's immersion in Futurism and Sanchez's Black Arts period are perhaps the clearest examples. Yet even in these cases, the involvement is either brief or ambivalent.

In this respect, my use of the term "avant-garde" challenges the ways in which avant-gardism itself has been conceptualized. These poets pursued their visions in relative isolation, alienated from both (largely male) avant-garde coteries and contemporaneous women's movements. This lack of group confederation thus epitomizes the difficulties they faced. Rather than rejecting the term "avant-garde" as inappropriate to such feminist poets, I prefer to claim it for their idiosyncratic visions. In fact, I propose that studying radical feminist poetries *as* avant-garde revises the category of avant-gardism itself—including the prevalent assertion of its death with the advent of the postmodern. Andreas Huyssen argues that the shift from modernist grand narrative to postmodern flux requires rethinking the fate and meaning of the avant-garde. Especially relevant to feminist poets, this sort of examination allows a revised conception of political/aesthetic engagement. I argue that these poets share a commitment to feminist transformation through radical art—a commitment that allows us to place the sex/gender system at the center of meaningful change to be sought through avant-garde art.[6]

I am also concerned throughout these pages with tradition—a concept as antithetical to the avant-garde as it is fundamental to recent feminist criticism.[7] Although it might seem contradictory, the notion of tradition informs not just feminist "re-visioning" but also many recent assessments of the avant-garde—particularly those that address contemporary poetics and its relation to "historical" avant-garde movements.

Huyssen describes a paradox at work in 1970s postmodernism: Ironically, "the postmodernist search for cultural tradition and continuity, which underlies all the radical rhetoric of rupture, discontinuity, and epistemological breaks, has turned to that tradition [the avant-garde] which fundamentally and on principle despised and denied all traditions" (Huyssen, *After the Great Divide* 169). Huyssen explains this attitude as an effort to redraw the map of the recent past, to locate "cultural formations not dominated by logocentric and technocratic thought" and create a history that might undergird contemporary values of diversity and difference (172).[8] In this book, I take the position that far from on its death bed, avant-gardism is thriving in the postmodern moment, albeit in different forms from those of the early twentieth century, and that new conceptualizations of the avant-garde are needed to understand radical art in the age of social and political decentering. Differing social climates necessitate new artistic and political strategies. Von Hallberg argues that the mainstreaming of the poetic avant-garde (dating at least from the sensational success of Allen Ginsberg's "Howl") not only has nullified the old techniques of novelty and shock but also has obviated avant-gardism itself, leaving only cultural "poseurs" in a world of "weakening political consensus" and trade presses eager to publish the latest literary trend.[9] But such a view ignores the emergent artistic/political tactics that have accompanied the new decentering. In a self-conscious revision of the avant-gardist aspiration to a pure position outside the bourgeois mainstream, feminist conceptual artists such as Jenny Holzer and Barbara Kruger have participated in the mass market and the mass media. Kruger employs the techniques of advertising in her polemical images, and she sells reproductions of her pieces in the form of mugs, refrigerator magnets, and other items of capitalist kitsch. Holzer's unadorned billboards similarly adapt the traditions of earlier avant-gardists to accommodate the postmodern experience of the market economy and media saturation. Influenced by theories of postmodern decentering, artists like Kruger have not abandoned the avant-garde. They've reinvented it.

Of course, the idea that neo-avant-gardism is alive and well does not address the paradoxical yearning for a *tradition* of the antitraditional "new." Here gender also must provide the terms of debate. Women poets have so often felt silenced and have so often been excluded from a place in American literary history, that far from being overwhelmed by tradition, they have suffered from its absence. In an ongoing process, feminist writers and critics continue to recover their "foremothers." Unfortunately, women avant-gardists have often remained invisible even in emerging canons of women's literature. Kathleen Fraser recalls that her excitement about the 1985 arrival of *The Norton Anthology of Literature by Women: The Tradition in English* was considerably dampened by the volume's "erasure of on-going and recent experiment in poetry and prose" (Fraser, *Translating the Unspeakable* 137; hereafter *Translating*); Fraser argues that even when a tradition of women's literature began to emerge, its formally radical wing was clipped. Writing in 1992, Fraser observed that "apparently, something remains troubling about women writers—even feminists, god forbid—working outside the tradition of the personal lyric or the classical epic forms"; the "myth" of women's writing requires "the safe hearth of the personal/autobiographical lyric" (*Translating* 134, 136). Herself instrumental in recovering the work of modernist women writers, Fraser notes that "Precisely because of this fragile and fairly recent path of regeneration, I am not yet ready to cut loose and move entirely away from . . . an 'older generation'" (*Translating* 95).

There remains an urgent need in the field of contemporary poetry to examine the range of women's traditions as they intersect with feminist politics—to extend the practice of what Elaine Showalter called gynocriticism, or the historicized study of women's writing. Over a decade ago, in examining experimental women's writing in light of theories of *écriture féminine*, Marianne DeKoven warned critics not to "elide the gendered signature"—to privilege so-called feminine (often male-authored) *writing* at the expense of actual women *writers*. The chapters that follow group texts under the category of women's writing, and in this respect I rely on the very biological dichotomy these antiessentialist feminists resist. But as Simpson points out, the commitment on the part of what she calls "language-oriented" women poets to overcome binary thinking does not preclude critical study of their work as *women* writers. Following DeKoven and Simpson, I attend to the gendered signature of the female author, even as I trace the evolution of an antiessentialist feminist poetic.[10]

In the remainder of this introduction, I would like to demonstrate in more detail why the theories that we might expect to see most fruitfully applied to feminist avant-garde texts are often inadequate to a full understanding of these writers' radical poetics and politics. Throughout *The Feminist Avant-Garde in American Poetry*, I find a theoretical analog for these writers' attitudes toward language and feminism in the work of theorists such as Monique Wittig and Judith Butler, who encourage the dismantling of binary divisions along the lines of gender, sexuality, and race, in pursuit of new, unimagined identities. I briefly examine these arguments as a way to position feminist avant-garde texts as works that *challenge* our culture's emphases on gender difference.

To begin to discuss feminist avant-garde poets is to consider the complex relationships women have experienced both within and outside of primarily male avant-garde groups. Typically, in the European experience, women have existed on the lines of what Susan Suleiman calls a "double margin." First, along with their male counterparts, they are at the edge of the mainstream culture from which they emerge—a position avant-gardists deliberately choose, the better to challenge the center. But often they also remain on the fringes of the very groups that seek sexual and psychic liberation, as is evident in the examples of the historical avant-gardes.[11] A similar pattern frequently holds true for American women poets: Women have rarely been the visible spokespeople, theorists, or anthologized representatives of such avant-garde groups as Vorticism, Black Arts, or even the more recent Language group; they have often been identified, however, as members of such coteries. I contend to the contrary that the avant-gardism of the poets in this study—from Loy's satires of Futurism to Howe's evocations of suppressed feminist dissidence—can be read as seeking a feminist practice that, often inevitably, involves considerable ambivalence toward existing avant-garde agendas.

In fact, the question of margins is particularly complicated for feminist avant-garde poets in America, for in the United States, avant-gardism and feminist poetics have frequently been seen in opposition to one another. As DeKoven has argued, experimental women writers in America have consistently lacked recognition because critics tend either to see avant-garde practice as a historically male phenomenon or to dismiss the gender of the author altogether and equate the avant-garde with the "feminine" in a manner that often erases the work of women poets: "It is not enough for a female/feminine/feminist avant-garde, or écriture féminine, simply to repudiate the dominant avant-garde," if we still acknowledge a debt only to artists in a masculinist tradition.[12] That this process has usually marginalized women experimentalists is apparent in the privileged position James Joyce, Antonin Artaud, and Stéphane Mallarmé, as well as other male writers, occupied in the work of Julia Kristeva and in that of other theorists and critics who embraced "revolutionary" poetic language in the same years that poets like Susan Howe, Rachel Blau DuPlessis, Fraser, Carla Harryman, Lyn Hejinian, and others were exploring just such a linguistic revolution. Similarly, although for many years feminist critics have debated the merits of the innovative writing proposed by French feminist theory, until very recently feminist avant-garde poets have gained almost no exposure. One reason for this neglect is that they do not celebrate either "female experience" or identity politics—the mainstays of much feminist poetry, which developed from the movement's powerful assertion that "the personal is political." There is, then, a third margin on which these poets are situated: The category of "women's poetry" in America, for an emphasis on personal voice—and the relatively transparent language that often accompanies it—supports an unspoken assumption that linguistic experimentation has little relevance to feminist writing.[13]

Alicia Ostriker's ground-breaking *Stealing the Language* exemplifies this tendency. Perhaps the single most important study of American women poets to date, Ostriker's pioneering account remains as crucial as ever to understanding that "women's poetry . . . has a history. It has a terrain. Many of its practitioners believe it has something like a language" (9). Nonetheless, despite its scope and diversity, the book posits an essentially Romantic view that privileges content and expression. Ostriker argues that women participate in a "powerful collective voice" (8):

> When a woman poet today says "I," she is likely to mean herself, as intensely as her imagination and her verbal skills permit, much as Wordsworth or Keats did, or Blake, or Milton, or John Donne of the Holy Son-

nets, before Eliot's "extinction of personality" became the mandatory twentieth-century initiation ritual for young American poets, and before the death of the author became a popular critical fiction. (12)

In fact, T. S. Eliot's "extinction of personality" (or Pound's disavowal of the Romantic ego) hardly became mandatory: The lyric—the short personal poem with a single speaker relating an emotional experience—is still the dominant mode for both male and female poets. But Ostriker's disavowal of such a practice is significant: Her assumption is that women poets are of interest precisely because they *don't* focus on linguistic experiment, but talk directly of the self, within the Romantic tradition.[14]

In one poem Adrienne Rich noted, "No one ever told us we had to study our lives." That personal reflection would make for a revolutionary feminist writing: "a whole new poetry beginning here."[15] Feminist avant-garde poets explore not Rich's "I" of personal experience but language itself—what Susan Howe, for example, calls the countermovement of two of her precursors, Emily Dickinson and Gertrude Stein, who "conducted a skillful and ironic investigation of patriarchal authority over literary history" by questioning the politics of speech and writing: "Who polices questions of grammar, parts of speech, connection, and connotation? Whose order is shut inside the structure of a sentence?" (Howe, *My Emily Dickinson*; hereafter *MED*, 11–12). Of late, there have been plenty of debates around the issues Howe raises. But until quite recently, discussions about women and language centered on the divide between Anglo-American and French feminist approaches. Feminist avant-garde poets tend to reject both models, defying established conventions even as they refute the notion that the symbolic is a masculine structure. In their uses of language, as in their feminisms, feminist avant-gardists seek to abolish the linguistic bases of gender binaries in a manner rarely seen among other feminist poets, who more often celebrate female difference.

Recent theories of the avant-garde have also contributed to the exclusion of women, and of gender, from consideration. Among theorists, as I mentioned earlier, debates have been dominated by other concerns: the death of the avant-garde (thus rendering it "historical"); the impossibility of reemerging neo-avant-gardes; and the failure of aesthetic and political revolution. What most fundamentally concerns me here is these theorists' notion of the political. Regardless of their positions on other questions, most theorists tend to follow the lead of the movements whose polemics they address by defining political activism according to narrow parameters that marginalize gender as a category and women writers as significant agents of change.

In addressing what he sees as the limited possibilities for any avant-garde venture in the flux of the postmodern, for example, Charles Russell, like other theorists, reveals a nostalgia for mass political movements that would supposedly transcend race and gender:

> To the extent that the political aspirations of these groups *can reach beyond their immediate populace*, the social changes demanded by minorities or women might revive a broader cultural faith in socio-historic movement. But if they remain the *circumscribed programs of the individual subcultures*, the success or failure of the political vision will remain functions of the all-embracing and enervating cultural pluralism that dominates contemporary society. (Russell, *Poets, Prophets, and Revolutionaries* 240–41, my emphases)

Russell's exclusion of the experimental, socially activist work of subcultures from a true avant-garde reveals his limited definition of the political, and of social change more broadly. If one writes from such a position, then the work remains circumscribed. As Craig Owens has argued, postmodernism's "enervating cultural pluralism" is depressing only if you are on the enervated side; in this instance, Russell's notion of politics is limited to a global attack on existing institutions, which in fact may *deny* meaningful social change.[16] His definition of the political is shared by most theorists of the avant-garde, and its prevalence provides the most important means of understanding the frequent exclusion of women and non-Anglo/European writers from its parameters.

Peter Bürger's *Theory of the Avant-Garde* is another case in point. For Bürger, as for Russell, what distinguishes avant-gardism from aestheticism is the artist's attack on the *institution* of art. Only avant-gardists, not modernists, insisted on blurring distinctions between aesthetics and polemics, art and practice. Bürger contrasts an allegiance to the aesthetic object with the avant-gardist use of shock to forward political aims: "Shock is aimed for as a stimulus to change one's conduct of life; it is the means to break through aesthetic immanence and to usher in (initiate) a change in the recipient's life praxis" (80). Yet of what does that praxis consist? Bürger's concern is with the critique of bourgeois institutions. Ironically, Bürger fails to acknowledge that the patriarchal quality of much avant-garde rhetoric positions it as the opposite of revolutionary. Although his description of avant-gardism could apply equally well to feminism, women (as well as other "subcultures") remain invisible because his model specifies capitalism as a totalizing system. Huyssen's *After the Great Divide* raises the inverse problem. Amid increasing "cultural diversity," belief in unity has given way to "notions of decentering and deconstruction" (171). Given such cultural flux, avant-garde shock is obsolete, attempted only by those suffering from "social and aesthetic amnesia." Ironically, though Huyssen names decentered movements as likely to be the most fruitful successors to the historical avant-gardes (15), he uses this very likelihood to argue that avant-gardism is dead. Preferring not to theorize multiplicity and difference, Huyssen remains enmeshed in the very grand narratives whose irrelevance he recognizes as inevitable.

Ironically, the same reliance on totalizing systems appears in the work of theorists frequently invoked in feminist readings of experimental texts. Julia Kristeva, for example, addresses sexual difference in experimental writing in *Revolution in Poetic Language*. But Kristeva's adherence to Marxism and Freudian drive theory in *Revolution in Poetic Language* and in "About Chinese Women" leads her to assert that women are psychologically unsuited to the use of semiotic disruptive rhythms or sounds because the risk of psychosis is greater for women than for men.[17] One of the most important women theorists of the avant-garde, Kristeva ironically excludes female subjects from the revolutionary speech she calls for and, true to her own model, has written largely about men.[18]

Narrow definitions of the political and the impossibility of speaking a feminine language in its structures—these are the problems Hélène Cixous and Luce Irigaray have brought to the fore, and, in this sense, they are obvious sources for a theory of feminist avant-garde poetics and indeed have received a great deal of attention as theorists of alternative women's writing.

The work of Cixous raises a rhetorical paradox. In her manifesto "The Laugh of the Medusa," she dismisses systemic thinking as inadequate to women's concerns, seeking to liberate an irreverent and powerful female laughter. Further, Cixous emphasizes the primacy of poetry to the possibility of a radical new language, linking the genre to the strengths of women: poetry engenders "strength through the unconscious," which Cixous calls "that other limitless country . . . where the repressed manage to survive: women."[19] Theorists have debated the extent to which Cixous's "writing the body" suffers from an essentialism that is at worst dangerous and at best flawed.[20] But there is an additional problem: insofar as Cixous's strategic essentialism grounds writing in the body, it equates feminine texts with unconscious drives: "I write woman: woman must write woman. And man, man" (247); "More so than men who are coaxed toward social success, toward sublimation, women are body" (257). As Diana Fuss has argued, strategic essentialism can be a powerful tool in the hands of the dispossessed, and Cixous can be seen as employing an effective rhetorical strategy.[21] Yet, insofar as Cixous identifies writing with the "white ink" of the female body, she risks undercutting possibilities for women's agency, for she implies that the repressed that is woman will *write herself*.

Irigaray's concern is also to liberate women's desire(s), and like Cixous she attacks not merely institutions of power (Marinetti's museum or Parliament) but a masculine dominance that, for her, characterizes *all* relations, especially those inherent in language. Deploying what Fuss calls an essentialist deconstruction, Irigaray explores the positionality of the female speaker, and she employs a series of bodily tropes to attack the fixed notion of "woman." Indeed, her manifestolike pronouncement "When Our Lips Speak Together" creates a plural feminine "we" based on an economy of abundance; her "you/I," which calls the female reader to a new relationship to the text and to language. Irigaray's provocative notions of mimicry and masquerade also illuminate the strategies of some feminist avant-garde poets, as my first chapter will show. Nonetheless, even as Irigaray explores as yet unforged textual politics, she focuses largely on the impossibility of articulating female desire in symbolic language.[22] Although "speaking (as) woman" (parler-femme) is a real, lived experience, it cannot be spoken in masculine language, and feminine syntax remains elusive. In terms of textual politics, Irigaray risks positioning feminist language so far outside of existing discourses that she ironically undermines the efforts she calls for.

Feminist avant-garde poets experiment with complex mixtures of linguistic and cultural propositions, including provocative hybrids of many theories I have alluded to. Among particularly helpful sources, Teresa de Lauretis offers a useful analog for the work of feminist poets like Mullen, whose mongrel poetics emerges at the intersection of divergent cultural idioms. De Lauretis holds that difference is constructed through a range of technologies and their accompanying discourses, from cinema to theory. Her notion of the "technologies of gender" emphasizes that a range of complex systems—including the political and the economic—inevitably contributes to conceptions of sexual difference. This link between language and the cultural construction of difference is highly relevant to writers like Stein and Loy, as well as, more recently, Sanchez and Mullen, all of whom attack these technologies in the interest of breaking down conventionally accepted notions of the feminine. Just as relevant to feminist avant-garde poets, Judith Butler's model of making "gender trouble" serves as a way to position the disruptions of language, as well as the rejection of binaries, that mark these texts. For Butler, gender trouble occurs whenever categories of difference are confused or subverted, and the resulting play with gender attacks assumptions about the foundational nature of identity. The sense that any fixed identity is nothing more than a potent illusion appears repeatedly in these poets' texts, whether in Loy's debunking of the English (feminine) rose, Howe's inquiry into the gendering of transgression in American culture, or Sanchez's struggle to combat stereotypical representations of black women. As in Butler's model of disrupting the conventions and codes that help define and fix difference, feminist avant-garde poets overturn the rules, questioning the nature of a presumptive, required coherence—of language and of racial and gender identities.

Finally, the work of Monique Wittig also provides a theoretical framework for the feminisms of these writers, since feminist avant-garde poets, like Wittig, see language as "an instrument or tool," "an institution that can be radically transformed" (*Straight Mind* 26) in its materiality. Wittig focuses on the relationship between linguistic gender and the (arbitrary) division of beings into two sexes in the social realm, and her work seeks to employ the novelty of avant-garde effects to overturn a fundamental given: that "gender is the enforcement of sex in language." For Wittig, this enforced bifurcation—the "mark of gender"—"deprive[s] women of the authority of speech" (79, 81) and impedes, if not destroys, their ability to function as subjects of and in language. This awareness—the parallel between gender division in culture and the basic structures of language—illuminates all the texts discussed in *The Feminist Avant-Garde in American Poetry*. Like Wittig, the writers in this study do not assume that language is a masculine structure. But they do assume that it reflects social constructions that they are determined to change.

Nonetheless, even these theories frequently assume a conception of gender that under-represents race and ethnicity, and in this respect these approaches must be seen as limited models. The intersection of race and experimental language still remains largely un-theorized. As Nathaniel Mackey points out, for any minority writer, a "willingness to risk obscurity" challenges both "mainstream notions of clarity" and "the prescription of such notions, in the name of political urgency, to writers from socially marginalized groups." The result is that "there has been far too much emphasis on accessibility" in the reception of work by writers outside society's mainstream.[23] Feminist avant-garde writing by women of color—including Theresa Cha, Mei-mei Berssenbrugge, Erica Hunt, and others—is too often neglected. The chapters that follow only begin to address this question, pointing the way toward future study.[24]

After reviewing poststructuralist language theories, Shari Benstock poses a question that all the poets in this book, in their varied ways, ruminate on as well: "If there is no escaping the Symbolic . . . is there a hope of transforming it?" (Benstock, *Textualizing the Feminine* 46). Of the many answers that feminists have proffered, Toril Moi's may be the most pragmatic: "We have to accept our position as already inserted into an order that precedes us and from which there is no escape. There is no *other space* from which we can speak: if we are able to speak at all, it will have to be within the framework of symbolic language" (Moi, *Sexual/Textual Politics* 170).

This is the view that most prominent women poets today would accept. Feminist avant-garde writers reject such pragmatism, even as they seek not to *deny* the power or uses of the symbolic but to make deliberate linguistic choices that they hope will redirect the very thought processes of their readers. Their various feminisms involve diverse strategies to overturn—and subtly reform—instrumental language. In this, they share a common vision: a world transformed by the act of breaking down—and remaking—the language that makes us.

In the chapters that follow, a first section ("Women Poets and the Historical Avant-Gardes") is devoted to the work of two modern poets who contest both contemporaneous avant-garde agendas and the discourses of the emerging fields of psychology, sexology, and eugenics. Both intrigued by and critical of a range of avant-gardist rhetoric, Stein and Loy engage in complex textual dialogues with the major proponents of avant-garde poetry and theory, critiquing the tenets of Futurism and Vorticism, and adapting the raw material of avant-garde revolution to feminist ends. The first chapter, which addresses Stein's *Tender Buttons*, delineates Stein's creation of an aesthetic that contested the masculinist rhetoric, as well as the formal strategies, of Futurism and Vorticism current during the writing of *Tender Buttons* (between 1910 and 1912). Whereas Marinetti and Pound emphasized the verb as poetic vehicle, Stein adored the noun. She developed a poetics devoted not to forward, linear motion but to circularity and repetition, to "knowing and feeling a name." Stein's language experiments in *Tender Buttons* embody fetishism, an object-love that focuses on the privacy of the domestic sphere. Stein's theory of caressing the noun is the source of her radical language experiments in *Tender Buttons*, in which a fetishization of the word emerges as a linguistic version of object-love. Evoking Freud's gender-specific theory of (male) fetishism, Stein parodies castration anxiety, even as she transforms conventional poetic usage to explore *lesbian* desire. In marked contrast to Marinetti and Pound, who made their art and rhetoric as public and vociferous as possible, Stein effected a private revolution of the word—a move that, as I discuss in my final chapter, provokes both homage and critique from later feminist avant-gardists.

In language less cryptic and more pointedly satirical than that of *Tender Buttons*, Mina Loy similarly launched a critique of avant-garde rhetoric and forged a new poetics as a feminist alternative. Loy's early fascination with Futurism led to disillusionment, evident in her satires of the group's luminaries, particularly Marinetti, and her later responses to the movement's infamous "scorn for woman." I focus on Loy's autobiographical mock-epic "Anglo-Mongrels and the Rose" (1925) as a feminist avant-garde *ars poetica*, a poem that illuminates Loy's radical sexual politics, as well as her odd linguistic strategies. In "Anglo-Mongrels," Loy voices her scorn for the highly "poetic" verse of her day ("the lyric / aroma of the rose") in a distinctive method that I call satiric overwriting. Loy attacks the (masculine) literary tradition in a comic overdoing of poetic effect and links the inheritance of an overwrought literary language to both racial and sexual identity: Loy uses the then-popular creed of eugenics to depict an oppressive hot-house femininity in an ironic rendering of her central female character's proper breeding. Parodying literary inheritance through this eugenical metaphor, Loy suggests that culture, not biology, determines gender differences and that language is a shaping force in identity. Loy's disorienting style is, I argue, an effort to dismantle for the female poet a delimiting cultural inheritance.

In the book's central chapter, I address conflicting "Agendas of Race and Gender" in the work of Sonia Sanchez during the late 1960s and early 1970s. I describe the Black Arts movement, in which Sanchez played an important role, as a neo-avant-garde group that provoked a familiar ambivalence in its women practitioners. This chapter thus suggests not linear progression but yet another new beginning for feminist avant-gardism: in terms of feminist precedents, Sanchez's poetic experiments cannot comfortably be traced either to Anglo-American feminist modernism or to the less confrontational poetry of women of the Harlem Renaissance. Sanchez confronts in the late 1960s many of the same difficulties Loy faced fifty years earlier in her effort to combine feminism with a militant avant-garde agenda. In her early work, Sanchez struggles to articulate a black feminist consciousness in the context of the revolutionary—and patriarchal—politics of Black Power and the Black Arts movement. I discuss two of Sanchez's books: *We a BaddDDD People* (1970; hereafter *Bad*), which follows the Black Arts agenda by using Black English to forge a public, often militant, communal voice; and *Love Poems* (1973; hereafter *Love*), a largely personal and seemingly apolitical collection of lyrics. I show that Sanchez's separation of public and personal voice parallels a split between racial and gender allegiances, and between the novelty of avant-garde forms and the pull of traditionalism. Sanchez's political and formal divides during the Black Arts years dramatize a woman poet's difficulty in voicing a feminist critique in conjunction with the nationalist politics of Black Arts, whose "straight / revolutionary / lines" impeded Sanchez's search for a feminist usable past. I argue that the emergence of *Love Poems* anticipates Sanchez's rejection of the masculinist elements of the Black Arts movement in favor of what she calls "a fo / real" revolution: one based on a more fluid sense of racial and gender identities.

The final section, "Traditions of Marginality," addresses the work of poets born a full two generations after Stein and Loy—writers who have developed new strains of radical feminist poetics. Here I emphasize the complex question of tradition. In Chapter 4 I discuss the disjunctive texts of Susan Howe, who establishes herself as the literary descendent of a hybrid set of precursors. My focus is Howe's belief in a feminized antinomian dissent in American history, variously embodied in Anne Hutchinson, Mary Rowlandson, and Emily Dickinson. Tracing in Howe's work Fraser's "tradition of marginality," I discuss Howe's *Articulation of Sound Forms in Time* (*Singularities*, 1987; hereafter *S*), whose allusions to Hutchinson, Dickinson, and H.D. announce a lineage that Howe links to the effort to dismantle gender difference: In *Articulation*, Howe explores tropes of gender crossing, recording the story of a Puritan minister who becomes lost in the wilderness he had set out to conquer, moving from masculine civic and religious leadership into the feminine domain of the "virgin" American landscape. In her fragmented text ("Poetry unsettles our scrawled defence," Howe says elsewhere), Howe likens the breakdown of gender difference to the dissolution of language, encouraging in her disconnected words "transfiguration beyond gender."

The last chapter further explores the question of inheritance by examining the work of Harryette Mullen, a writer who mixes avant-garde modes too often considered only in isolation. I first address the influence—and revision—of both Steinian and Black Arts poetics in *Trimmings* (1991), in which Mullen modifies the speech-based Black Arts legacy by fusing it with the prose poem form of *Tender Buttons* and abundant Steinian allusions (Stein's famous "rosy charm," among others). Mullen's "tender girders" repeat, with a crucial difference, the language of *Tender Buttons* and the thematics of Black Arts poetics. I go on to discuss a similar hybridity in Mullen's long poem *Muse & Drudge* (1995). Mullen questions, like Mackey, those presumptions that identify avant-garde writing solely with traditions of highly textual innovation, while coding the work of writers of color as emerging from an oral tradition. Merging visual and speech-based poetries, classical and contemporary sources (from Sappho to Bessie Smith), *Muse & Drudge* illuminates language as a locus of a hybrid culture, one in which feminist avant-garde writing has become conscious of its predecessors.

Finally, in a brief epilogue I observe that such varied texts bear witness to the growing richness of feminist avant-garde poetry and to an increasing sense of its complex traditions, reinvented over a century of American cultural history. All the poets in this study explore feminist consciousness in new forms. Their ambition is nothing less than to transform the gendered landscape of American culture.

WOMEN POETS & THE HISTORICAL AVANT-GARDES

I

1

"REPLACING THE NOUN"

Fetishism, Parody, & Gertrude Stein's *Tender Buttons*

n "Poetry and Grammar," Gertrude Stein writes, "Poetry is concerned with using with abusing, with losing and wanting, with denying with avoiding with adoring with replacing the noun." Kin to her inimitable styles, Gertrude Stein's theories of the noun, and of language in general, are like no one else's, and *Tender Buttons*, which is like no other text, is Stein's great experiment with the noun. Stein challenges conventional models of signification and explores the relationships among language, consciousness, and sexuality independent of movements, programs, or manifestos — in fact, in divergence from most of the preoccupations of her avant-garde compatriots at work on seemingly similar experiments. For in the minds of its most important practitioners, the rhetoric of avant-garde groups of the 1910s and 1920s was linked to the rise of a powerful new technology. Whether in F. T. Marinetti's infatuation with the automobile and airplane or Francis Picabia's renderings of intricate mechanical designs, avant-garde artists (Futurist, Vorticist, or Dadaist) emphasized the seductive potency of the machine. By contrast, Stein's prose and poetry reflect not the forward thrust of the mechanical but a pace slowed by repetition; further, the recurring linguistic motifs in her writing center on domesticity, erotic exchange, and a fascination with ordinary objects. Stein's early interest in portraiture (along with her friendships with such artists as Picasso, Matisse, Picabia, and Juan Gris) links her work in the 1910s to Cubism and to collage, as well as to elements of Dada.[1] But the domestic motifs of *Tender Buttons*, and of Stein's other poetry, set it apart from the preoccupations of the modern sensibility, with its imagery of the train, the airplane, and the engine.[2]

Of particular significance to *Tender Buttons* is Stein's obsession with the noun. In distinction from the forward motion of the verb emphasized by both Marinetti and Pound, Stein's theories of the noun represent an entirely different sense of physicality, as well as of poetic language. Stein writes in "Poetry and Grammar" that "the noun must be replaced . . . by the thing in itself" (Stein, *Lectures in America* 246; hereafter *LIA*). *Tender Buttons* enacts a wish to get back to material experience in a gesture similar to Marinetti's lyric "obsession with matter." Yet Stein's preoccupation with replacing the noun, with substituting one "thing" for another, is more than a variation on the predominant avant-garde theme of materiality in the new art. To the contrary, the well-documented presence of lesbian experience encoded in *Tender Buttons* suggests an erotic form of substitution. It is this sexual inscription that concerns me here: *Tender Buttons* implements a linguistic strategy that I describe, in light of recent feminist theories, as lesbian fetishism — an anti-Freudian, and anti-Futurist, version of object-love. Stein's theory of the noun as loved object is the basis for an idiosyncratic avant-garde practice. Stein affirms the erotic charge of words and objects, contesting the presumption of sexual difference propounded in Freud's writings and in masculinist avant-garde rhetoric.

Drawing on debates in the new psychology, which fascinated her from her studies with William James onward, Stein selects as point of departure a philosophy that was indeed new — and certainly revolutionary — but which was largely rejected by avant-garde writers from Marinetti and Pound to Tristan Tzara, all of whom abjured the focus on personal subjectivity in the late Romantic sensibility. I assert that Stein's erotic investment in the objects named in *Tender Buttons* parallels fetishism as theorized by Freud. Stein's play with the materiality of language suggests what has been called the strategy of the fetishist, a double consciousness of something at once absent and present, of language as both symbol and object. As some critics have pointed out, "perversion" suggests choice—that of either a rhetorical strategy or, more sweepingly, an irreverent aesthetics. According to one definition, perversion involves "a mental strategy that uses one or another social stereotype of masculinity and femininity in a way that deceives the onlooker."[3] Similarly, in *Tender Buttons* Stein diverges from the Freudian notion of fetishism by using objects to parody the male fetishist's anxiety and disavowal, to attack rigid views of sexual difference, and to suggest the possibility of an object-love based on plenitude rather than loss. I argue that this alternative model of sexuality is the basis of Stein's revolutionary art.

If Stein's idiosyncratic visions are distinct from both Freudian and contemporaneous avant-garde pronouncements, they also diverge from the two predominant schools of thought advanced in what was then called the "woman movement." The first, social purity, asserted that women were morally superior to men, in the process disavowing the existence of sexual desire in women. By contrast, the second — "pro-sex" radicalism — opposed sexual repression and championed a woman's right to sexual pleasure.[4] The social purists saw women and men in terms of binary difference: they identified lust as a male quality opposed to women's more asexual, spiritual natures, while the pro-sex minority, whose roots were in the nineteenth-century free love and utopian movements, "challenged the identification of sexual desire as masculine" (DuBois and Gordon, "Seeking Ecstasy on the Battlefield" 16). Stein's erotic poetry clearly has far more in common with the sex radicals' new openness. Yet the sex radicals, like the social purists, hardly invited the liberation of "female inverts."[5] Even these most daring advocates of the newest brand of free love tended to reject "intense female friendships as adolescent" (DuBois and Gordon 18), and their strong ties to the new movements in sexology and psychology — including Freudian theory — led to heterosexual norms. Feminist radicals from Victoria Woodhull and Tennessee Claflin through Dora Marsden asserted only heterosexual desire as normal for females; as Linda Gordon points out, the "sexual revolution" of the 1910s in effect intensified taboos against homosexuality.[6] Stein's lack of identification with the woman movement (largely synonymous with the Suffrage movement in the 1910s and dominated by social purists) is thus hardly surprising.[7] Stein's "perverse" desire had no contemporaneous feminist exponents; in fact, it was the importance of child rearing that provided progressives with the rationale for education (including sex education) for women.[8] The opposing positions of purity and sexual radicalism effectively limited women to just two alternatives: heterosexual reliance on men or a life of abstinence. In this climate, Stein and Toklas adhered to a socially acceptable emphasis on privacy and opted for a pragmatic approach to contemporary views of same-sex relations.[9] Stein's poetry — particularly its treatment of words and objects — represents a highly private feminist liberation.

A number of feminist critics explore Stein's sexual motifs as a version of an essentialist "writing the body." Other critics have argued more convincingly, however, that for Stein, gender and identity are fluid. Stimpson provides insight into Stein's gender politics: Stein attempts to show how gender might be eliminated outright, its tropes and codes broken. *Tender*

Buttons offers us a degendered world.[10] Following this general view, I suggest that in *Tender Buttons*, as in much of her other prose and poetry, Stein plays with language, fetishizing the word to subvert gender division through the signs of a radical experimental language.

Stein's fetishization of the word offers us an early model for feminist avant-garde practice — and, as the last chapter of this book demonstrates, a highly influential one for recent poets. In this chapter, I first explore the various theoretical implications of Stein's replacing the noun, contrasting her practice to that of contemporaneous avant-garde pronouncements. In a second section, I demonstrate the ways in which Stein refutes the gendered narrative of Freudian fetishism through parody, and I link that parody to Stein's poetic experiments with language and her radical sexual politics in *Tender Buttons*. I argue that lesbian fetishism is the basis of Stein's linguistic practice, while Freudian (male) fetishism is the target of her parody. Stein's assertion of lesbian sexuality in radical new forms can be seen as the basis of an avant-garde poetics devoted to realizing a new subjectivity through a newly conceived word.

In the heady years before the First World War, male avant-garde writers from Marinetti to Guillaume Apollinaire and Pound tried to capture the speed of the new urban landscape, and, in particular, both Marinetti and Pound focused a good deal of their theoretical writings on the verb as poetic vehicle. Throughout his manifestos and polemical writings, Marinetti extolled dynamism, virility, and a technological sublime, calling for the new art to convey "the lyrical obsession with matter" and to embrace the project of capturing "the life of a motor, a new instinctive animal" to replace the outworn fin de siècle obsession with subjectivity. Marinetti's technical agenda for writers involved substituting mathematical symbols for syntax (to convey speed in written form) and using only the infinitive form of any verb (Marinetti, *Let's Murder the Moonshine* 92). His linguistic program also included abolishing adjectives and adverbs as superfluous and imprecise. Pound, borrowing from Marinetti, embraced the new sciences revolving around the concepts and uses of energy. In his manifesto "Vortex. Pound.," he declared that "The vortex is the point of maximum energy, / It represents, in mechanics, the greatest efficiency." In this same document, Pound headed one section of the manifesto "The Turbine" (*BLAST* 153). In poetic practice, Pound (influenced in this instance by Ernest Fenollosa) believed as well that superposition would transmit the engine's speed, and that "The verb must be the primary fact of nature."[11]

The Vorticist manifestos in the 1914 issue of *BLAST* curse "THE BRI-TANNIC AESTHETE" (15) and "BLESS ENGLAND, / Industrial Island machine," "FOR ITS SHIPS [and] PORTS" (22–23). "Machinery is the greatest Earth-medium," one manifesto declares (39). Praise for the matter of industry and technology in such rhetorical flourishes (advanced early on in T. E. Hulme's denouncement of Romantic "softness" in favor of the "hardness" of classicism) finds a counterpart as well in much Dada visual art. Francis Picabia's "Portrait d'une Jeune Fille Américaine dans l'état de Nudité" wryly replaces the female body with the more durable goods of nuts and bolts — a mechanism with the phrase "FOR-EVER" inscribed on its hexagonal surface. Picabia's machinist works, like Duchamp's ready-mades, revel in the intricacy of mechanical reproduction, as in the two interconnected cogs labeled "Femme" and "Homme" in "Machine Tournez Vite." Like other works of the period, this one slyly hints at sexual and psychological entanglement while replacing the body with man-made materials.[12] With characteristic irreverence, artists associated with Dada play with the inanimate as a substitute for human, flawed bodies, often in moments of sexual arousal.

Like visual artists of the 1910s, Marinetti and Pound linked their theories to a futuristic technology. Both writers also represented their new poetics as an extension of an improved biological essence — the male body as metaphor for a unique, modern form of reproduction that would happily sidestep the biological reproduction that depends on the *female* body. In the new world, masculine potency would eliminate the female and certainly the feminine. Marinetti provides a seminal metaphor for his concept of a timely, matter-loving literature: "Art is a need to destroy and scatter oneself, a great watering can of heroism that drowns the world" (97). Pound's new man of the vortex practiced a similar masculinized form of birth: "You may think of him as DIRECTING a certain fluid force against circumstance, as CONCEIVING instead of merely observing and reflecting" (*BLAST* 153). Ironically, Pound saw the Futurism he was clearly indebted to as a failed, bombastic enterprise ("Marinetti is a corpse," he announced [154]) in which the male seed of creation was spilled and wasted: "Futurism is the disgorging spray of a vortex with no drive behind it, DISPERSAL." By contrast, the birth of the new would emerge from a vibrant tradition: "All the past that is vital, all the past that is capable of living into the future, is pregnant in the vortex, NOW" (153).[13]

Marjorie Perloff describes the extraordinary optimism of these machine-age avant-garde stances which, in the case of both Futurism and Vorticism (as distinct from Dada), preceded the First World War. These were visions in which the forging of new forms and the advent of liberating new technologies would extend human capacity.[14] By contrast, Stein was largely uninterested in the technological changes taking place in Europe and the West, drawing more (from her studies with William James and later in medical school) from the fields of psychology and biological science that, despite extraordinary recent developments, Marinetti labeled all but moribund.[15] In contrast to the speed and forward motion championed by Marinetti, Stein was fascinated with repetition and circularity, the retrograde motions Futurists and Vorticists combated with the powerful thrust of the contemporary. Stein's love of circularity acquired linguistic and sensual components that claimed poetry for her own brand of feminism: Poetry would be concerned "with avoiding with adoring with replacing the noun"—that is, with substituting for the "name" of things words that would somehow, in an entirely different way from the methods of either Marinetti or Pound, "make it new."

Stein's attitudes toward the failings of more militaristic avant-gardist rhetoric is apparent in "Marry Nettie" (1917, in *Gertrude Stein Reader*, ed. Ulla Dydo; hereafter *GSR*), an amalgam of poem and disjunctive narrative, which sheds light on Stein's attitude toward Futurism in general and Marinetti in particular. The predominant feature of the title is Stein's feminization of the ultramasculine Futurist by means of the imperative to "Marry Nettie." Just as provocative is the statement "They don't marry," which, as Perloff notes, refers on several levels to Futurism: Futurism's rejection of the bourgeois institution of marriage was a hallmark of Marinetti's movement; the year 1916 offered Stein a bitterly ironic perspective on Marinetti's militarism afforded by the deaths of a number of Futurists killed in the war they had extolled; and, further, "They don't marry" refers to pairs like Stein and Toklas, barred from the institution of marriage by virtue of their illicit love. Perloff's reading situates "Marry Nettie" as Stein's counter-Futurist manifesto, in which "the day-to-day relationship" and "ordinary language" triumph over Futurist pretension.[16] I would argue further that "Marry Nettie" is a direct expression of Stein's disgust with the violence of the war the Futurists rallied for, and an articulation of the remedy of object-love. "Marry Nettie" lampoons warmongering and, refuting Marinetti's condemnation of "Amore," proffers an experience of the sublime based on shared domestic life.

In "SPANISH NEWSPAPER," Stein satirizes the workings of the new killing machinery: "A Spanish newspaper says that the king went to a place and addressed the artillery officer who was there and told him, artillery is very important in war" (*GSR* 310). The omission of a specific, identifiable place deflates the king's prowess and stylizes Stein's account, just as the obviousness of the officer's statement renders the newspaper account wasteful and irrelevant. Here and elsewhere Stein underlines the connection between the culture of war and a journalistic prose ("The soldier what is a soldier. A soldier is readily given a paper" [311]) that her own writing purposefully disrupts. Nonetheless, important artillery is quite capable of instilling fear and denial: "She said I was nervous. I said I knew she wasn't nervous. The dear of course I wasn't nervous. I said I wasn't nervous" (311). This "nervous" repetition reveals the dislocation, felt by both lovers, induced by the war — the result of a military technology.

What serves as comfort against the terror of war in "Marry Nettie" is the presence of objects — goods of the sort earlier celebrated in *Tender Buttons*, including food and clothing, elements of survival and aesthetic pleasure. In "A NEW SUGAR BOWL WITH A CROSS ON TOP," loving attention to an ordinary domestic object serves to deflect the "nervousness":

> We said we had it. We will take it to Paris. Please let us take everything.
> The sugar bowl with a cross on top now has sugar in it. Not soft sugar but the sugar used in coffee. It is put on the table for that.
> It is very pretty. (311)

The utility and the beauty of the object please and reassure; yet the link to food — sugar, being especially treasured in times of rationing — suggests that bodily sustenance and domestic detail are life affirming, in stark contrast to the hierarchy of organized violence. Against the carnage of the Great War, Stein offers the consolation of common objects and the private affections they signify. Pound satirized women and commodity. His "Women Before a Shop" reads: "The gew-gaws of false amber and false turquoise attract them. / 'Like to like nature.' These agglutinous yellows!" (*BLAST* 49). Stein presents shopping as a sign not of women's silliness but of succor. Shopping is linked to eating, and both to romance. The ironically titled "PAPERS" requests: "Buy me some cheese even if we must throw it away. Buy me some beets. Do not ask them to save any of these things. There will be plenty of them. . . . Will you give me some of the fruit. It is thoughtless of me to be displeased" (312). The passage sounds like a condensation of the "Food" section of *Tender Buttons*, but with the crucial difference of the implied mood of nervousness that pervades "Marry Nettie."

Rebelling against the hardships imposed by the war, the speaker mends the strained relationship by food shopping, reaffirming the most mundane ties of romantic life.

Linked to such basic acts of survival are names themselves. The text bears the subtitle "Alright Make It a Series and Call It Marry Nettie"; the issue of naming, of what the series will be called, appears immediately — a self-consciousness integral to Stein's theories of the noun. The question of names includes, of course, a partner, evoked in a highly efficacious marriage: "Marry Nettie. Which Nettie. My Nettie. Marry whom. Marry Nettie. Marry my Nettie" (313). In contrast to either Marinettian (or the sex radicals') cries for free love, Stein's command deflates the grandiose Futurist's name to a simple imperative to marry — anathema to Marinetti, who declared in "Against *Amore* and Parliamentarianism" that having

> watched the takeoff of a Blériot plane, panting and still held back by its mechanics, amid mighty buffets of air. . . . before so intoxicating a spectacle we strong Futurists have felt ourselves suddenly detached from women, who have suddenly become too earthy, or, to express it better, have become a symbol of the earth that we ought to abandon.
>
> (Marinetti 83)

Stein plays on Marinetti's name, creating the homey female "Nettie" from the male proponent of technological revolution. Her linguistic legerdemain suggests the love for language and names that *Tender Buttons* practices, reclaiming from the rhetoric of violence the force of a romantic sublime.

Stein's disgust with the public disaster of war is apparent in "Marry Nettie" in the attention to material sustenance in the private sphere of marital union and the love of both ordinary objects and the word itself. Yet even more markedly than in "Marry Nettie," the earlier *Tender Buttons* suggests a love of the object status of language and its relation to naming one's beloved. As many readers have shown, in *Tender Buttons* Stein substitutes private codes, predominantly of erotic experience, evoking, as in "Marry Nettie," domestic pleasures. In this respect, Stein not only suggests the sacredness of the private sphere but also signifies on a different register from that of conventional, instrumental language. Stein makes use of the plasticity of words, explores their materiality, their relation to the orality of speech; in *Tender Buttons* she "caresses" them as nonreferential objects. Stein challenges the very rules of signification, for while she refuses to abandon the symbolic function of language, she also evokes the pleasures of words as things. Accordingly, signification coexists equally in Stein's text with materiality.

This double experience of language, a poetic means of refusing to choose, contrasts with theories of the new forms poetry should take, as proposed by other avant-gardists of the period. In different ways, both Marinetti and Pound theorized a sort of hypersymbolic — a sped-up, mechanized poetic communication that gave primacy to signification over the materiality of language. In "Technical Manifesto of Futurist Literature," a "whirring propeller" (replacing the Muse) inspires Marinetti in the poetics of matter. Although "an uninterrupted sequence of new images" will "destroy the *I* in literature" and "finally put matter in [its] place," the material of language itself is speedily dispatched, relegated to nothing *but* signifying: words are even to be eliminated altogether when possible, replaced by more efficient mathematical and musical symbols, or strung together in chains of analogies "condensed and concentrated into one essential word" (92–95). Less extreme in his poetic measures, Pound focused as well on the ideal of instantaneous transmission of information in poetry. The economy of Imagism ("direct treatment of the 'thing,'" employing "absolutely no word that does not contribute to the presentation" [*Literary Essays* 3]) led to the more forceful vortex, which spun itself less through a poetic love of the word (as in the Tennysonian mode of savoring highly wrought, musical phrases) than toward the efficient conveyance of the signified by means of verbal superposition. Both approaches sacrifice the materiality of the signifier. At the other extreme, Tzara's Dada experiments championed radical nonmeaning, highlighting the absurdity of war and the nonsense of speech precisely through a renunciation of the signifying function of words. Stein rejects such models, for they all require a choice between the roles language plays. At once signifying and utterly palpable, Stein's words, like her objects, function on both levels addressed by these poet-theorists — the symbolic as well as the experience of rhythm and sound through the body.[17] In this way, and in contrast to her compatriots, Stein forges an avant-garde practice that claims an eroticized, material language for private "revolutions."

In "Poetry and Grammar," Stein describes this linguistic doubleness, focusing on the materiality of language and at the same time clarifying that her interest is not in an experience of pure sound (that would frustrate efforts to extract meaning) but in having it both ways. Stein relishes the symbolic function of words — the numerous puns and syntactic plays in all her poetry reveal her fascination with the double potential of words to *mean* as well as to be *felt*. Yet in her discussion of the noun, Stein seeks to dislocate the relationship between meaning and sound so that, through a process of substitution, language becomes material. In her theory, one word-as-thing substitutes for another one whose meaning has been lost through overuse in expected contexts. In prose, this tiredness of particular words means that nouns are essentially uninteresting:

> A noun is a name of anything, why after a thing is named write about it. A name is adequate or it is not. If it is adequate then why go on calling it, if it is not then calling it by its name does no good. (*LIA* 209–10)

But in poetry, Stein's practice as she explains it is to make the named thing new by renaming it, or, rather, by circumventing the original name: "I too felt in me the need of making . . . a thing that could be named without using its name" (*LIA* 236). This need is explored in the new kind of poetry Stein was to write:

> And so in Tender Buttons . . . I struggled with the ridding myself of nouns, I knew nouns must go in poetry as they had gone in prose if anything that is everything was to go on meaning something. (*LIA* 242)

Stein's interest is clearly in signifying — in engaging the reader in the process of "meaning something," not simply in the material pleasure of the signifier. As Harriet Scott Chessman notes, Stein said that making sense of language while writing is inevitable: "Any human being putting down words had to make sense of them."[18] At the same time, though, Stein refuses to give up the palpable existence of the noun as an object, physically felt: "poetry is . . . a state of knowing and feeling a name" (*LIA* 233). And to know and to feel involves not just the intellect, which responds to the symbolic, but the body and its passions.

The difference between poetry and prose is that poetry involves the state of being in love:

> if you love a name then saying that name any number of times only makes you love it more, more violently more persistently more tormentedly. Anybody knows how anybody calls out the name of anybody one loves. And so that is poetry really loving the name of anything.
>
> (*LIA* 231–32)

Marinetti — enemy of "*Amore*," the force that "hinders the march of man, preventing him from transcending his own humanity . . . and becoming what we call *the multiplied man*" (80) — rejected any such open expression of obsession with "anybody one loves." Moreover, Stein's theory privileges the noun as loved object, and in this it is at odds with Marinetti's views that "every noun should have its [analogical] double" and that infinitives, not nouns, "provide a sense of the continuity of life" (92). For Stein, that continuity can be grasped only through repetition, by "loving the name of anything."

Yet the experience Stein describes is not just amorous. It is also fetishistic. If Stein distanced herself from Marinetti, her avant-gardism also distinguishes itself in relation to, and difference from, emerging Freudian narratives. As I will explain in the second part of this chapter, Stein was certainly familiar with Freud's theories, and the resemblances between Freudian fetishism and Stein's object love are striking. Although Stein opposed elements of this revolutionary new discourse (the gender specificity and heterosexism in Freud's model), her embrace of romantic love aligns her with the erotic investment crucial to Freudian theory. Stein was drawn to Freudian thinking (in contrast with both Marinetti and Pound) as a model for innovative poetic language. I argue that, in Freudian terms, words in Stein's practice function as fetishes: Just as the fetishist substitutes a newly beloved object for the "missing" phallus of the mother, in Stein's explanation a violent and persistent passion is invested in the name as substitute.

Clearly, "saying that name any number of times" is a favorite device in Stein's earlier poetry[19] as well as in *Tender Buttons*, which is all about names — the relationship between the things one loves (for Stein, the material world in general, and Alice Toklas in particular), and the names that they possess. This loving exchange of names — often in dialogic form — appears in much of Stein's erotic poetry. The final section of "Ada" ends with an encomium relating the acts of speaking and listening to love and both to endless, pleasurable repetition of the word of the beloved: "Some one who was living was almost always listening. Some one who was loving was almost always listening. That one who was loving was almost always listening. That one who was loving was telling about being one then listening" (*GSR* 102–3). "Lifting Belly" similarly uses repetition and circularity to link language to both the loved partner — engaged in playful erotic dialogue — and the act of "lifting belly": "Kiss my lips. She did. / Kiss my lips again she did. / Kiss my lips over and over and over again she did" (19). Here "Lifting belly is a language. . . . Lifting belly is a repetition" (17), and such acts of circular definition give distinct pleasure. In the midst of sensual enjoyment ("It gives me a great deal of pleasure to say yes" [5]), the "name" is invoked, along with the delectation of food: "What is my another name. / Representative. / Of what. / Of the evils of eating. / What are they then. / They are sweet and figs" (5). Such sweetness is wonderfully compatible with language: "In this midst of writing there is merriment" (54).

Passion makes poetry. In "Poetry and Grammar," Stein recounts the anecdote of her older brother who fell in love and, as comical as the resulting poetry was, "he knew the poem was funny but he was right, being in love made him make poetry" (*LIA* 236). Stein herself discovers, supposedly during the writing of *Tender Buttons*, that passion must be invested in the noun — and in the things one sees:

> I called them by their names with passion and that made poetry, I did not mean it to make poetry but it did, it made the Tender Buttons, and the Tender Buttons was very good poetry. (*LIA* 235)

This emphasis on passion, as well as on names, clarifies the way we should read *Tender Buttons*: The logic of love in connection to words and objects makes good poetry. Stein didn't care for the simple act of using language merely to label (*Wittgenstein's Ladder* 88–89), yet that Adamic role of words has little to do with loving the proper name of "anybody one loves."

Immersed in the amorous syntax Stein describes, we need to adopt an utterly unorthodox means of reading Stein's text — one that I liken to a strategy of fetishistic oscillation. In Freud's model, the fetishist, unable to accept the new knowledge of the mother's castration, selects an object to represent *both* the maternal phallus itself and, implicitly, its absence, evident in the act of substituting a shoe, for example, for the missing organ. The erotic investment in the fetish that Freud describes parallels Stein's relation to the "tender buttons" of language in her poem — whose opening section, we might remember, is called "Objects." The name functions as erotic substitute. Yet Stein resolutely refuses to choose between the registers Kristeva calls the symbolic and the semiotic, and in this respect her text embodies a fetishistic approach to language. Like Stein, we experience words as signs and material things at the same time.[20] Engaging with the necessarily symbolic nature as well as with the materiality of words — the pleasure they offer through the physical experience of speech — Stein makes her words into fetishes, linking questions of sexual identity to those of language and delivering a multiplicity of both sensuality and sense.

Stein's fetishistic desire for both the material and the symbolic in poetic language is apparent throughout *Tender Buttons*. The constant play between sensuality and semantics, materiality and meaning, begins with the title and the subsequent disjunction between headings and text.[21] As a title, *Tender Buttons* initiates the reader into the fetishistic strategy. The near paradox of a hard object that is tender is evocative on several planes. One apparent reference is to a domestic activity that seems to pay tribute to the Victorian sensibility: Just as boxes and dresses pervade Stein's "Objects" section,[22] so buttons are the implements of the feminine activity of sewing. At the same time, the plurality of these small objects suggests her words themselves, and perhaps even the multiple geometrical shapes used in Cubist painting. Yet these buttons also suggest sexual arousal, a body become multiple, pluralized, in pleasure.[23] The more conventional meanings cover the sensual one in Stein's displacement of the erotic onto the objective world, the fetishized buttons of her domestic landscape. The same strategy is effected linguistically by the back-and-forth between the headings and the text. For the most part, the headings bear witness to the transparent function of language; with a few exceptions ("A Little Called Pauline," "A Leave," "Suppose An Eyes"), objects are conventionally named in the headings. Oddly, though, they become the backdrop for disruptive texts in what would normally be a hierarchical relationship. Instead, the symbolic language in the headings merely provides the reader with a false sense of security, of stable ground that Stein will shift throughout the writing of *Tender Buttons*.[24]

Within the text, the essence of Stein's linguistic practice involves the experience of reaching after fact and reason and of discovering pleasure at the same time. In "A Substance in a Cushion," for example, the text can only be read by experiencing the materiality of the language at the same time as the multiplicity of possible significations at play with one another:

> A closet, a closet does not connect under the bed. The band if it is white and black, the band has a green string. A sight a whole sight and a little groan grinding makes a trimming such a sweet singing trimming and a red thing not a round thing but a white thing, a red thing and a white thing. (*TB* 462)

Here language functions under two imperatives — polyvalent signification and semiotic release, impossible to separate from each other. Moments of sense introduce speculative ideas: "A closet, a closet does not connect under the bed" raises the question of what it means to connect, in (or under) the bed or elsewhere, as well as the pervasive issue in *Tender Buttons* of embeddedness and enclosure. At the same time, the heading "A Substance in a Cushion" suggests needles and pins in their cushion (the passage continues, "The disgrace is not in carelessness nor even in sewing it comes out out of the way," creating syntactic ambiguity that multiplies meanings around the motif of sewing). The band surrounds a part of the piece of clothing, just as a sash (mentioned later) surrounds one's waist. Labor produces "a trimming" through arduous activity — "a little groan grinding." Briefly, then, the passage becomes a portrait of sewing. So the text is readable, or, rather, decipherable; if we want to push and pull at it, like a piece of cloth, we can cut it into shapes of meaning.

Yet these meanings cannot account for the materiality language takes on here. It is not simply that poetic devices create onomatopoeic effect or decorate a discursive content. Stein evokes the physicality of the words.[25] Rhythmic insistence and sonic repetition suggest sensual experience. As in some of Stein's other erotic poetry (such as "As a Wife Has a Cow: A Love Story" and "Susie Asado"), this section is propelled by imperatives other than those of semantics, particularly in the long final sentence. Stein orchestrates phonemic shifts through which sounds evolve and resolve: "sight a whole sight" lightens into the short "i" of "trimming such a sweet singing trimming and a red thing," while the long "o" of "whole" and "groan" evolves into the diphthong of "round" and the higher sounds of "a red thing and a white thing." The recurrence of particular words (sight, trimming, red, white, thing) exemplifies Stein's theory of the relationship between "love" and repetition: that "if you love a name then saying that name any number of times only makes you love it more" (LIA 232). The sentence lightens into a kind of ecstasy of repetitive sound. There is no way to render such release in discursive terms. The multiple meanings work on a completely different plane from the eroticized experience of the words as sounds. Having become material "things," carrying not just symbolic but sensual content, Stein's words are fetishes, even as the reader — forced to see doubly, through the lenses of the mind's meaning and the body's knowing — must become a fetishist to read Tender Buttons.

In this important respect, Stein's fetishization refuses to choose between sense and sensuality. In "A Waist," for example, she suggests the motif of sewing, as in other sections of "Objects," yet she also creates of language not a container for meaning but an emphatic physical presence:

A star glide, a single frantic sullenness, a single financial grass greediness.

Object that is in wood. Hold the pine, hold the dark, hold in the rush, make the bottom.

A piece of crystal. A change, in a change that is remarkable there is no reason to say that there was a time.

A woolen object gilded. A country climb is the best disgrace, a couple of practices any of them in order is so left. (*TB* 471–72)

"A Waist" evokes feminine dress. But the disjunction between the heading and the content (which, except for the word "woolen," evokes the natural world) forces the reader to examine individual words to decode the symbolic workings. The word "disgrace," for example, will recur in "A Petticoat," in a parodic version of lesbian transgression. And a "star," "crystal," and "gilded" may be drawn from Stein's lexicon of that which "shines" — a code word for sexual pleasure in *Tender Buttons*. "Grass" suggests the envy of "greediness," and the green of money, conflating nature and the fiduciary, the natural object and symbol. Categories are dismantled, as in the heading, where the pun on "waste" questions distinctions between physicality and social coverings (the waist of a dress). There is also a different kind of meaning in the heightening of tone ("Hold the pine, hold the dark, hold in the rush"), which impels the writing toward emotional climax, only to end in bathos: "make the bottom."

And yet we need to curb our irritable reaching after fact and reason. Any efforts at "encoding" are complicated, if not foiled, by moments that refuse grammatical rules. "A couple of practices any of them in order is so left" could be pinned down only with punctuation — a confusion similar to "object that is in wood" (a location, a material?). With such syntactic indeterminacy, no single meaning will yield itself. Instead, there are sonic repetitions: "a single frantic sullenness, a single financial grass greediness" uses sounds hypnotically (the liquid "l," for example), independent of semantic content. And, though this is no ecstasy of the mellifluous, even discursive statements (like the much-cited "Act so that there is no use in a centre" [*TB* 498]) provide only momentary resting points. It is tempting, for example, to read the following autobiographically: "in a change that is remarkable there is no reason to say that there was a time" (during a favorable change in one's life, there is no reason for nostalgia). Perhaps this is a cryptic allusion to the change of ménage when Alice moved in to 27, rue du Fleurus, and Leo eventually moved out. But such a reading, while possible, seems hopelessly reductive if asserted as a kind of translation — especially juxtaposed as the passage is with the more surreal "A woolen object gilded." Stein's breach of our expectations makes her play apparent: The pleasure of this text is in the continuous doubling of words as names or symbols, and as material things.

It is this ability to see and to write both ways that makes *Tender Buttons* so disruptive a text. Stein disassembles existing systems of language, yet she does so without sacrificing the pleasures and functionality of the symbolic.[26] Stein's practice offers not only a joyful multiplicity but also a model for the feminist avant-garde text. Embracing language as thing and symbol at the same time, with a sense of both the signifying function of language and the disruptive release of prelinguistic pleasure, *Tender Buttons* shows us a poetics of fetishism, an eroticized, liberated objective world. For this reason — the subversive nature of the word in *Tender Buttons* — a description of Stein's poetics must take into account the other register of doubleness in her text: the parody that similarly claims an altered fetishism for a feminist avant-garde poetics.

From all available evidence, Stein was cognizant of Freudian theory by the time she wrote *Tender Buttons*, and in this respect there is support for her parody of the sexual difference on which Freudian theory (along with the sexologists' models) depended. In addition to Stein's extensive connection to William James and his lectures on psychology at Harvard, Lisa Ruddick has documented Stein's familiarity with Freud well before the writing of *Tender Buttons* (which Ruddick dates between 1910 and 1912) — as early as the time Stein was at work on *The Making of Americans*, between 1906 and 1908. Around 1909, when her brother Leo became absorbed in the theory of the unconscious, the terms "conscious" and "not-conscious" appear in Stein's chapter on love in *The Making of Americans*, which, according to Ruddick, associates the unconscious with sexuality and the infantile — a prominent and controversial feature of Freud's thinking (Lisa Ruddick, *Reading Gertrude Stein: Body, Text, Gnosis* [Ithaca, N.Y.: Cornell U. P., 1990], 93). A shift away from Jamesian psychology and toward Freud is evidenced, in part, through Stein's embrace of the notion of repetition, linked to that of the unconscious. Ruddick quotes a notebook entry in which Stein declares both that she is "not a pragmatist" and that "I believe in repetition." The notion of repetition suggests Freud's view of the functioning of the mind (96) and is further apparent in *Lectures in America*, where Stein writes about the repetition of the name of "anybody one loves."[27]

Passages of *Tender Buttons* provide evidence that Stein was engaging with the Freudian narrative of male fetishism, along with a variant of it —

a version of object love that is multiple and playful, rather than fixated on the singularity of the (one) "thing." What many critics see as the submerged erotic plot of *Tender Buttons*[28] involves a parody and lesbian revision of the male fetishist's sexual pleasure in his personal objective world. In her playfully erotic and multiply-punning treatments of objects, Stein retells the Freudian story with a difference — that of the lesbian sexuality necessarily absent from Freud's theory of the fetishist.[29] In this sense, Stein contests not just Futurist rhetoric but also the emerging cultural discourse of the talking cure — itself oppositional — whose radicalism Stein implies is marred by lacunae.

Freud's essay "Fetishism," in which he describes the fetish as "a substitute for the [mother's] penis" (152) was not published until 1927, but versions of the theory appear as early as 1905, in "Leonardo da Vinci and a Memory of his Childhood."[30] The Freudian narrative runs as follows: Fetishism, strictly a male perversion, begins with the boy's devastating loss of belief in the mother's phallic power and his attendant anxiety about his own possible castration. For some boys, this trauma is so profound that a deliberate self-deception ensues. The fetishist forges a strategy: He substitutes an object for the mother's missing penis. The defining feature of Freudian fetishism is thus its gender specificity. According to Freud, the fetishist, who cannot accept the mother's castration, chooses an object in which to see *both* the maternal phallus and, implicitly, its absence from the mother, evident in his substitution of this object (a shoe, for example) for the missing phallus: "the fetish is a substitute for the woman's (the mother's) penis that the little boy once believed in and . . . does not want to give up." He empowers the fetish object with symbolic significance, so that its presence allows him to retain his belief in the phallic mother even as he acknowledges her lack. Freud calls this maneuver "a very ingenious solution of the difficulty" of confronting reality and still minimizing castration fear. Girls, on the other hand, share the mother's anatomy, and as a result they would derive no benefit from disavowing her castration. Hence the impossibility of female fetishism.[31]

In *Tender Buttons*, Stein projects desire onto diverse objects, rather than choosing a single substitute, as in Freud's male model, or glorifying the nonsentient world as masculine fetish object, as in Marinetti's and Pound's "seminal" poetics. The subject in Stein's scenario experiences the sensuality of the objective world without the threat of castration, the need to invest the fetish with purely symbolic potency, or the association of matter with force. In articulating her own form of object love, Stein also stages a parody of her masculine counterparts — particularly the gender specificity of Freud's model. Whether in Luce Irigaray's concept of mimicry or Judith Butler's interest in gender confusion, parody in various forms has offered avant-garde women writers a way to show how women can benefit from asserting a different kind of power by subverting an overbearing original. Butler, in fact, links parodic gender practices ("subversive bodily acts") directly to an effective politics.[32] In this context — the potential parody offers to feminist politics (and its links to avant-garde practice)[33] — I am making a strong claim for Stein's lesbian fetishism: In *Tender Buttons*, Stein both asserts the difference of lesbian sexuality through a redeemed and revised fetishism and, at the same time, parodies the *male* versions of that same object love. Both highly serious and highly irreverent, Stein's text suggests the ways in which feminist avant-garde texts exploit parody and appropriate existing cultural norms to attack the mechanisms of gender difference.

Overturning the Freudian scenario, parody in *Tender Buttons* turns the rules of gender typing inside out. Like Joan Riviere's and Luce Irigaray's notions of masquerade and mimicry, Stein's parody is based on a strategic *performance* that suggests the material conditions that necessitate certain strategies.[34] Yet if Stein's parody in *Tender Buttons* attacks masculine views of the feminine (as does Irigaray's notion of the speculum and Wittig's creation of Amazon fantasies),[35] a crucial difference is that in her relationship with another woman, Stein refuses to be the object of masculine desire. In affirming lesbian sexuality, Stein is free to express a nonphallic desire that can only be mimed in heterosexuality. Attacking the Freudian economy, through which women are claimed for a masculine norm, Stein asserts the experience of lesbian pleasure through parodic revision.

Tender Buttons as a whole is clearly parodic — and not only where Freud is concerned. In Elizabeth Fifer's view, Stein both encodes sexuality and offers us moments of parody, including send-ups of romantic love itself (Fifer, "Is Flesh Advisable?" 477–79). Throughout *Tender Buttons*, Stein also takes shots at the Victorian earnestness that dictates strict sexual roles. In "Objects," for example, "A Time to Eat" can be read as a parody of Victorian domestic ritual in which the voice of the patriarch betrays its reliance on strict order: "A pleasant simple habitual and tyrannical and authorised and educated and resumed and articulate separation. This is not tardy" (*TB* 472). The whole notion of creating a time to eat suggests a need to control the raw energy of the appetite; in appointing a time for the consumption of food, the patriarch places limits on the satisfaction of desire. The notion of control over the body is reinforced by the tyranny of Latinate adjectives here. (Stein condemned the adjective as "not really and truly interesting" [*LIA* 211]). "Pleasant" and "simple" suggest the psychological need for decorum; like Edith Wharton's Mrs. Welland, whose life strategy was to avoid anything unpleasant, the paternal figure institutes a ritual of decorum, "resumed and articulate," to protect himself and those he is responsible for. In defense of the importance of honoring this time to eat, the patriarch chides the members of the family that "This is not tardy," that the law is to be respected and that, at the same time, the ritual itself is not tardy — outmoded. And yet, amid what is authorised appears the protest, the renaming of the father as tyrannical and the notion of time as articulate, in opposition to a more organic sense of the body and time as Bergsonian (or Jamesian) duration. The humor of "A Time to Eat" lies in its combination of parody with quick shifts in voice that alter the tone even from one word to the next.

Yet this parodic word-play is most cutting in the crucial passages where Stein contrasts masculinist views of sexuality with a lesbian alternative. The erotic encodings in *Tender Buttons*, as I have noted, have been explored extensively, but Stein's parody in these same passages has often been overlooked. *Tender Buttons* metonymically substitutes eroticized objects for the female body and yet also impersonates the masculine perspective on both lesbian and heterosexual sexuality. The fetishistic functioning of language in *Tender Buttons* in this way provides the means of achieving this kind of double-seeing.

One of the densest examples of Stein's parody of masculinist attitudes is the close of the "Objects" section. "This Is This Dress, Aider" signifies on multiple levels, parodying a masculine view of heterosexual intercourse, as well as representing lesbian sex and one kind of masculine response to its supposed perversion. It demonstrates Stein's use of puns and linguistic play to parody one thing and pay tribute to another:

THIS IS THIS DRESS, AIDER
Aider, why aider why whow, whow stop touch, aider whow, aider stop the muncher, muncher munchers.
A jack in kill her, a jack in, makes a meadowed king, makes a to let.

(*TB* 476)

William Gass astutely points out the contrast between male and female sexuality that emerges in the space between the first sentence and the second.[36] What Gass and others have noticed fits the model of Stein's textual fetishism, for the multiply signifying — punning — heading sets up an even broader range of meanings. "This Dress" is often read as "distress," and "Aider" as both a pun on Alice (Ada was one of Stein's names for Alice Toklas, evident in "Susie Asado," among other works), and an elision of "aid her." Thus the possibility of both distress and pleasure emerge right away, coupled inextricably in the same signifiers. "This Is This Dress" also picks up on the domestic motif of sewing for a final time in "Objects" and implies a play with identity and difference (this is this), central to all sexuality.

Given the confusion between calling for "aid" and receiving pleasure from "Aider" (evoked in the ecstatic sounds of "why whow, whow stop touch"), Gass, despite his cogent reading of the movement from female orgasmic pleasure to more violent (male) sexuality ("A jack in kill her"), misses the double perspective Stein creates. The second sentence, as Ruddick points out, critiques the male sex act in which a "jack," who, through patriarchal law becomes a "meadowed king," "makes a to let" — a toilet or a rented or used vessel — out of the female body. The second sentence seems less polyvalent than the first; clearly the meadowed king is crowned at the expense of the female, "her."[37] In this sense, Stein satirizes the meadowed king.

Yet the same kind of parody occurs from the very beginning of "This Is This Dress." The play between lesbian sexuality and "distress" clearly calls up the patriarchal law; since "Aider" is the source of pleasure, distress would be felt only by the *male* onlooker — who, fetishistically, watches and labels what he sees with a symbolic value, one he associates with a threat. The lesbian experience of pleasure — which need not involve the phallus at all — causes distress to the "king," who, as patriarch, longs to aid the female gone astray. He displaces his phallic anxiety (for the two women represent the insignificance of his own sexuality) onto chivalric concern for a woman in distress. There is a fetishistic substitution of castration fear with paternalistic regard that Stein brilliantly parodies through punning — sheer signification.

Meanwhile, however, the text registers on the other level as well — that of pleasure. "Aider, why aider why whow, whow stop touch" presents several possible decodings. "Aider" is the lover's name (and "saying that name any number of times" makes one "love it more" [*LIA* 232]), but it is also a question: "Aid her?" The response is, in fact, "*why* aid her?" That is, the lovers don't need the intervention so anxiously posited by the patriarchal onlooker. As the sentence unfolds, the masculine perspective drops out, giving way to pleasure ("whow stop touch"), and ending with a humorous

version of mutual satisfaction (a single "muncher" — suggesting oral grati-
fication — becoming plural, "munchers"). The final reflection that occurs
in the second sentence interprets the masculine response to the lesbian ex-
clusion of the phallus and ends the "Objects" section with what is at once a
satire of masculine panic and, at the same time, a representation of an or-
gasmic lesbian experience. Stein's invention of a fetishistic language — at
once satiric and shot through with erotic pleasure — thus aids her in creat-
ing a parody of the very fetishism she appropriates and renews in a radical
poetics that contests the "normal" in sexuality and language alike.

Elaborate encodings of sexual experience occur throughout "Objects"
and continue in "Food" and "Rooms."[38] Yet the first part of Tender Buttons
exemplifies most clearly Stein's parodic versions of Freudian fetishism that,
at the same time, seek to represent sexuality. Stein begins with the material
world. Stein's process of composition involved a consciously fetishistic re-
lationship to the objects she chose to paint in prose.[39] Her strategy was to
focus on an object and through this visual relationship liberate herself to
name it without using its already-given name. Three times in "Portraits and
Repetition" Stein describes the importance of such looking in Tender But-
tons: "I was trying to live in looking, and looking was not to mix itself up
with remembering" (LIA 189); and later, "I did express what something
was, a little by talking and listening to that thing, but a great deal by look-
ing at that thing" (LIA 190). She even goes so far as to explain the substitu-
tion of objects for living subjects: "I had the feeling that something should
be included and that something was looking, and so concentrating on look-
ing I did the Tender Buttons because it was easier to do objects than people
if you were just looking" (LIA 198–99). According to Freud, the child "be-
gins to display an intense desire to look, as an erotic instinctual activity"
even before he discovers the mother's castration, and the awareness of cas-
tration is based on his visual encounter with the female body. Stein delib-
erately repeats the fetishist's scopophilia (love of looking) that invests the
object with erotic significance and then focuses on it to achieve orgasm, or,
in Stein's appropriation, a pleasure of the text.[40]

This fetishistic process at once mimics male fetishism and substitutes a
feminist version — a release into the sensuality of the material world and
of language that asserts independence from masculine norms and controls,
and from men as sexual partners. Within an economy of plenitude, the
lesbian fetishist sees language as presence. She is liberated to experience
the sensuality of the objective world without fearing castration.[41] In writ-
ing that refuses to link language and lack, Stein irreverently appropriates

Freud, parodying his theory of fetishism by toying with the notion of castration. From start to finish, many of the items featured in "Objects" are fetishistic favorites, metonymically associated with the female body: a box, an umbrella, a long dress, a hat, a purse, a petticoat, a handkerchief, shoes, a shawl.

The most clearly parodic of these sections is simple enough, and its very clarity is, in this case, a result of its reliance on a predominantly symbolic use of language. Here signification supplies the tools for parody:

A PETTICOAT
A light white, a disgrace, an ink spot, a rosy charm. (*TB* 471)

In Freudian terms, a petticoat would be a perfect candidate for a fetish, since it is likely to be the last object glimpsed before the boy discovers his mother's castration; then, too, there is both a metaphoric and a metonymic logic to the choice of the petticoat, encircling as it does the female body, even bearing its traces, its shape. Stein plays on the likelihood of male fixation on feminine clothing, much as she does in "This Is This Dress, Aider" (and, clearly, the petticoat is part of the study of dress in *Tender Buttons*) through the word "disgrace," akin to the pun in "distress" in the later section. Ruddick points out the specifically female nature of this "rosy charm," for the "disgrace" that taints the "light white" of the undergarment is, on one level, menstrual blood.[42] Thus the fetishistic narrative functions doubly. In Stein's rendering of the male fetishist's perspective, for a moment the fetish is ruined — stained by the female genitals that the fetishist finds loathsome. At the same time, Stein substitutes a feminist narrative, one that rejoices in the erotics of disgrace, of a mistake that becomes charming because it represents a transgression of the virginal white of the petticoat. For Stein, the petticoat does, in fact, take on an erotic charge; just like the "Red Hat" (*TB* 467) that becomes eroticized through the fact of its color, this tainted garment is a source of joy to the lover who identifies its familiar color. The male, on the other hand, sees blood as other, perhaps even a sign of the castration he has sought to forget through the process of fetishizing a newly beloved object. In the paratactic list of "A Petticoat," Stein at once creates a male fetishist's nightmare and a lesbian fetishist's revision: Taking pleasure in the rosy charm, this alternative economy recovers (or avoids in the first place) the loathing of the female body that obsesses the male fetishist.

At once parodic and erotic, using both semantics and suggestion, "A Petticoat" represents the female laugh in *Tender Buttons*, what Cixous would later see as a version of the Medusa, an image she appropriates to recast male castration fear. For Cixous, castration should elicit only women's laughter: "Too bad for them if they fall apart upon discovering that women aren't men, or that the mother doesn't have one" (255). Just as Cixous takes Freud's interpretation of the Medusa as a figure for male castration fear (the head enveloped by phallic snakes) and invests the image with beauty, Stein invests the rosy trace with the appeal of a charm. And laughter — at once joyous and vengeful — is part of Stein's strategy. In the case of "A Petticoat," Stein's laughter mocks and celebrates at once, cutting both ways. We could well apply Freud himself, on the function of humor: "Humour is not resigned; it is rebellious. It signifies not only the triumph of the ego but also of the pleasure principle, which is able here to assert itself" (Freud, "Humour" 163). Stein's strategy bears out Freud's insights, "asserting itself" against masculine anxiety and domination, and, by so doing, Stein's becomes an example of feminist practice, fomenting both rebellion and a triumph of the ego.

Stein's alternative view of the material world emerges as well in other sections of "Objects" that contrast male fetishism and lesbian sexual experience. In "Shoes," as in "This Is This Dress," Stein uses the relatively simple structure of two sections to create a marked contrast:

SHOES
> To be a wall with a damper a stream of pounding way and nearly enough choice makes a steady midnight. It is pus.
> A shallow hole rose on red, a shallow hole in and in this makes ale less. It shows shine. (*TB* 474)

The object is common to male fetishists because of the boy's (supposed) act of glancing up the mother's skirt only to discover her lack and substituting, for the phallus, her shoes. Stein contrasts male and female anatomy, reversing the polarity by displaying a disgust for the former and celebrating the latter. The first section contains the phallic images of "a stream of pounding," and its residue of seminal "pus." There is a resistance to motion, a stifling of the body (a version of the patriarch's control of the appetite in "A Time to Eat"). A "wall with a damper" suggests the hindering of fluid movement, while violent "pounding" leads only to "a steady midnight," a (spiritual) obscurity. The shoes, as fetishes, represent fixation — the lack of choice characteristic of the male fetishist. Whatever pleasure might be taking place in the closet, its climax is deflated.

By contrast, brightness and multiple punning erupt in the second section as Stein substitutes pleasure for the male fetishist's unappealing relationship to the shoes. Crucial to the reversal of the male fetishist's mechanism is a bilingual pun. Ruddick points out that the French "chose" is slang for "vagina" ("Rosy Charm" 227), punning on both "shoes" and "shows." The change of perspective, then, takes place on the level of the signifier itself: The same object, and the same word, are perceived from different points of view. "A shallow hole rose on red" serves as an alternative depiction of the "chose," one that rejects the male fear of the female genitals. The sensory and symbolic qualities of "red" and "rose" — associated with the female body — are played with rather than feared, while assonance and alliteration return the language to its materiality. The repetitions Stein delights in ("a shallow hole," "in and in") link the love of words to a delight in the "rose" of the female body. And, of course, the code for Alice ("ale less") evokes Stein's difference from the male paradigm. In this movement from fear to pleasure, "midnight" becomes "shine" — a term which, along with other words for brightness in *Tender Buttons*, signifies sexual satisfaction. Rejecting the male's fixation on the object in the closet, Stein brings the shoes into the light; even as she retains a private textual code, Stein takes a specifically lesbian pleasure in the heterogeneity of the material world, the body, and the word.

The same eroticization of language and objects appears in "A Little Called Pauline," one of the few headings that is as disjunctive as the text itself. The act of naming ("calling") with affection (the diminutive "little") results in a new name — Pauline, the feminized version of the masculine (perhaps apostolic) Paul. Stein evokes several different objects in the game of naming what one desires; the plurality (rather than the fetishist's singular choice) suggests a polymorphously perverse pleasure. The sexual image with which the section opens ("A little called anything shows shudders" [473]) can be glossed by Stein's comments on the noun, conflating language, love, and object in Stein's poetic world. Since poetry is "really loving the name of anything" (*LIA* 232), naming an object (a little called anything) is an act of love — it "shows shudders." Throughout this section, Stein refuses to choose *one* object. Rejecting patriarchal symbols ("There is no pope"), Stein also escapes the obsessive singularity of the male fetishist, as in this punning reprise of "Shoes": "little dressing and choose wide soles and little spats really little spices." From "soles" and masculine "spats" come "little spices," elements of a rather feminine oral pleasure that refuses to be singular. Instead, Stein evokes male fetishism ("A little lace") and its possible punishment (it "makes boils") only to shed such fear ("This is not true") in favor of "her": "A peaceful life to arise her, noon and moon and moon." Perhaps the most explicit sexual "rise" is "I hope she has her cow." Fifer has noted that "cow" denotes orgasm in Stein's lexicon, here associated with "Bidding a wedding" and thus with Stein's own romantic sublime (480–81). The unnamed "she" places "A Little Called Pauline" in a realm of concern for — rather than objectification of — a loved woman,[43] suggesting a version of fetishism based on adoration, not loathing, of the body.

Such an embrace is suggested by "A Shawl" whose comfortable intimacy counters the Freudian fetishist's fixation: "A shawl is a hat and hurt and a red balloon and an under coat and a sizer a sizer of talks" (*TB* 475). The hat has already emerged in Stein's erotic lexicon, especially in being red, while "hurt" is itself a metonym for shades of red (in "A Carafe, That Is a Blind Glass," it suggests wine). A "red balloon" becomes an eroticized shape. Most significantly, "A sizer" reads as "a scissor," a feminine aid to sewing that can be both a threatening instrument to the male fearful of castration and, conversely, a potent tool for the fetishist who cuts women's hair. Yet the reflexive language here bears further examination, as in the following: "It was a mistake to state that a laugh and a lip and a laid climb and a depot and a cultivator and little choosing is a point it." The "mistake," like the fortuitous "disgrace" in "A Petticoat," is a matter of language ("a mistake to state"). It is a mistake to state that this list "is a point it," that is, "disappointed," or, possibly, has a point or logical closure, as in traditional syntax. "Point" suggests a directive; Stein returns to the questions with which "Objects" began — the carafe, an object that is "an arrangement in a system to pointing" (*TB* 462). Meditating on her relationship to the covering of language, Stein refuses to rely simply on making a point; at the same time, she is not disappointed with the nouns she "addresses and caresses." Instead, Stein takes joy in the material that is language.

In *Tender Buttons*, Stein combines object love with her own encoded sexuality, rejecting both the hard realities of the technological sublime and the primacy of the masculine in Freudian discourse. Her object love claims Freud's version of the fetishist's intriguing oscillation for a joyful multiplicity rather than the perception of absence. Rejecting Freudian difference, Stein assumes a nonphallic view of the objective world and of language.

The Freudian fetishism whose narrative Stein explored relies on what Freud called "genital deficiency" — the notion that women's bodies lack what is apparent in the male anatomy.[44] We might argue that, like Sarah

Kofman and other recent feminist theorists, Stein explores what Naomi Schor calls a "paradigm of undecidability" in her play with fetishism, "a *strategy* designed to turn the so-called 'riddle of femininity' to women's account." Any such subversive revision of psychoanalysis might serve as a means to assert a necessary ambivalence toward Freud — to salvage aspects of his theory for feminist ends.[45] In this respect Stein counters the heterosexual and masculinist elements of Freudian theory. Still, Stein does not express a singular version of "the feminine." Rather, she refutes contemporaneous theories of women's sexuality, encoding a taboo lesbian desire into the most common, seemingly innocuous words. *Tender Buttons* sets the stage for experiments like Monique Wittig's *Lesbian Body*, which attacks dominant conceptions of lesbian desire (and identity) by deconstructing syntactic norms. Wittig asserts the existence of an Amazonian lesbian culture. Since the lesbian is "illusionary for traditional male culture," this lived reality includes no distinctions among "fictional, symbolic, [and] actual." For Wittig, as for Stein, "The body of the text subsumes all the words of the female body," achieving "affirmation of its reality," so that "To recite one's own body, to recite the body of the other, is to recite the words of which the book is made up" (Wittig, *Lesbian Body* 9–10). Wittig wrests the lesbian body from heterosexual linguistic control: Because the "generic feminine subject can *only* enter by force into a language which is foreign to it," Wittig invents a pronoun, employing a visual sign for the split lesbian subject — "j/e." As in Stein's model, Wittig not only rejects dominant narratives of female sexuality but also literally creates an alternative feminist language.

In its radical signs, *Tender Buttons* attests to Stein's belief in the intersections among the objective world, language, and sexuality, in contrast to the fascination with the power of the inanimate, and the ambivalence about the human body, that spurred the writing of so many male avant-garde writers of her day. Stein's "revolution" insisted on the intimacy of domestic life and the preeminently private experience of an encoded language. Yet Stein's experiments differ as well from those of other feminist avant-garde writers working during the years of the historical avant-gardes. Stein's cryptic encodings cannot be likened in formal terms to Mina Loy's feminist satires, yet Stein and Loy share the ambition of distinguishing their experiments from the work of the vocal avant-garde groups of their day. Like Stein, Loy was in dialogue with Futurist rhetoric. And like Stein, she voiced dramatic divergences from Marinetti's aesthetics and politics. Hers is an even more pointedly satiric poetics that announced an idiosyncratic feminist avant-garde agenda of its own.

2
"CRISIS IN CONSCIOUSNESS"
Mina Loy's "Anglo-Mongrels and the Rose"

When Mina Loy met Marinetti in Florence in 1914, she developed an enthusiasm for his then-thriving movement. Her "Aphorisms on Futurism" (1914) explodes with a new vision: "THE Future is limitless — the past a trail of insidious reactions." Kin to Marinetti's own insistence on forward motion ("we want no part of it, the past, we the young and strong *Futurists*!" [51]), this passage is followed by the imperative to "ACCEPT the tremendous truth of Futurism / Leaving all those / — Knick-knacks" (Mina Loy, *Lost Lunar Baedeker* 152).

This "tremendous truth" — a rejection of the knick-knacks of contemporary culture — complements issues she raises in her "Feminist Manifesto" in *The Lost Lunar Baedeker* (New York: Farrar, Straus and Giroux, 1996; *Lost* hereafter), also written in 1914. "The first & greatest sacrifice you [women] have to make," Loy asserts, "is of your '<u>virtue</u>,'" a "knick-knack" of the male marriage market. In this feminist challenge to outmoded Victorian values, Loy rejects romantic love and urges a celebration of pure desire: "Women must destroy in themselves, the desire to be loved —"; "there is <u>nothing impure in sex</u> — except in the mental attitude to it" (*Lost* 155–56). The arguments parallel not only Breton's later declarations of the liberating power of sexuality but, more specifically, Marinetti's attack on property ("We want to destroy not only the ownership of land, but also the ownership of woman" [86]), his rejection of the family ("a legal prostitution powdered over with moralism" [85]), and his diatribe against Romantic love ("There is nothing natural and important except coitus" [80]). "In this campaign of ours for liberation," Marinetti argues, "our best allies are the suffragettes, because the more rights and powers they win for woman, the more will she be deprived of *Amore*, and by so much will she cease to be a magnet for sentimental passion or lust" (81). However ironic his "feminism," Marinetti agreed with Loy on one crucial point: that the ideology of romantic love was a social ill affecting men and women alike.[1]

Yet in voicing more fully the feminist politics that was only just emerging in her "Feminist Manifesto," Loy ultimately demonstrates as much revolt against as indebtedness to Futurism and its rhetoric of revolution. Elizabeth Arnold argues that Futurism spurred Loy to both her later satires and what Arnold calls a more "determinate poetic" than that of avant-garde radicalism.[2] Loy's brief immersion in Futurism clearly reveals the difficulties women experienced in forming alliances with the prominent figures — and philosophies — of avant-garde movements in the 1910s and 1920s, despite parallels between such projects and those of a number of contemporaneous women poets, including Stein, H.D., and others. Like Arnold, I see Loy as moving toward quite different conceptions of both language and gender than those Marinetti expounded, in defiance of a masculinist avant-garde agenda. But the result is hardly determinate: Coopting Marinetti's provocations to her own feminist ends, Loy develops an avant-garde poetics to combat the linguistic and cultural determinism she believed were destroying women's lives.

Loy's poetic practice reveals attitudes toward language that, compared to Marinetti's, are considerably more attuned to the intransigence of social custom and the elusiveness of revolution. Loy urges change not by unleashing "words in liberty," but by using a satiric voice to parody existing literary genres. The poetry that emerges after Loy's education in Futurism reflects the fundamentals of the avant-garde text: Here language plays dual roles as functional social tool and persuasive aesthetic instrument. Loy shares with Marinetti, Tzara, Breton, and other avant-gardists a belief in the interconnections among language and consciousness. This awareness leads her to develop a style less shocking, but no less singular, than that of any avant-garde poet of her day. Combining the rhetorical lessons of Futurism with her nascent agenda — a quest for female sexual and psychic liberation — Loy forges a feminist avant-garde poetics that illustrates the urgent need for women's self-determination. Nonetheless, the crisis in consciousness proved resistant: Although Loy's manifestos lay out blueprints for radical change, her poetic texts reveal doubts about how to realize her feminist vision.

Early on in her writing career, Loy merged idiosyncratic feminist beliefs with Marinettian "revolution." Almost immediately, poetic satires start to measure her distance from Futurist grandiosity. But perhaps the best example of Loy's divergent agenda appears in her autobiographical mock-epic, "Anglo-Mongrels and the Rose." I view "Anglo-Mongrels" as a feminist avant-garde ars poetica, a story fundamentally about women and language. Although "Anglo-Mongrels" certainly offers insight into Loy's early years — detailed in Carolyn Burke's biography, *Becoming Modern* — the poem is perhaps most significant as a mythic construct, an articulation of Loy's attitudes toward language, identity, and gender: Loy explores the intersections of gender and racial identity and applies both to the category of the "woman poet" whose status remained uncertain even during the years of burgeoning experimentalism and openness in the arts in the 1910s and 1920s. In this allegory, Loy's most ambitious work, Loy seems to cast her life history in a deterministic mold, tracing the biological inheritance of the mongrel Ova, the poem's central character. Yet for the female poet Ova represents, the problem is culture, not nature, and this conviction is at the center of Loy's aesthetic activism. Loy demonstrates the inadequacy of the literary inheritance available to the woman writer of her day. Making detailed use of the tropes of racial determinism and the then-thriving eugenics movement, Loy portrays the inheritance of language itself, and a female subject's entry into its symbolic, social system. Although the references to racial breeding that appear throughout the poem may make the text seem deterministic and even racist, in fact what Loy struggles against in "Anglo-Mongrels" and elsewhere is not biological but cultural determinism: the belief that language, culture's arm, so shapes consciousness that it has the power to govern perception and even individual destinies[3] — to determine female identity.

It was this sense of outrage about linguistic and gender determinism that necessitated and defined Loy's feminist avant-garde stance, defined in both theory and practice in distinction from the vociferous militance and technological obsessions of Futurism and Vorticism. As seen in "Anglo-Mongrels," Loy opted against the rhetoric of violent overthrow, endorsing not destruction but what she hoped would be an equally effective irreverence. The result in poetic terms is parody — an attack on the cultural symbols Loy found most pernicious. Like her satires, the semiautobiographical "Anglo-Mongrels" exploits the traditions it critiques, investing poetic idiom with an irony adopted to demonstrate to her readers that language is a sign of culture — a potentially determining system, yet one that can also be challenged.

The motivations for Loy's avant-garde strategies have frequently been misunderstood. Even Yvor Winters — an early defender of her work — was puzzled by what he called her "unexciting method" and "the clumsiness which one can scarcely help feeling in her writings" (Yvor Winters, "Mina Loy" 499). He failed to see that this clumsiness is satiric, a means of exploiting both literary tradition and rhetorical language. Fascinated by the connections between language and culture that inform any avant-garde poetics, Loy differed from Stein (whom Loy greatly admired). Far from exulting in the sensuality of words or the playful encoding of meanings, Loy runs to irony rather than ebullience.[4] Hers is a highly deliberate method I call strategic overwriting: an overdoing of poetic technique to the point of parody, an overdeterminacy of meaning in verse saturated with polysemy, alliteration, inflated diction, punning, bathos, and ironic rhyme — a ragbag of techniques that mimic poetic convention.[5] This overdetermination of words, the inverse of Stein's sensual fetish-making, provides a different surplus of signification: Deliberate and ironic overwriting undermines the literary tradition as a whole, which Loy saw as confining, even hostile, to the female speaker.

Loy's strategic overwriting appears in much of her poetry. But its origins and rationale emerge most clearly in "Anglo-Mongrels and the Rose," a mythologized account of Loy's parentage and childhood in turn-of-the-century London. The daughter of a Hungarian Jewish father and an English Protestant mother, Loy uses her national and religious inheritance to detail a story of emigration and ethnic difference: Loy describes the early struggles of the mongrel Ova, whose father and mother (Exodus and Ada) bequeath her precisely this mixed inheritance. It is a story of the female subject's language acquisition — her entry into the medium of a Darwinian contest in which race and class threaten to determine not just social status but identity itself. Adapting the epic device by which exterior qualities suggest a psychic dilemma, Loy uses this apparent eugenical history to cast herself not just as an ethnic mongrel but as a hybrid of male and female traits, a child born into a culture that disdains the powers (and bodies) of women as much as it does those of racial others.

The central fact of Ova's mongrel status is that she inherits a masculine intellect in a female body. Through this adaptation of gender and racial inheritance, Loy demonstrates the paradoxes of her position as woman poet, as well as a woman of mixed national, religious, and linguistic inheritance. Loy's mongrel poetics attempts to breed feminist politics from racist and patriarchal rhetoric, grafting a feminist subjectivity onto a masculine tradition of heroic narrative. Adopting overwriting to mock, even as she practices, high art, Loy demonstrates her prowess by exaggerating the limitations of literary and social conventions, particularly the nationalist ethos of the English epic. While the *mock*-epic satirizes its subject matter, generating humor through the unlikely combination of grand rhetoric with banal subject matter, Loy's overwriting satirizes the epic *itself*, and the culture it promotes, by lampooning her own literary birthright. By implicating the high art of (masculine) epic with the racism of eugenics, Loy deflates literary tradition and offers an explanation of her strategic war on language as a means of exploring the social construction of gender identity.[6]

Like the other avant-gardists of her day, Loy believed that altering language could alter consciousness, thus changing identity itself; this fundamental belief in the power of the medium of language to effect political change makes her work an exemplar of the avant-gardist work of art. The nature of the transformation she sought is nonetheless debatable. It could be argued that the use of eugenical, hereditarian rhetoric in "Anglo-Mongrels" implicates Loy in the most perniciously racist beliefs of the twentieth century. Loy's more polemical texts in fact do not offer consistent positions about her attitudes toward race, and she sometimes shows a predilection for the very eugenical thinking that she lampoons in "Anglo-Mongrels." One passage from her "Feminist Manifesto" advocates an elitist cleansing of future generations: "Every woman of superior intelligence should realize her race-responsibility, in producing children in adequate proportion to the unfit or degenerate members of her sex —" (*Lost* 155). Here Loy promotes a eugenical, Sangeresque doctrine.[7] Yet as I see it, in "Anglo-Mongrels" and other texts as well, she sought to assault institutions that foster inequalities of both class and race.[8] Loy explores a materialist approach to cultural identity, in which society threatens to determine the nature of individuals, yet in which there is hope to undercut misogyny and class hierarchy through language itself. Satirizing English culture, "Anglo-Mongrels" attacks racial and gender typing and opposes hereditarian attitudes, which Loy saw as ingrained in "the subconsciousness, that rubbish heap of race-tradition" (*Lost* 152) — the realm of consciousness that her radical art sought to change.

Not unlike Marinetti and Wyndham Lewis, Loy hoped to popularize a new discourse, to create through artistic activism a new future. In "Anglo-Mongrels," she emphasizes the potential of language to determine subjectivity, and, like that of other avant-gardists, her poetry and polemics show

how much faith she placed in the reverse procedure — that altering language might create a *new* consciousness and liberate the reader from the fetters of outworn ideas. "TODAY is the crisis in consciousness," she asserts in "Aphorisms on Futurism":

> CONSCIOUSNESS cannot spontaneously accept or reject new forms, as offered by creative genius; it is the new form, for however great a period of time it may remain a mere irritant — that moulds consciousness to the necessary amplitude for holding it. (*Lost* 151)

According to Loy, the poet creates the "irritant" of the new, jolting the reader out of a language that stutters over anything but time-worn forms. Futurism's power — as Loy conceived it then — was its disruptiveness:

> TO your blushing we shout the obscenities, we scream the blasphemies, that you, being weak, whisper alone in the dark.
>
> . . .
>
> THUS shall evolve the language of the Future.
>
> THROUGH derision of Humanity as it appears —
>
> TO arrive at respect for man as he shall be — (*Lost* 152)

There is no clearer explanation of Loy's own avant-gardist "derision"— its origins in an anticipatory respect for the new. According to Burke, when Loy was in Florence, she read the first Futurist manifestos "as if they were news from the front" (*Becoming Modern* 153). Her early infatuation with the movement reflected her own emerging views about language and cultural politics. Like Marinetti, Loy believed that language embodies ideology. Yet unlike Marinetti, she eventually saw her task not as inventing a "new" language of the future, but engaging in the earlier step of disrupting traditional language, remaining skeptical of commonly spoken words, even as she continued, by necessity, to make use of them.

Loy's short satires, written throughout the 1910s, as well as her important (and highly ironic) "Love Songs," all reveal her renovation of traditional, often male-dominated, poetic genres to voice a feminist agenda in an altered tongue, specifically through the technique of overwriting. Several of these pieces lampoon gender roles both in bourgeois culture (as in "Virgins Plus Curtains Minus Dots") and in avant-garde circles, as in "One O'Clock at Night" (in "Three Moments in Paris"), where a male "pugilist of the intellect" (*Lost* 15) holds forth, and the female listener feels the marked divide between her "personal mental attitude" and her identity as a woman. Most notably, concerning Futurism, "The Effectual Marriage" and "Lions' Jaws" pillory Loy's erstwhile influences. "The Effectual Marriage or the Insipid Narrative of Gina and Miovanni" makes full use of Loy's affair with Futurist artist Giovanni Papini to poke fun at the strictness of gender roles even in the most bohemian circles: Miovanni's artistic pretensions are posited on a woman's residing "among his pots and pans / Where he so kindly kept her / Where she so wisely busied herself" (*Lost* 36).[9] Although the poem hardly goes so far as to announce a new consciousness, it does more than hint at gender difference as the point at which changes in what Loy called "psychic evolution" might start.

Loy's feminist satire, then, goes hand in hand with her more specific critique of masculinist avant-gardism. Although she initially admired Marinetti's iconoclasm and sheer forcefulness, she also called him early on a "bombastic superman" and argued with him about his infamous "scorn for woman," objecting to his low opinion of women (*Becoming Modern* 156–57). Despite her romantic entanglements with Marinetti and Papini, Loy remained skeptical — an attitude that turned to renunciation in her bitterest satires.[10] "Lions' Jaws" assaults both ends of the aesthetic spectrum in the figures of "Danriel Gabrunzio" (Gabriel D'Annunzio) and "Raminetti," founder of "the Flabbergast Movement," along with his cohort "Bapini" (Papini). For Loy, the male bombast on both sides cries out for feminist satire, through which she showcases her overdoing of poetic effect:

> The antique envious thunder
> of Latin littérateurs
> rivaling Gabrunzio's satiety
> burst in a manifesto
> notifying women's wombs
> of Man's immediate agamogenesis (*Lost* 47)

As Burke points out, some time before her affair with Marinetti, Loy knew of, and found ridiculous, Marinetti's novel *Mafarka*, in which the hero gives birth to a son (*Becoming Modern* 171) — a variation on the process Marinetti describes in "Against *Amore* and Parliamentarianism": "We have even dreamed of one day being able to create a mechanical son, the fruit of pure will" (83). Loy rebels against Futurism's appropriation of birth — whether biological or mechanical. In this biting passage, Loy piles up abstractions and alliteration at her subject's expense, until the irony of positing a revolutionary manifesto on "antique envious thunder" (envying, of course, both literary rivals and the more significant "women's wombs") can't be missed. Here and in a number of other narrative poems, Loy uses a novel form of satire to expose the pretensions of masculine avant-gardism, and of Futurism in particular.

Yet Loy's critique of avant-gardism didn't imply an orthodox feminist agenda. Loy's vision differed substantially from that of prominent feminists in the 1910s. "The feminist movement as at present instituted is / **Inadequate**,"[11] Loy contends in her "Feminist Manifesto." She advises "**Absolute Demolition**": "Cease to place your confidence in economic legislation, vice-crusades & uniform education — you are glossing over **Reality**" (153). She sent her declaration to Dodge, asking her, "Have you any idea in what direction the sex must be shoved — psychologically I mean?" (*Becoming Modern* 179). She also added, "bread and butter bores me rather" (Virginia Kouidis, *Mina Loy* 27). Her rejection of "bread and butter" reflects impatience with the more practical considerations of politics, including, by implication, the legislative agenda of the Suffrage movement. This sentiment is echoed in a letter to Carl Van Vechten: "What I feel now are feminine politics — but in a cosmic way that may not fit in anywhere" (*Becoming Modern* 187).[12] Loy was caught between avant-gardist rhetoric largely hostile to women and a feminism she saw as "inadequate" to women's "evolution." Loy's feminism focused, at least in part, on the ties between gender and language.

In "Anglo-Mongrels," Loy's choice of epic as intertextual companion emerges from her desire to voice her frustration with overdetermined gender roles and, at the same time, to explore literary alternatives to violent avant-gardist rhetoric. In this case, however, the target is less her former avant-garde friends than the larger culture both sides are rebelling against: The epic, with its heroic, nationalistic overtones, provides both form and object of scrutiny here. Certainly Loy's revisionist epic has parallels in other efforts of the day. James Longenbach argues that the Great War forced poets to examine the ethical implications of making death and destruction into poetry and, at the same time, provided a wake-up call to reject the minimalist aesthetics that dominated the early years of the century.[13] This imperative was more complex for women whose exclusion from the predominantly masculine concerns of epic was only underlined by the advent of world war. Melita Schaum details Loy's feminist response to the developing genre of the long poem, particularly *The Waste Land*, the *Cantos*, and *The Bridge*. For Schaum, Loy's focus is on the *Bildüng* of the *female* poet, and her genre is the female autobiographical epic, a form initiated as well by Lola Ridge and Laura Riding Jackson.[14] Loy clearly takes on the epic as cultural symbol in "Anglo-Mongrels." Yet her response to romantic (and military) conquest is not so much to create a female genre informed by ideas of sexual difference as to advocate a feminist avant-garde aesthetic to enlighten women and men alike. Loy's use of the epic emerges from her desire to transform the genre's nationalistic role and attack the "normal" culture, which E. M. W. Tillyard has argued it represents.[15] In "Anglo-Mongrels," then, the social categories that shape us all (class, race, and gender) are figured in language, which the poet must necessarily alter in order to alter consciousness for both genders. As Megan Simpson has argued, Loy holds that "linguistic freedom and sexual freedom are closely connected" even as gender and self are never essential or permanent.[16]

The plot of "Anglo-Mongrels," drawn from events of Loy's childhood, provides an index to Loy's assault on the cultural factors that determine identity, and insight into the origins of her strategic overwriting. The first part of the poem concerns Ova's origins and her entrapment by feminine forces against which she must define herself in order to develop her art. Seemingly, language holds the promise of escape, the social channel for her creative instincts — and the instrument of an avant-garde medium of expression available to other rebels, figured in the outrageous hijinks of the avant-garde infant, Colossus. Yet the final episodes of the poem revoke what appears to be Ova's salvation and possibility for self-definition. These final episodes center on betrayal — by the father — through language. Thus the very linguistic system Ova inherits is finally inadequate; the question that remains is how to forge a poetic strategy of cultural survival (if not "revolution"), a means of allowing a new feminist consciousness, somehow, to exist in symbolic language.

From the very opening of "Anglo-Mongrels," Loy presents culture as dangerously deterministic, and she implies that literature is a powerful tool in an ideological agenda. Loy's title hints at this determinism by linking mongrelization — a term used for miscegenation — to national symbolism and literary tradition (the rose of England and of courtly love).[17] As against an elitist allegiance to purity or high culture, Loy places Ova with the many, the masses; as child of Exodus and Ada, she is the mongrel, certainly not the pure-bred and singular "Rose." Epic tradition supports the breeding of social and literary purity, resulting in idealizations like the Rose — identified here with both England and Ada, Ova's mother. Through the character of Ova, Loy thus positions herself (as poet) with her father, Exodus, also a mongrel of sorts, having bred his original national and religious identities with those of England, his adopted country. Loy's title suggests that something hidden contaminates the high seriousness that characterizes epic; in this way it offers a point of departure for Loy's feminine infiltration of high (masculine) art. Yet this same gesture also signifies the limitations of Loy's feminist vision, for it initiates as well a plot of female disavowal of the mother and identification with the father. In biographical terms, Loy's identification with her father apparently emerged early in childhood, when she conceived of her image in a mirror as that of an "exile" w— the quality she associated with her father.[18] Both Ova's mixed inheritance (masculine mind, female body) and Loy's open attacks in the poem on gender dualism anticipate Butler's gender trouble, through which subversion might effectively rewrite the binary roles of our cultural script. Yet as I will demonstrate, Loy implies that the solution is not so readily to hand. Unlike contemporaneous exemplars of vanguard sexuality (Stein, H.D., and Djuna Barnes among them), Loy seems to reject female identification as a source of power; self-definition would come only through alliance with the masculine.[19]

The dilemma is evident in the opening of "Anglo-Mongrels," where Loy presents Ova's cultural pedigree and highlights — from her very birth — Ova's difficulty as a developing female artist. Unlike Joyce, whose moo-cow episode opens *Portrait of the Artist as a Young Man* by setting the stage for a *künst roman* about the formation of a creative mind, Loy cannot simply begin at her own beginnings — that is, with the birth of the poet's imagination. Instead, "Anglo-Mongrels" presents an intimidating genealogy of patriarchs, mixing scriptural allusions to recast her story of inheritance. From Ova's father, Exodus, we move backward to *his* father, the "Patriarch" who "erected a synagogue / for the people" — empty rhetoric, since there are problems in this class-bound society when "His son / look[s] upon Lea / of the people" and falls in love. As Burke shows, the story is accurate — Loy's great-grandfather disinherited her grandfather for marrying beneath him (*Becoming Modern* 17). In Loy's revisionist mythology, though, the biblical parallel is crucially altered. The Leah of Genesis competes with her younger sister Rachel as the proper mate for Jacob but she fails to win his favor; this Lea is rejected by the Patriarch because of her social position. Loy shifts the focus of the Genesis story to posit a *dis*inheritance that will be passed down to Ova: Because Exodus's father disrupts class structure by choosing a woman "of the people," he sacrifices Exodus's legacy. "Disinherited," the Patriarch's son "begat this Exodus."

Biblical language confirms the role of patrilineal descent, but the story is fundamentally about class hierarchy: Romance is quickly passed over in favor of the unhappy childhood of Exodus and his lack of social standing. Instilled with the "secret patriotism" of nation-state, burdened with "his forefathers' ambitions," he is damaged by a drop in status when his higher-born father dies, leaving him with "sinister foster parents" who decide that he will be "hired / . . . in apprenticeship." His resulting "paralysis of / the spiritual apparatus" is not a result of any racial trait but is, instead, "common to / the poor." The emigration that results begins not from his breeding but its economic implications. Ironically, his pursuit of the "promised land" (the issue of the book of Exodus) is a search for economic independence: He longs for the "paradise of the pound-sterling" (112), a desire that undercuts the validity of the father's birthright.

Yet Ova's ancestry reveals more than the politics of pedigree. At issue is how social status relates to language — a central concern to Ova later. Part of Exodus's wandering is linguistic — he is caught among the lessons of "Imperial Austria," nationalism ("secret patriotism / the Magyar tongue"), and religion ("the father / stuffed him with biblical Hebrew"). The linguistic mélange represents a mixture of cultural allegiances that will be repeated in Exodus's "migration" to English upon his (physical) emigration. By then the "long unlistened to Hebrew chants" will be "A wave / 'out of tide'" (117). In fact, Loy's father did repress his Jewish heritage — and certainly his familiarity with Hebrew — to attain English middle-class status for his family. By multiplying the father's languages and cultural inheritances, Loy casts Exodus in the role of refugee through cultures whose conflicting demands exile him from the start. Through the father-figure of Exodus, Loy presents the building blocks of identity as cultural and linguistic; language is *both* determining and diverse in its forms, inextricable from cultural identity.

The issues Exodus confronts — the question of inheritance, the puzzle as to how individual identity is shaped — reflect debates in the early part of the century about eugenics — discourses that are relevant to Loy's cultural politics and her idiosyncratic avant-gardism. Like Stein, Loy experimented with a linguistic grafting. Playing with the terms of a highly charged debate, she incorporates a dominant cultural discourse — in this case the lexicon and rhetorical figures associated with eugenics — as a means of forging an idiosyncratic poetics, one defined by its investigation of gender politics through innovative poetic form. Before discussing the linguistic strategies of "Anglo-Mongrels" further, then, I will need to describe Loy's idiosyncratic philosophy of personal evolution — and its relation to, and divergence from, the eugenics movements of her day.

In her manifesto "Psycho-Democracy" (*Little Review* 8.1 [1921]; hereafter *LR*), Loy articulates one of the central points of her radical vision, in distinction from the rhetoric of pre–World War I avant-garde disruption. She calls for cultural evolution as an alternative to the "Criminal Lunacy" of militarism: The only sensible move would be "to replace the cataclysmic factor in social evolution WAR" and "establish *a new social symbolism, a new social rhythm, a new social snobbism* with a human psychological significance of equal value to that of militarism."[20] Loy counters the emphasis on political might with a feminist politics of regeneration, underlining the need for new cultural symbols and systems. Resisting militaristic avant-garde rhetoric even in the form of the manifesto itself, Loy was clearly intrigued by social *and* personal evolution, adapting social Darwinism to a utopic vision of her own — a view of culture in which new national symbols would eliminate the emphasis on war and allow the evolution of the race. "The Aim of Society is the Perfection of Self," and since "Human imagination is illimitable," "'Self' is the covered entrance to Infinity."[21] Combining Jungian collective consciousness with personal growth, Loy promotes "a movement to focus human reason on THE CONSCIOUS DIRECTION OF EVOLUTION." Her "Democracy of the Spirit" is "The Substitution of consciously directed evolution for revolution, *Creative inspiration for Force* . . . Human psychology for Tradition" (15). Loy rejects not only nationalism and militarism but also more anarchic forms of revolution — whose exponents in the arts were Loy's Futurist and Vorticist acquaintances, clearly positioning herself against the day's familiar avant-garde destruction, and aligning herself with the likes of William James, not Tristan Tzara.[22]

But Loy's use of the word "evolution" in relation to social and individual development suggests the then-popular discourse of racial determinism and eugenics. That Loy should be aware of eugenics is not surprising, given the prevalence of the various groups promoting some form of it in the 1910s and 1920s. The ideas of Sir Francis Galton (1822–1911), the founder of England's eugenics movement, had been in the air since the turn of the century in England and America, and they spawned a prevalent xenophobia, most markedly in New York, where Loy had been living out the war years before moving to Paris.[23] Daniel Kevles's account of eugenicists' goals seems to reflect Loy's philosophy in "Psycho-Democracy": Eugenics would "manipulate evolution to bring the biological reality of man into consonance with his advanced moral ideals" (12). Yet Loy's emphasis on self-realization and democracy counters the most crucial features of that movement. As I will show, Loy appropriates the discourse of contemporary science and social engineering in order to articulate a far different vision of cultural change.

An offshoot of Darwin's theory of evolution, eugenics emerged as "the science of the improvement of the human race by better breeding."[24] Eugenicists posited the ideal of the purity of racial types, with a racist hierarchy of stock. They also favored controls over reproduction that would prevent the physically or mentally unsound from having children through sterilization or other methods, to ensure the proper evolution of humankind. Spanning the realms of science and social policy, eugenics legitimized (and sought to institutionalize) racism, even as it influenced some reforms in the Progressive Era, including such issues as prohibition, the burgeoning peace movement, the development of contraception, and the treatment of the mentally ill and indigent.[25] But despite this role in some progressive policies, eugenics was racist and protectionist: Its hey-day coincided with racially motivated restrictions on immigration in the United States,[26] which Loy may well have had in mind when she wrote in "Psycho-Democracy" of a "Cosmic Neurosis, whose major symptom is Fear [which] takes the form of international suspicion and the resulting national protective-phobias" (LR 16).[27]

Loy was clearly influenced by eugenical rhetoric, particularly by Sanger's concern over birth control. Indeed, her version of evolution in "Psycho-Democracy" is closest to what Kevles calls "social-radical eugenics," in distinction to "mainline" eugenics — thinking aligned with Fabian Socialism, the movement for sexual liberation, and other liberal causes, whose proponents included George Bernard Shaw. The social-radical eugenicists deplored class distinctions and held that women should be able to have children outside the institution of marriage. There was a working alliance between socialism and feminism instructive in considering Loy's politics, for whether in the destruction of the class system or the advent of the radical concept of sex education, both sets of beliefs underlined the need for new social structures to transform gender roles and sexual behaviors. In fact, many intellectuals gravitated toward topics such as birth control, because these daring notions tended to legitimize the radicalism of their own social circles.[28]

Yet Loy did not sign on to this agenda. Instead, she constructs an idiosyncratic theory of her own. "Psycho-Democracy" espouses an individualistic self-creation that has little to do with breeding the fittest at all. Loy emphasizes the psychic (the movement is based on the laws of "psychic evolution" [*LR* 15]), as opposed to the purely biological, revealing the influence of Freudian and Jungian psychology.[29] For Loy "'Class' is a psychological condition," and "*Cosmic Neurosis*" is her term for "the destructive element in collective consciousness induced by inhibitive social and religious precepts that ordain that man must suffer and cause to suffer and deny the validity of Man's fundamental desires" (*LR* 17, 16). Loy's polemic concerns the damage experienced by repressing the drives, which are linked to "collective consciousness." It was the advent of this new thinking in psychology (and sexuality) that helped lead to the decline of hereditarian attitudes, since any theory that posits childhood and socialization as the source for adult behavior puts the burden on nurture, not nature.[30] Much like Stein, Loy thus both appropriated and redefined psychological theorizing in order to advance a feminist agenda of her own creation.

As Rachel Blau DuPlessis argues, Loy's celebration of hybridity clearly challenges notions of racial purity.[31] Addressing the question of Loy's concepts of race, I suggest an inverse conclusion: In "Anglo-Mongrels" Loy emphasizes the powerful determinants of culture and class, exploring their realization in literary tradition and their crippling effects on the female artist. This set of concerns motivates Loy's linguistic experiments, for only the disruption of existing laws can liberate such future creations as Ova.

Loy's disgust with feminine "breeding" is evident in the character of Ada, Ova's mother, the first female character to appear in Loy's narrative. Ada — the "rose of the hedges" — calls up both national symbol and literary reference (*Roman de la Rose* is only the most obvious), as well as the appropriated tropes of eugenics: We soon see that Ada is a "well-bred" hothouse flower. Appropriately, Exodus first spies her in a cultivated garden: "The terrestrial trees shades / virgin bosoms and blossoms / in course of his acclimatization / a hedge-rose" (Mina Loy, *The Last Lunar Baedeker* 119; hereafter *LLB*). The natural object (the rose) is really artificial; and, conversely, womanhood is scarcely distinguishable from the prettiness of cultivated flowers (in the mere shift of phonemes from "bosoms" to "blossoms"), while the hedge-rose puns on the orderly rows that use nature to create social boundaries.[32] Eugenicists used such agricultural analogies to argue for purity and the dangers of hybrid breeding, a position Loy lampoons by ridiculing the pure-bred product, indicating that, if she endorsed any eugenical thinking, it was in favor of what was known as "hybrid vigor."[33] This rose represents how cultural "currency" creates identity in a shift from foliage to guineas: "The parasite attaches to the English Rose / at a guinea a visit / he becomes   more tangible to himself."

The "English Rose" acquires, too, heavy literary baggage. Following convention, it inherits a Blakean threat (the worm as the less romantic, more scientific "parasite"). Yet money is the primary instrument of power here, a more potent tool than chivalry. Exodus's wooing of the cultivated hedge-rose is more a matter of guineas than of romance. Most important, the purity of the bred rose is already violated by economic contingencies:

> through
> stock quotations
> and Latin prescriptions
> for physic
> filters the lyric
> aroma of the rose. (120)

Even its natural trait — its aroma — is filtered through an economic and cultural verbiage that usurps bodily experience; the body, in fact, needs "physic," and "lyric aroma" (the sickly-sweet smell of the poetically overblown) can do little to heal it. Instead, literature's lyric conventions define its very aroma. In this the hedge-rose, which is anything but pure, Loy uses Ada to subvert the romance of the rose and sully the national symbol of England, which, she implies, merely covers over the economic realities that confront — and define — its people.

Loy's farcical rose is an expression of literary rebellion. Forcing onto the rosy purity of the English national symbol associations of outworn literary traditions and banal (though pressing) economic realities, Loy participates in the modernist rejection of time-worn tropes. DuPlessis points out that William Carlos Williams mocks the stock figure associated with courtly romance and sentiment, which he also links to the feminine. Instead of abandoning it he reclaims it — by making it masculine:

> The banal "rose is obsolete" (S&A 107). But if "to engage roses becomes a geometry," if roses can be "copper roses / steel roses" (S&A 108), then powers of science and technology are grafted to the rose. The sotto voce

> gender narrative in Williams will offer the banal feminine back as the
> property of the despised female artist. . . . He will . . . take hold of, claim,
> the female power grafted to masculine codes.
>
> (Rachel Blau DuPlessis, *The Pink Guitar* 54–55)

The same breeding of feminine and masculine (it is interesting that Du-
Plessis chooses the metaphor of grafting) can be said of Pound, whose rose
takes on the dynamism Pound craved only when it is shaped in steel dust
("Hast 'ou seen the rose in the steel dust?"), magnetized, removed from the
emotive feminine (*Cantos* 463).

Williams and Pound might successfully modernize — read "masculin-
ize" — a tired literary symbol. But, as DuPlessis observes, gender was an
obstruction in their vision. The natural object might have been the ade-
quate symbol in theory, but in practice, when it came to women, both
Williams and Pound not only used symbols in their writing but did so in
highly conventional ways (43). Loy similarly rejects overbred Victorianism,
and she does so by equating it with the rose, sign of the unhealthy hege-
mony of the feminine in English culture.[34] The irony of this stance illus-
trates the complex dilemma Loy faced: striving to become modern, in
Burke's phrase, even as she becomes feminist. If Pound, Williams, or the
strident Wyndham Lewis were to serve as models, Loy would have to ab-
jure female identity in order to assume the stance of (masculine) modernist
innovator. The modernist trope of despised conventionality as feminine —
signaled by the wearily symbolic rose — threatens a crisis of identity and
voice for the female poet.

In my view, however, it was a useful difficulty. It was incumbent on Loy
to develop an idiom that could merge modernist condemnation of the fem-
inine with a feminist consciousness sorely lacking in such avant-garde rhet-
oric as that of Lewis's journal *BLAST*, with its vitriol against the "effeminate
lout within" the ailing English nation. Refusing both the feminine sweet-
ness of conventional lyricism and masculinist avant-garde misogyny, Loy
arrives at a middle ground. She writes herself out of the difficulty through
parody — an over-determination of the very tropes that cause the female
poet so much trouble. It is no coincidence that Loy's section on Ada, "En-
glish Rose," is the first that employs her strategy of satiric overwriting:

Early English everlasting
    quadrate Rose
    paradox-Imperial

trimmed with some travestied flesh
tinted with bloodless duties dewed
with Lipton's teas
and grimed with crack-packed
herd-housing
petalling
the prim gilt
penetralia
of a luster-scioned
core-crown (121)

Here, surely, is an instance of the quality Pound saw in Loy that led him to invent the term "logopoeia," a writing that is a "dance of the intelligence among words and ideas." Loy presents the English woman as bloodless, bodiless, and, in effect, mindless, attacking the English "paradox-Imperial" as the source of English womanhood. At the same time, however, this over-writing deflates through abundance; assonance and alliteration over-whelm to the point of parody. The stylistic fault of "verbal inflation" (in-cluding hyperbole and extravagant figures) was commonly denounced by nineteenth-century literary critics. Loy seems to exploit just such forays into overtroping for satiric effect.[35] The heavy assonance of "Early English everlasting" mocks the pompous presumption of the everlasting hegemony of the empire, and, in "trimmed with some travestied flesh," alliteration un-derlines the idea that flesh itself is travestied in women like Ada, who do not value the body, who should, instead, use their "unbiased bravery to de-stroy the impurity of sex — for the sake of [their] self-respect" (271).

The elaborate use of effect reveals a mastery of poetic technique. But Loy's overdoing of technique trivializes it, in a parody of English self-seriousness. Neologism and hyphenation provide a superfluity of asso-nance and alliteration — "paradox-Imperial," "crack-packed," "prim gilt / penetralia," "luster-scioned / core-crown." Such lines assault the conven-tions of ornamental, Tennysonian sound-play.[36] But beyond the parody of Victorian aesthetics, this overdetermined poetic emphasizes that linguistic practice — in poetry or in common speech — effectively, if subtly, deter-mines the parameters of appropriate gender behavior. The densely ironic "prim gilt / penetralia," for example, is a euphemism for "genitalia," ap-parently omitted by any "prim" speaker of English, even as it puns on sex-ual penetration, superficial efforts at grandeur ("gilt"), and culturally ingrained sexual "guilt." Such moments alert the reader to the ways language usage influences perception — as it has determined the identity of the well-bred English rose.

Pound missed the political import of Loy's word-play, calling her writing "poetry that is akin to nothing but language," seemingly divorced not just from lyric emotionalism but from contemporary culture. Yet he was right in identifying Loy's poetics as avoiding "the stupidity beloved of the 'lyric' enthusiast," for that is precisely her target in "English Rose."[37] Attacking the feminine, as did Pound and Williams, Loy uses word-play to achieve the distance she needs, as a woman poet, from the overly lyrical rose, and to insert, instead, an oppositional feminist avant-garde aesthetic. Her target throughout is the culture that produces well-bred women like Ada, whose minds are so shaped by the twin forces of romance and misogynistic fear of the body that they are nothing more than ornamental "Blossom[s] Populous."

Further, this jab at English mores mocks a form of cultural, not biological, breeding that impedes self-development, the "covered entrance to Infinity" (*LLB* 281): The English Rose — both female and nation-state — is "self-pruned / of the primordial attributes," possessing "a tepid heart," having been bred to the point of "mystic incest with its ancestry," existing in a stifling "pink paralysis." Equating this feminine cultivation with English imperialism, Loy describes "A World-Blush / glowing from / a never-setting-sun / Conservative Rose," invoking the cliché (England's "never-setting sun") to satirize the imperialist project that is also at the root of women's "blushes" at home.[38] Loy condemns the masculine "trouser-striped prongs of statesmanship" as well as the breeding of women into a "post-conceptual / virginity" supposedly "of Nature."

Gender typing — the separation of masculine and feminine traits — is evoked here not just in the narrative but, more significant, in the recourse to stylistic disruption. Loy embraced a Jungian sexual complementarity that has political and aesthetic implications: "For the harmony of the race, each individual should be the expression of an easy & ample interpenetration of the male & female temperaments" (*Lost* 155); she described herself as both "the most female thing extant" and "somewhat masculine" in the same breath (*LLB* lxviii). Here she implicates the imperialism of the state in the vapidity of English womanhood, for England *is* the "Conservative Rose / storage / of British Empire-made pot-pourri / of dry dead men making a sweetened smell / among a shrivelled collectivity" (122). The lovely scent of feminine potpourri is created by the Empire, the "dry dead men" whose statesmanship supports the "shrivelled collectivity" Loy bemoaned in "Psycho-Democracy." Loy thus uses the rose to mock the feminization of national identity — the same target Lewis aimed for in his Vorticist manifestos in *BLAST*. Yet Loy creates a critical difference from male avant-garde writers' perspective on femininity, or from Modernists' masculinization of the rose. She implies that England must take responsibility for the "ideological pink" (124) that divorces women from their bodies, dulls their minds, and belies the fundamental androgyny of both individual and collective identities. Most crucial, the "shrivelled collectivity" must unfasten the link between language and gender.

The ideological role of literature is one of Loy's central concerns. Ada ("Albion") and Exodus ("Israel") are shaped by cultural imperatives, bred to particular desires through the ideology of romance. Exodus's first view of the "insidious pink" flower is an introduction to "Albion's ideal" (122), a type the émigré can hardly resist. His desire parodies that of the hero of the *Roman*, who sees the rose in a garden reflected in a pool and instantly begins his quest. This "rose / rises / from the green / of a green lane / rosily-stubborn / and robustly round // Under a pink print / sunbonnet" (123). Domesticated, ordinary, in the pink print of English girlhood, the rose is ridiculous as the object of an epic desire that will propel Exodus and Ada toward each other: "the alien Exodus," in courtly form, "lays siege / to the thick hedgerows / where she blows / on Christian Sundays." Modern-day epic siege (military and erotic) consists of no more than a weekly pilgrimage to the private park protected by hedgerows. Deflating romantic quest, Loy reduces the dialogue between lover and beloved to the psychology of haves and have-nots. The outsider to the English class system inevitably conflates money and desire: He is "loaded with Mosaic / passions that amass / like money." As in Loy's account of the economic basis of marriage in her "Feminist Manifesto" (*Lost* 155), this courtship shows heroic love to be a front: Even a "pearl beyond price" (126) can be bought with guineas. "Men & women are enemies," Loy writes, "with the enmity of the exploited for the parasite, the parasite for the exploited" (*Lost* 154).

"English Rose" testifies to the unhealthy power of the romantic ethos — what Loy called "sexual dependence" — on women. Her avant-garde innovations in "Anglo-Mongrels" are a means to intervene in the ideological workings of such convention. We learn that Ada is the pawn of romance, whose myths have helped alienate her from her own sexuality. Nourished on the novel (heir to both epic and romance), Ada lives not for a real lover but for an ideal script of chivalric attentions:

Maiden emotions
breed
on leaves of novels
where anatomical man
has no notion
of offering other than the bended knee
to femininity

. . .

For in those days
when Exodus courted the rose
literature was supposed to elevate us (124)

Desiring only symbolic gesture — the bended knee — Ada is horrified by the body, the "anatomical man" whose sexuality she finds revolting, having been bred on "the Anglo-Saxon phenomenon / of Virginity" and trained to treasure her chastity, "the fictitious value of woman as identified with her physical purity" (*Lost* 154). The cult of virtue leads women to devalue their bodies and to allow their "maiden emotions" to "breed / on leaves of novels" rather than in response to flesh and blood. While Exodus covets the "pearl beyond price" of national acceptance through marriage, Ada "expect[s] / the presented knee / of chivalry" and is alarmed by "the sub-umbilical mystery" (126) of sex. The insistent rhyme here strains the lines along, mocking the poeticism of Ada's romantic (certainly not sensual) conceptions. And in the last judgment, Loy informs us, "Jehovah / roars 'Open your mouth! / and I will tell you what you have been reading'" (125). Exodus and Ada are no more than the sum of the day's cultural imperatives — "people / who know not what they do / but know that what they do / is not illegal" (127).

That these two decide to "unite their variance / in marriage" (126) furthers Loy's indictment of social engineering and sexual repression. But language is the potent and elusive instrument of the gender ideology Loy deplores. Ada's actions are dictated by "ideological pink," so that "an impenetrable pink curtain / hangs between [the rose] and itself" (128), keeping all men but those "possessed / of exorbitant incomes" at abeyance. Language is the fabric of the veil. "[T]he ap parent impecca bility / of the

English" is manifest in speech, which Loy picks apart on the page. "Impec-
cability" is derided, divided into syllables that invoke other meanings: The
role of "parentage" in social status, the "sin" which is the root of the word,
and the petty sound of "peck" emerging from the "impeccable."[39] Loy's
final reflection in "English Rose" concerns the tyranny of class — returning
to Exodus's father's transgression of class boundaries and anticipating Ova's
difficult inheritance. The petals of the now-dissected national rose are
"hung / with tongues" that "may never sing in concert":

> for some
> singing h
> flat and some
> h sharp "The Arch
> angels sing H"

> There reigns a disproportionate
> dis'armony
> in the English Hanthem (130)

Loy's logopoeia is anything but *purely* about language, as Pound asserted,
for language is the arm of gender and class ideology. In her "Futurist Man-
ifesto," Loy prophesies that the "language of the Future" will evolve only
from the "obscenities" and "blasphemies" through which "sounds shall dis-
solve back to their innate senselessness" (*Lost* 152) and take on new, as yet
unthought-of meanings. For now, however, h flat and h sharp speak the
"dis'armony" of a hierarchical society whose very "Hanthem" is sung with
class difference encoded in its very pronunciation. For this very reason, Loy
closes "English Rose" by referring to a satire as disruptive as her own:

> And for further information
> re the Rose —
> and what it does to the nose
> while smelling it
> See *Punch* (130)

The businesslike memo deflates the Rose again, dwelling bluntly on its un-
healthy effects, while the vibrant blasphemy of *Punch* suggests that satire is
a healthier manifestation of English culture than the dying "Hanthem."

Revealing the rationale behind Loy's fusing of feminist politics with
avant-garde poetics, "English Rose" illustrates the need to resist gender
norms. In response to the repressions of English culture, evident in roman-

tic myth and literary conceit, Loy implies that only a Butlerian subversion of gender norms might liberate the indoctrinated. And yet, this daring is hardly apparent in either Ada or Exodus. For the moment, only Loy's poetics itself — the avant-garde disruption effected by the style of strategic overwriting — allows the reader the distance to imagine a world freed from the stifling stench of the sickly English rose.

Loy's poetics, constructed to alter the reader's consciousness of linguistic and gender norms, complements the plot of "Anglo-Mongrels," which embodies defiance and radical change in the person of Ova, who is — literally — a result of a taboo cross-breeding that threatens the purity of the race. Eugenicists classified hybrids as "disharmonious"[40] and, according to that definition, this "Mongrel Rose," product of divergent national strains, would be an unfortunate birth. But Ova's travails, unlike those of the hothouse Ada, promise a model of how to mock, if not altogether escape, even the most powerful ideological control. Ova's birth symbolizes the arrival of feminist consciousness — and the female body — in English culture and poetry. The mixed-breed girl-child personifies the disruptions in Loy's texts, the uncouth mixing of stylistic elements, whose blasphemies jar existing traditions. A possible agent of much-needed derision, Ova has the potential to resist cultural and linguistic harmony — to clear the way for a new inheritance through the sanguine effects of feminist avant-garde intervention.

The crucial aspect of Ova's disharmony is that it is gender-based. In emphasizing gender, Loy moves her heroine's story away from eugenics, which generally did not invoke gender specificity; rather, the traits passed on to future generations came from either parent, and specific qualities were not attributable to either sex.[41] Yet as Christine Battersby has demonstrated, genius has never been a gender-neutral term, and the power of *logos*, from Stoic philosophy through biblical sources, is associated, quite literally, with the male seed: *Logos spermatikos* permits the father to pass down the attributes of the species, a concept repeated in the patrilineal descent upheld by the Church fathers.[42] For this reason, Battersby argues, the great artist, from Romantic rhetoric through Jungian androgyny "is a *feminine male*," a "genius" capable of benefiting from his own inner femininity, whereas, to the contrary, "the masculine woman merely *parodies* the male Logos." Thus "feminine" is often positive when applied to male writers, while the term remains derogatory when applied to women writers, effectively excluding women from creative genius (7–8). It is this version of inheritance that Loy draws on, in biological terms, to represent Ova's cultural dilemma. Loy's parody of the male logos presents Ova's mongrelization as a mixture of sex-specific attributes summed up in the very term "female poet": she is disharmonious in her makeup because she inherits the male brain in a female body. In Wittig's terms, an inescapable mark of gender will determine Ova's speech and language. Her very being (emblematic in her name) evidences "a primitive ontological concept that enforces in language a division of beings into sexes." Like Wittig, too, Loy reveals that "there is nothing natural about this notion" (*Straight Mind* 76–77).

Loy's narrative thus posits the female poet's status as mongrel — a position that both enables and stalls her creative powers. Albion and Exodus produce a "composite / Anglo-Israelite" (132) whose legacy has as much to do with gender as with race: Ova receives a Jewish (masculine) brain in an English (female) body. While Ada offers Ova the undesirable birthright of the female body, allegorically represented in her name, the godmother "Survival" bequeaths her a masculine intellect: "Curse till the cows come home / Behold my gift / The Jewish brain!" (132).[43] "The mystic absolute / the rose" is cursed with "the computations / of the old / Jehovah's gender"; Ova is purely neither English Protestant nor Hungarian Jew, neither "true" woman nor man. Ova, in fact, should be a most productive woman; as Loy argues in her "Feminist Manifesto," sexuality, intellect, and the maternal function cannot be divorced: "the woman who is a poor mistress will be an incompetent mother — an inferior mentality — & will enjoy an inadequate apprehension of **LIFE**" (*Lost* 154). Yet such a woman, in English culture, is a misfit; hence the invocation of a Darwinian survival that threatens to extinguish Ova — a merely incipient life, a culturally premature "egg" — altogether.

By contrast, we have Esau Penfold, Ova's counterpart, the pure-bred male reared for literary genius. Based on Loy's first husband, Stephen Haweis, this "infant aesthete" inherits the birthright denied Ova — a guaranteed spot in the mainstream of English literary life. In "Enter Esau Penfold," Esau's mother is seen breeding her male-child for a high culture career. She is "authoress" both of him and the instructional book that predicts his future:

Patricia Penfold's preface
from the publishers
the "author's
copy" circulating at the small

and informal reception
for wiseacres and waisted-women
"To view" Esau and his authoress
in their accurate draperies (133)

In Loy's satiric turn on the subject-rhyme between creation and birth, Esau's authoress (a parody of the literary patroness) has engendered "only" a life. Her greater ambition will be realized through Esau, who will father a purer birth, "Beauty" (143).[44] The scenario corresponds to Battersby's account of the gendering of genius; literary creation is reserved for the son, that of (literal) procreation for the woman/mother.[45] Complete with "fifteenth-century / andirons" and "treasures of Tibet" (134), "the Penfold residence" (135) provides Esau with a cultural birthright that the mongrel Ova, whose house boasts only "an oleograph / of 'The Cat's Fancy Ball'" (135), is denied. Loy seems to assume that such cultural cachet is necessary to the poet — that the individual talent must engage with tradition — and paints Ova as culturally deprived. Loy even alters her actual address in middle-class West Hampstead to Ova's working-class Kilburn, as though to emphasize her deprivation (see *Becoming Modern* 352). Yet Loy also implies that Ova's exclusion fuels her creations — predicting Loy's own idiosyncratic and irreverent art.

Given her gender, Ova's best bet is to play Jacob to the poem's Esau — to dress up as the favored son and steal the words necessary to succeed to her inheritance.[46] Taking account of the powerful cultural forces against her, Loy doesn't easily grant Ova Jacob's success. In fact, language acquisition only brings an awareness of the feminine dissociation from the body that characterizes Ada, even as, ironically, the body seems to be Ova's primary inheritance.[47]

Socialized early, Esau is articulate, precocious, and satisfied: At five, Esau "suavely smiles / to a professor of anthropology" that he has everything "'to delight the heart of a child'" (134). By contrast, Ova's prelinguistic existence harbors a promise of imaginative flight sadly dashed by her entrance — or fall — into language. Depicting a poet's emerging consciousness, Loy describes a Paterian exploration, a genderless creative process. Coaxing "the caryatid of an idea" (135), the wandering consciousness "quickens / to colour-thrusts / of the quintessent light" (136). The abstractions and sensory evocations in the passage are closer to Joycean epiphany than to the topical irony of "English Rose." Here, Loy implies, is early consciousness in the prelinguistic state that DuPlessis brilliantly captures in an account of her daughter's language acquisition. This realm is far from silent:

> there is babble and pulse, intonation, mark and sign. There is everything of language in it but specificity and form. It is the place that could be any language. . . . If this area represents the mother, it is a mother visualized as a font of linguality, as well as a mother (they say) repressed by virtue of the transfer of power and allegiance by means of oedipalization: the learning of gender asymmetry, inequalities, one's place in a gendered order. (*Pink Guitar* 85)

It is precisely this "learning of gender asymmetry" that awaits Ova — with the fall into language, and the return of Loy's own strategic overwriting.

The exploratory mind, along with Loy's Joycean verse, are quickly cut off, representing the disjunction between body and word — and between mother and daughter. Ova's quickening mind thrives

> until a woman's
> ineludable claws of dominion
> lift her above the Elysian
> fields of flame
>
> in a receding
> prison
> of muscular authority (136)

This entrapping female does little besides mirror patriarchal domination; Loy's overwriting (as in the inflated diction of "Elysian / fields of flame") emphasizes that female "claws of dominion" assert an imperial, "ineludable" power over the child. That the mother should be seen as "a receding / prison / of muscular authority" points not to pre-Oedipal union but to a fear of the maternal, like that of male avant-garde writers from Marinetti to Georges Bataille:[48] Ova must escape the maternal "prison" of the feminine, flee from "the heavy upholstered / stuffing" of their bodies, a sort of Victorian furniture without sensuality or fluidity — a position Loy certainly felt in regard to her mother's strict Victorianism. Loy's text thus diverges from theories that propose a pre-Oedipal union that the daughter retains even *after* acquiring language. Margaret Homans, for example, discusses female "bilinguality": the daughter "has the positive experience of never having given up entirely the presymbolic communication that carries over, with the bond to the mother, beyond the preoedipal period. The daughter therefore speaks two languages at once."[49]

mina loy's "anglo-mongrels and the rose" 53

Homans's bilingual female speaker seems to escape the *cultural* associations of language that Loy is conscious of — the forces that make women of one generation differ from those of the next, or, in Ova's case, make the mother, already indoctrinated into a misogynistic culture, a threat rather than a comfort. Loy's poetic dilemma is closer to the question DuPlessis poses: "How can we 'deconstruct' a language we 'never' possessed before?" (*Pink Guitar* 60). At this point, then, Loy reverses poles: Having lost the pre-Oedipal "quintessent light," might she steal the language of Esau — and be free of the maternal "claws"? Signifying this hope, the "curious glare" Ova indulges in is coded as masculine — it is "virile," a word for which there is no feminine equivalent (135–36).[50]

Finally, despite her need to reject the overcultivated feminine, language acquisition is still riddled with disappointment, for it entails a patrilineal inheritance that threatens to determine her very consciousness.[51] Moments before her first awareness of words as symbols, Ova senses mystery:

> The child
> > whose wordless
> > thoughts
> > grow like visionary plants
>
> > finds
> > nothing objective new
> > and only words
> > mysterious (139)

Ova's imagination returns us to the natural — unlike the sequence about the all-too-artificial rose. Her thoughts are Coleridgean, organic — "visionary plants." Although Ova finds nothing new, she connects with the mysterious *through* words, for they have not yet lost their palpable quality. Here Loy's overwriting gives way to a simpler and more expressive representation of an emerging consciousness, with plainer diction and less extravagant craft.[52]

Yet irony reemerges almost immediately, for the disjunction between Ova's *experience* of language and its *signification* forecasts the trouble the female poet will encounter in forging a new consciousness. The mystery she believes she is privy to, the magical sound of words, is belied by their meaning, which leads in the crudest fashion back to the body that Ova's name signifies; unlike the "infant aesthete" Esau, who already exists in a sophisticated linguistic world, the girl-child is trapped between symbol and thing. Ova yearns to explore the physical quality of words. She watches for a word's "materialization." In Loy's tragic-comic account, its incarnation is no more than the sound "iarrhea" (139). Truncated, not even fully signifying, the word represents waste, the physical run amok, illness, the abject. The beauty of pure sound — the vowels, the internal rhyme, the rhythm of two perfect trochees — appeals to the soon-to-be poet, yet the word can never match her expectations once the symbolic attaches meaning to it. Nothing, Loy seems to say, is pure — not breeds of humans or roses, and certainly not words. Instead of an initiation into power, the moment of language acquisition reaffirms the domination of male-appropriated women, severe "armored towers / [. . .] bending / in iron busks / of curved corsets / consulting" (140). Strategic overwriting returns with the fall into the symbolic, as the ironic alliteration of "curved corsets / consulting" debunks the task of nurturing. The new baby "lies / in the young mother's / arms of indignation." The mother loathes her bodily function, and Ova is powerless as before.

Rather than a liberation, language acquisition is part of Ova's disappointing inheritance. The child overhears and records talk — "It is / quite green." In Lockean fashion, she will associate two distinct sensations: the word, however mangled ("iarrhea"), and the color (green). Her mind is not unlike the substance described, a "cerebral / mush convolving in her skull / an obsessional / colour-fetish // veers / to the souvenir / of the delirious ball / deleted / in the ivied / dust" (140–41). The quest for meaning has begun, as a "simultaneity / of ideas // embodies / the word" (141). Ova searches for the ball — the "orb of verdigris" her new understanding has given her. The "globe terrestial [*sic*] / of olive-jewel / dilates" (142). Here again, inflated diction captures the gap between words and objects, the failure of the thing and the sound to connect for the young female poet; through euphemism, we avoid what the word really embodies, and the recourse to the Latinate ("verdigris") and the overblown ("olive-jewel") renders ironic the child's first search for meaning in the form of a lost ball. The quest, ironically echoing that of the *roman*'s hero, ends in disappointment: disappearing under the furniture "to look for it // She is pulled out by her leg" (142). Like Jacob — the one who usurps Esau's birthright, and who emerges from the womb clutching Esau's heel — Ova is born into language in a moment of contest.

The prison of the Exodus household that Ova is now a part of leads Loy to suggest ironic kinships between the battle-royal of marriage and the tenets of the then-popular notion of Darwinian survival, which, just as powerfully, must lead to breaking culture's rules in an avant-gardist performance. Loy's writing becomes far more discursive, markedly less disruptive, as she asserts the conviction that informs her poetics and politics:

> Oh God
> that men and women
> having undertaken to vanquish one another
> should be allowed
> to shut themselves up in hot boxes and breed
> spirits of prey
> ceaselessly
> on the watch in their cruel privacy
>
> Seizing upon occasion
> for crippling the personal
>
> to test the law of the craftiest for survival
>
> . . .
>
> until at last the vanquished mate dies
> of modification (143–44)

The eugenical sentiment in this passage might well reflect the liberal view that preventing the feeble or deficient from being born was kinder than providing for them once they enter society.[53] Yet far from preaching about the appropriate breeding of men and women, in which the issue (for eugenicists) was finding suitable mates, Loy shows that culture itself is killing England. It is the institution of marriage that imposes a Darwinian imperative on offspring and "mates." These "hot boxes" are not unlike the cages and boxes that appear in Loy's unpublished memoir, *The Child and the Parent*, as images for the bonds of marriage. In both cases, the "spirits of prey" do battle, and the "boxes" succeed in "crippling the personal," until only the "craftiest" survive.[54]

The result of a psychic disharmony, an alien speaker of her culture's tongue, Ova must strive to "[make] moon-flowers out of muck" (142), to negotiate a male aesthetic in her female body: The "mongrel-girl / of No-man's land / coerce[s] the shy / Spirit of Beauty / from excrements and physic" (143). In the "Noman's land" of the female speaker, and the female body, Ova is doomed to an impossible alchemy. Esau, like Pound's Mauberley, is "out of key with his time," striving to "flatten" the multiplicity of life "to one vast monopattern"; rather than plunging into the future, he is trapped in a fin-de-siècle aestheticism through which he "absorbs the erudite idea / that Beauty IS nowhere / except posthumously to itself / in the antique" (143). But Ova is threatened far more profoundly, for the mother's obsession with her girl-child's "vile origin" makes "subliminal depredations / on Ova's brain" (147), impeding the "intuition" on which Loy based "Psycho-Democracy":

> Lacking dictionaries
> of inner consciousness
> unmentionable stigmata
> is stamped
> by the parent's solar-plexus
> in disequilibrium
> on the offspring's
> intuition (148)

Even intuition is shaped by cultural imperatives; even inner consciousness must have its dictionaries. Lacking adequate language, Ova finds the stigmata inherited from her Christian mother "unmentionable," for there is no language with which to articulate the dilemmas of the female body. Ideological "disequilibrium" (like the disharmony of the English class system) is passed down from mother to offspring through ideology, and the wound threatens permanently to affect the daughter's intuition.

Interestingly, an outsider to the drama emerges as the avant-gardist hero — and instructor — in this story about the emerging *female* artist: Colossus, "the male fruit / of a Celtic couple" who understands early that "'All words are lies'" (150). His gender allows Colossus to muster strength against the feminine middle class: "he sits up / devouring his pap / it is as if a pillar of iron / erects him," and, conquering the female body, he "communes within himself." In defiance of "his ancestors" and "His gracious little lady-bird / of a mamma" (150), Colossus flouts convention and assaults the culture he inherits, scorning the feminine ("throwing the tea-pot / at Mme Fallilot") and discarding religion ("pissing into our reverend pastor's hat" [151]) in avant-gardist acts of rebellion. Loy's relish for Colossus's high-jinks must come, in part, from her model for the role — her great love, and second husband, Arthur Cravan, the "poet-pugilist" who outraged and intrigued European and American artistic circles for a decade.[55] It is in fact only through Colossus that Loy can depict her fantasy of irreverence, realized through his masculinity: "when his governess offers him a bun / 'Bring me a bifteck de femme / — and under done!'" His distaste for the entrapping feminine is released in wild displays unavailable to Ova, until "These women run / in all directions," their forces scattered by the Rimbaudesque "criminal" (151). Unlike Ova, Colossus suffers from no gender disharmony: the outlaw-poet, Loy implies, must be a man.

Wittig puts the problem simply: "Gender then must be destroyed." The job will require "a transformation of language as a whole" (*Straight Mind* 81). Loy would have agreed wholeheartedly. But "Anglo-Mongrels" indicates that she was far less sanguine than her postmodern successor. Instead of leading, like Odysseus's travels, to an inevitable return home for a triumphant hero, Loy's epic ends with inconclusive flight: Loy evokes the tyranny of cultural indoctrination for women into a sacrosanct tradition, one difficult to escape. Yet "Anglo-Mongrels" also demonstrates Loy's more mature politics and poetics — and in this way, if no others, Loy allows us to witness her own evolution toward belief in the marriage of radical feminism and avant-garde activism.

The final sequences of "Anglo-Mongrels" center on Ova's betrayal — through language — by the father, and her subsequent, if only implicit, move toward another kind of language use. First, "The Surprise" and "The Gift" connect cultural determinacy to the workings of a male-dominated language, through which Exodus betrays Ova. The surprise is a basket of cotton Japanese fishes from the jovial "Miss Bunn."[56] Father and daughter create a bond with an illicit act: "'We will not tell Miss Bunn' / says father 'what we have done / peeping in the basket'" (162). The promise of not telling cements a pact between them. Yet when Ova is asked "'Have you peeped in the basket?'" she must either lie or betray them both. Choosing the former, reinforcing their bond, she is not rewarded but betrayed by the father, who has no compunctions about sacrificing her: he "snaps," "'you opened that surprise / under my eyes'" (162). The real surprise comes when she is transformed from compatriot to "'Liar.'" The same forces she and her father subverted demand her exile:

> She is turned into a liar
> by father
> they push her
> out of the front door with their hands (162)

Her banishment becomes literal; expelled from the house, she "decides to travel" (163). But "a hand upon her shoulder / jolts her / with mocking laughter / bolts her / to smoulder / once more / behind the door" (163). Imprisonment in the confines of the house, and within the narrow confines of the existing language, is inevitable. Having learned to distrust the father, she also learns that language is the instrument of lies.

Centering on puns on the word "sovereign" (king, father, autonomous agent, unit of money), a later section emphasizes "the pockets of the Father" (165) — his financial and social power — and the humiliation of the daughter in "a sullen / economic war." She is enjoined to "obey him" so that, according to his discretion, "he can bestow / upon her whatever she pray him" (165). "He seems a sovereign / The maximum / of money / A golden octopus / grasping," while she longs for the world of her imagination:

> She is asking
>
> for a sovereign
> to buy a circus universe
>
> Laughing
> he gives her a shining coin
>
> She is exalted
> in spontaneous knowledge of beauty (165–66)

She discovers his trick only when she uses the coin as though its power were hers. When the sovereign is revealed to be "'a new farthing'" and she a "'little fool'" (166), she understands the complicity of father, money, social exchange — the tyranny of the social contract:

> How evil a Father must be
> to burst a universe by getting
> so far into a sovereign (167)

The position of patriarch and the monetary exchange it affords him convert him to "evil," and he "bursts" her imaginative universe. Ova, representing the female body, is initiated into the social, and her first lesson is her powerlessness in language and finances alike.

Social breeding in such episodes represents a perverse alchemy: The lead of the child is transformed into the gold of (the father's) culture. Caught in a system she longs to escape, Ova reaches toward liberty and "her heritage of emigration" (170), ironically adopting the terms of monetary success to define her rebellion against the "sovereign": She

"sets out to seek her fortune"
in her turn
trusting to terms of literature
dodging the breeders' determination
not to return "entities sent on consignment"
by their maker Nature
except in a condition
of moral
effacement (171)

Her turn must indeed be on her own terms, if she is to avoid the destiny mapped out for her (or determined for her, in Loy's pun on "determination") by the "breeders" intent on holding on to her, a commodity on consignment. For the female protagonist, epic return must give way to anti-epic escape. If Tillyard is right in asserting that epic expresses the norms of its society and reestablishes its codes, then the genre must be revised — if not rejected — by the female poet.[57] Ova's future depends on her ability to re-create the "terms of literature" — to steal Esau's birthright. But the social world depends on the continuance of its rules. Hence her recapture "into the hands of her procreators" (171). Unlike Joyce's Stephen, Ova will find escape impossible. Like the gazing and mute subjects of Loy's early poem "Virgins Minus Dots," Ova is condemned to be inside, to fulfill the race destiny of her procreators.

Ova's mongrel nature bespeaks the imperatives of the feminist avant-garde: Although her fate seems sealed, her story anticipates the oppositional art of "Anglo-Mongrels." To get there, the woman poet takes recourse not to violent overthrow but to more subtle subversion, to clear the path for the evolution of gender. The final meditation in "Anglo-Mongrels" marks the difference between male avant-gardist gestures of rebellion — like those of Colossus or "Raminetti" — and the divergent methods available to the female poet. Loy advocates a pragmatic strategy of linguistic subversion — one that co-opts the culture's devices to challenge its legacy.

Loy concludes "Anglo-Mongrels" with the ideal of androgynous creation, finding a metaphor in the tailoring that is Exodus's profession. In a reversal of Loy's depiction of the sovereign father/law, Loy ironically chooses the father as prototype for feminist avant-garde poetics.[58] There is, at any rate, no question of Exodus's outsider status: "despised / distrusted" for his manufacture of "fig-leaves" that remind the wearer of the body beneath, "he chose / an occupation all too feminine" (*LLB* 175) — indeed, an occupation that even by Loy's day had long served as a trope for female artistic production. Loy's invocation of the tailor suggests Loy's ideal of the artist, one that combines the feminine and masculine.[59] The covering that is language — the social fabric — can never be discarded; it can simply be recut. The tailor remakes what is given; in the problematic of body and language, the tailor is the conjurer of pragmatic solutions, the priest of the real. Loy's apologia for her poetics implies that change emerges from cutting, hemming, and trimming language — an antiessentialist position more tempered than Loy's early, Futurist desire to use "blasphemy" and "obscenity" to destroy conventional language. It is an explanation for her impulse to alter language even as she exists in it, to embrace not violent rebellion but individual acts of evolution, retouching the social fabric by unraveling and respinning the material of the word. And, although Loy's final figure is not Ova — the allegorical female body — but the exiled, male/female tailor, she still refuses to idealize the androgyne as a utopic ideal, as did many avant-garde writers of her time. Loy's figure parallels Woolf's androgynous ideal in *A Room of One's Own*, a notion explored by other innovative women writers, including Djuna Barnes and H.D. (André Breton also bases part of the revolution in consciousness in the "Manifesto of Surrealism" on androgyny).[60] Tailoring is no easy task, and it is clearly a thankless one; the androgyne is ever despised, never embraced, and the sewing the creator accomplishes is a restitching of culture, neither overthrow nor fresh making. This is the best Loy has to offer in answer to the inheritance of language. Ova must be multilingual, and she must, like Exodus, stitch her own inheritance.

At the close of "Anglo-Mongrels and the Rose," Ova's destiny hangs in the balance, and Exodus's social status remains precarious. Loy's parodic account of the birth of a feminist avant-gardist seems to conclude that the categories "female" and "poet" may never be viewed as mutually inclusive — at least not in light of existing literary traditions. Loy never undertook the larger project of forging an alternative *feminist* tradition, as did such modernists as H.D.; nor did she locate a source of myth or history that would enable a more radical vision, obviating her satire of familiar tropes drawn from a predominantly masculine tradition. Indeed, by 1927 Loy had already refused various editors' solicitations of her work. After leaving Paris for

New York, Loy increasingly withdrew from artistic circles altogether. Asked years later to consider issuing a book of poems, Loy responded, "I was never a poet" (*LLB* lxxviii).[61]

But although her critique of racist and sexist ideology leaves Ova's fate uncertain, Loy offers avenues of resistance to the feminist avant-gardist intent on altering consciousness through an altered tongue. Her satiric overwriting assaults literary tradition in an entirely new breed of feminist poetics, and her attack on gender binarism is far-reaching. As my next chapters show, resistance to gender difference — which draws Stein and Loy together — continues to play a central role among recent feminist avant-gardists. But while writers like Stein, Loy, and Barnes share concerns about the "new woman" in the modern age, a shift into the 1960s and beyond reveals still more diverse expressions of feminist avant-garde poetics — from the theorizing of race and revolution to the search for a feminist avant-garde tradition with a diverse history of its own.

AGENDAS OF RACE & GENDER

II

3
"a fo / real / revolu /shun"

Sonia Sanchez and the Black Arts Movement

Writing at the height of the Black Power movement of the late 1960s, Amiri Baraka (LeRoi Jones) called for a "Black Art" packing heat — for "dagger poems," "Poems that shoot / guns." With activist Larry Neal and others of the Black Arts movement, Baraka issued manifestolike declarations of war on "wite" America. This militant black nationalism was hardly intended to bring to mind the old news of European avant-garde coteries. But in theorizing that a new aesthetic could foment revolution, leaders of the Black Arts movement indeed shared the assumptions of their radical precursors: Baraka's "assassin poems" are in fact adapted from Guillaume Apollinaire. The connection is one of ethos, if not specific agendas: Black Arts theorists believed, like their radical predecessors, that innovative art has the potential to draw cultural and political battle lines, to transform consciousness, and ultimately to play a role in revolutionizing the world.[1]

Like other women involved in the Black Arts movement, Sonia Sanchez revealed ambivalence about the nature of that struggle. Like Loy before her, Sanchez experienced conflicts as a woman poet both working within, and remaining resistant to, a revolutionary avant-garde rhetoric. Sanchez's work reveals a tension between two often-conflicting causes — those of black unity and of a specifically black *feminist* consciousness. This struggle is apparent not just in her subject matter — which focuses on racial oppression and rage — but in her poetic form and idiom. Sanchez's first books, published in 1969 and 1970, resonate with the language of black empowerment and the liberating potential of black rage, and her work of this period is dedicated to the Black Arts project: it fosters the awareness that "the black artist is dangerous" (Claudia Tate, ed., *Black Women Writers at Work* 135) and asserts that "the most fundamental truth to be told in any art form, as far as Blacks are concerned, is that America is killing us." Through its disruption of poetic business as usual, Sanchez's writing will be "a clarion call to the values of change" (Evans, in *Black Women Writers* 416). Even the use of Black English, as in Black Arts poetry generally, is a political gesture that testifies to the primacy of language in a rebellious cultural politics. At the same time, the very characteristic that epitomizes the movement's avant-gardism — its pursuit of political overthrow through the shock of a new aesthetic — impedes Sanchez from asserting a feminist agenda in concert with Black Arts revolution.

In much of this early work, if not her more tempered recent writing, Sanchez endorses the notion of a violent transformation that would be carried out by maintaining racial unity and avoiding internal conflict — including feminist critiques of masculinist black power. Elsewhere, however, Sanchez voices a feminist alternative for change — in particular, to address the problems of gender relations and roles both within the movement and in the larger spheres of black *and* white America. In this chapter, I start by identifying Black Arts as an avant-garde movement to help elucidate its goals and rhetoric and also to challenge the association between the term "avant-garde" and a solely European-derived art. I then focus on Sanchez's avant-garde writing of the period as both practicing and diverging from a masculinist rhetoric of violent overthrow. The Black Arts movement, with its strengths and its failings, is the source of Sanchez's own powerfully divided poetic rhetoric and her emerging feminism in the late 1960s — a feminism largely ignored by the predominantly white, middle-class second-wave feminist activists. Along with Jayne Cortez, Nikki Giovanni, and Carolyn Rodgers, Sanchez writes at the intersection of a number of competing identities: that of a black writer for whom feminist concerns were often suppressed in the interests of racial unity; that of an experimental writer whose early efforts were to score the space of the page as musical composition (and in this way exert the influence of the black vernacular and performance in a written medium); and that of an emerging black *feminist* writer who explored black female subjectivity — one that often has been overlooked in favor of more recent black feminist poetry, written since the advent of both Black Power and the increasingly diverse contributions of black feminist criticism.

To shed some light on the agendas that mark Sanchez's feminism and her avant-gardism, I focus on two of her early volumes. Although these books hardly represent Sanchez's most significant poetic achievement, they do illuminate her avant-garde agenda and the complications of her attitude toward the Black Arts movement. Published just three years apart, these two books differ so widely in language and tone that they might easily be mistaken for the work of two different poets. Sanchez's second book, *We a BaddDDD People* (1970), is clearly the product of a Black Arts sensibility and the politics that the movement endorsed. Declamatory and enraged, it urges revolution against white economic and political interests and does so through experiments with Black English, rendered on the page in a highly visual form. By contrast, the later *Love Poems* (1973) consists of brief lyrics whose intimate, meditative voice expresses the essence of the personal — celebration, grief, and loss recur in these poems about the intricate dance that takes place between two lovers. These poems (many in the strict forms of haiku and tanka) have shed both the spoken quality and the visual appearance of the black vernacular, as well as the high pitch of revolt and invective that characterize the earlier book.

Addressing Sanchez's revolutionary rhetoric, the poet Haki Madhubuti (formerly Don L. Lee, who wrote an introduction for *Home Coming* [Detroit: Broadside P., 1969; hereafter *Home*], Sanchez's more confessional first book) holds that Sanchez made a wise choice in dropping her early experimentation in the later *Love Poems*.[2] In terms of feminist avant-garde practice, however, and of the articulation of black female subjectivity, more than formal choice or aesthetic achievement is at stake in the divergence between these two volumes: The earlier work is public, overtly political, and self-consciously experimental, whereas the latter is markedly private, apparently apolitical, and formally more traditional. A problematic divide appears between black nationalism and a proto-black feminism; Sanchez's own ambivalence takes the form of opposing idioms and even poetic forms — divergences that raise questions about the nature of avant-garde politics and the practice of black feminist poetics.

Sanchez's selections in *I've Been a Woman: New and Selected Poems* (Chicago: Third World P., 1985; first published in 1978), might seem to suggest that the three-year publication gap between *We a BaddDDD People* and *Love Poems* represents a change in sensibility and agenda over a short but volatile period of time: Sanchez the Black Arts revolutionary seems to retreat from political poetry in favor of more lyrical and traditional forms. Among other differences, the latter book is largely devoted to a more personal perspective, which is mainly absent from the communal voice evident in the revolutionary *We a BaddDDD People*. But in the original, complete *Love Poems* (now out of print), Sanchez dated each poem. The chronology shows that these poems were composed not after but during the writing of *We a BaddDDD People*, and even during the same period as the earlier, more confessional *Home Coming*. The divergence hardly reveals a change over time. It shows instead a decided split between public and private idiom, between the revolutionary and the personal.

Certainly the disjunction between public and private discourse dramatizes the political division faced by Sanchez and other women involved in the Black Arts movement — between the powerful rhetoric of black nationalism and a still-emerging feminist identification. In the discussion that follows, I demonstrate, however, that these easy divides — between public and private, and between experimental and traditional writing — are based on critical assumptions about what revolution, blackness, and feminism might constitute. Despite her allegiance to Black Power, Sanchez challenges the easy affiliation between revolution and violent overthrow, and, before black *feminism* emerged in force, she challenged sexist avant-garde rhetoric in order to consider seriously questions about gender. In keeping with 1960s black nationalism, Sanchez situates the black body at the center of her poetics. But though the promotion of racial unity is apparent in Sanchez's work of the period, her critique of Black Power challenges the deployment of a fixed notion of the black woman. Monique Wittig would write later of women's oppression, "We have been compelled in our bodies and in our minds to correspond, feature by feature, with the *idea* of nature that has been established for us. . . . in the end oppression seems to be a consequence of this 'nature' within ourselves" (*Straight Mind* 9). Sanchez combats just such a predetermined idea — one of "the" essential black woman, a depiction all too often drawn by black men. Arriving at the very moment of the sway of Black Power and the burgeoning of white, middle-class feminism in the United States, Sanchez's work allows us to reconceptualize both feminist poetics and American avant-gardism more broadly — to address the emergence of feminism in the context of Black Arts poetic revolution. In both her oratorical poems and her more intimate lyrics, Sanchez clearly engages with the Black Arts agenda. But she also challenges what constitutes aesthetic — and political — innovation. Her goal throughout this period is difficult indeed: to forge a feminist avant-gardism that would voice the concerns of African-American women without betraying the "revolution."

Alice Walker, June Jordan, Lucille Clifton, Ntozake Shange, Audre Lorde —
these are the poets most often associated with the emergence of black fem-
inism.[3] It is an Alice Walker poem, for example, that opens the collection
*All the Women Are White, All the Blacks Are Men, But Some of Us Are Brave:
Black Women's Studies*. Simply called "Women," the poem about "My ma-
ma's generation" strives to encapsulate and honor a historical notion of
black female identity in a way Sanchez rarely undertakes. Included in this
important collection of essays on black feminism is work by Alice Walker,
Barbara Smith, Gloria T. Hull, and Mary Helen Washington, but Sanchez's
work is treated only in an annotated bibliography of black women play-
wrights.[4] In fact, Sanchez has most often been seen not as a proponent of
black women's consciousness but as an activist for black liberation more
generally. In a tribute to her work in a book devoted to black feminist criti-
cism, Houston Baker concludes by saying that "There may well be more cel-
ebrated Afro-American women writers integral to a woman's movement."[5]
It is because Sanchez has most frequently chosen to emphasize racial unity,
in keeping with Black Power and black nationalist concepts of the 1960s,
that she is less frequently represented, or anthologized, as a feminist writer.
This construction of her work reveals the gap between feminism and black
revolutionary politics, between the agendas of race and gender, that San-
chez tackled in her earliest publications, along with such writers as Jayne
Cortez, Carolyn Rodgers, and Nikki Giovanni.

Sanchez's early rhetoric certainly exemplifies Black Arts theories and the
underlying militance of Black Power. The goal was to promote black unity
in the face of white supremacy, to be "blk / & ready" (*Bad* 54), to be "full of
remembered [/] deaths" (*Bad* 55), "for the time is [/] coming soon" (*Bad*
56) when the battle will begin.[6] In this call to arms for the nascent black
warrior, addressing black women's needs and concerns was a matter of dic-
tating their place. Feminist writing or activism of any sort was perceived as
undermining the revolution by exposing intraracial conflict. Yet even
within the rhetoric of Black Arts, in the battle cries of *We a BaddDDD People*,
Sanchez begins to make oppositional gestures that voice a black feminist
agenda divergent from that of the movement she endorses. How are we to
view Sanchez's ambivalence toward black revolution, a still emerging (and
unquestionably white middle-class) feminism, and a radical new poetics?
To locate Sanchez's emerging feminism in what I see as a militaristic, mas-
culinist rhetoric, I first describe the concepts and goals of Black Arts, and

why I define that group as an avant-garde movement. I then place San-chez's poetics in the context of Black Arts theory, as well as more recent black feminist criticism, characterizing her writing as an ambivalent expression of feminist avant-garde poetics.

Despite parallels between the historical avant-gardes and the Black Arts movement, among critics of postwar American poetry only Robert von Hallberg discusses Black Arts as an avant-garde — one that provided both art and theory together to advance a "dream of social and cultural opposition" ("Avant-Gardes" 83). For von Hallberg, Black Arts practitioners manifest the four elements found in any avant-garde: producing an art geared toward the future, forming a public confederation (involving various media), rebelling against establishment art, and asserting "an explicit view of the relation between art and society." As I argue throughout this book, I believe this conjoining of radical politics with formally innovative art contains a causal element not stressed in von Hallberg's account: The avant-gardist creates a radical aesthetic specifically to advance a political vision that can be realized fully only if the public psyche is transformed. As I will show, Black Arts fits squarely in this rubric, for its focus was a social and political revolution that could be successful, its practitioners believed, only through a fundamental change in consciousness.

Still, calling Black Arts "avant-garde" may seem to ignore the very real problem faced by those writer-activists who originally sought a name for this new sort of black writing. "The Black Aesthetic" was one that emerged, but it was criticized by many — including Baker — for its reliance on the conceptual frame of the Anglo-European tradition the movement was striving to overthrow; the term "aesthetic" called to some minds an art-for-art's-sake sensibility.[7] The problem of definition, of labeling, remained. Clarence Major voices this dilemma when he explains why he defines Black English words with European concepts in his *Dictionary of Afro-American Slang*: "the evolution of this mode of speech defies linguistic interpretation — so far. If, for example, I have characterized a phrase like 'O-bop-she-bam' as 'existential' it is my own attempt to define as closely as I can what no one else can define any closer" (14). Major might seem to be in the business of approximation, or translation. But Major does make a powerful claim for such whimsical expressions as "O-bop-she-bam": This language, too, he implies, can claim "existential" status or be defined in terms of an existing vocabulary, however different its assumptions might be. It is a strategy of appropriation: Rather than cede territory to the (Anglo-European) powers that be, Major co-opts their terms. Calling on such examples, I would like to examine further the parallels between theories of avant-garde practice and those of the revolutionary Black Arts activists, emphasizing the limitations too frequently applied to the notion of avant-gardism and claiming that term for an often-neglected revolutionary movement in American literature.

Like the Futurists and Surrealists before them, Black Arts thinkers held that culture determines consciousness, and that only an art unifying politics and aesthetics could create the "new world."[8] As Michael Bibby summarizes it, "Where Civil Rights activism had advocated an end to 'race-thinking' in American society . . . Black Liberation activism repudiated the existing systems and sought to change the fundamental structure of U.S. society" (*Hearts and Minds* 76). Their art was determined by the new Black Power concept. In the wake of the assassination of Malcolm X and increased disillusionment with the nonviolent tactics of the Civil Rights movement, the revolutionary agenda of Black Power burst on the scene in 1966. In a speech in Greenwood, Mississippi, Stokely Carmichael asserted the futility of Civil Rights tactics: "We been saying freedom for six years and we ain't got nothin'. What we gonna start saying now is Black Power!" The exclamation led to the audience's chanting the term in unison — a moment emblematic of a new approach to black activism that resulted in a diverse range of militant agendas.[9] The arts would be a crucial tool in creating what Don L. Lee called "the newness of it all" — the time when "We'll become owners of the New World."[10] "Shapers of the future reality," Black Arts activists positioned themselves as the first and last black vanguard, the ones who understood that the "artist and the political activist are one," whose art would usher in the revolution. "We want a black poem. And a / Black World," Baraka explained. Claiming the position of vanguard, Black Arts poets proffered the rhetoric of the future, a separatist ideal achievable only through uprising: "We must make our own / World, man, our own world, and we can not do this unless the white man / is dead."[11]

The avant-garde stance of Black Arts rhetoric is evident not only in the theorization of a distinct and separate black culture but also in the way its proponents defined their goals against those of all previous black literary production. Geneva Smitherman reminded readers in 1973 that "the contemporary rediscovery and legitimizing of the Black Cultural Heritage is not new in this century. Nor is the political protest stance of the Black writers." Among others, writers of the Harlem Renaissance — Claude McKay and Countee Cullen, for example — "wove both themes of protest and beauty-in-Blackness into their works" (Geneva Smitherman, "The Power of the Rap" 259). Certainly McKay's enraged black men "Pressed to the wall, dying, but fighting back" are prototypes of 1960s defiance of "the potent poison of [white] hate."[12] Pointing to this crucial lineage, Lorenzo Thomas argues that the Black Arts movement does indeed derive from the Harlem Renaissance, for it was the earlier movement that first explored the link between folk or popular culture and progressive politics.[13]

But in a climate of crisis throughout the country and markedly within black politics, Black Arts theorists rejected virtually everything associated with Harlem Renaissance writers, believing that "Rather than bashing the bourgeoisie, [they] were attempting to create one" (Baker, *Afro-American Poetics* 4). The earlier movement shamefully sought to "prove the cultural worthiness of African Americans by demonstrating their aptitude for cultivation, development, and progress in terms understood by white American society" — an attitude labeled all but devilish by Larry Neal, who denounced the "temptation" of merging with "the oppressor" and courting "not merely integration of the flesh, but also integration of the spirit."[14] According to Smitherman,

> Today's Black artist is not content to be simply a *writer*, sounding his protest only through his art. He sees himself as a Black *man* first, and thus as an active participant in the struggle for Black Liberation. . . . [R]ejecting the elitist tendencies of the Renaissance literati, the new Black writer is making Herculean efforts to create a literature that will reach and reflect common Black folks. ("Power of the Rap" 259–60)

Fighting for the souls of the new black folk, writer-activists like Neal opposed the elitism of the "talented tenth" and vowed to create art that would "be functional and relevant to the lives and daily struggles of Black people." The new "total art form" would never — like its precursors — proffer "exotic entertainment for white America."[15]

It was with this goal that Black Arts advocates sought immediate power over their cultural productions. Ron Karenga, a central spokesman for the black aesthetic, argued for the importance of culture to self-determination.[16] Neal (one-time Black Power education director) emphasized the same message in his repeated call for cultural revolution.[17] "New constructs will have to be developed," he contended. "The dead forms . . . will have to be destroyed." Only then would the "New Black Poetry" become "the appropriate artistic counterpart to Black Power," achieving "a redefinition of the role of the artist and a new perspective on what constitutes Art" — a perspective Major labeled the "black criterion."[18] Consistent with this vision, Black Arts theorists saw theirs as a mass movement giving birth to a mass art. Rejecting as "individualistic" the black authors lauded by the white literary establishment of the 1950s — particularly Ralph Ellison and James Baldwin — Baraka felt that black American folk culture had yet to gain literary voice.[19] Thomas notes one source of 1960s nationalism as an "underground of unknown artists — mainly sign painters and street-corner musicians" in the 1950s. For Thomas, "the assertion of a *communal tradition* over . . . literary (read 'white marketplace') concerns" was critical (*Extraordinary Measures* 137). Hence the affirmation of cultural difference — of a community that shared both heritage and an underlying identity that transcended linguistic and national boundaries. One version of this identity was what Johnetta Cole called "soul," a marker of difference that Baraka and Karenga urged writers to incorporate into a specifically black art, one that would express the contemporary realities of the largely urban African-American population. For Cole, "soul" has a number of elements — "long suffering" or weariness, "deep emotion," and "the ability to feel oneness with all black people."[20] Giving artistic expression to soul — or other aspects of black culture — required rejecting the "wite" aesthetic in favor of a new language and new forms. However reductive such a view might be, its goal was transformation through new modes of artistic practice — an avant-garde radicalism in a time that favored the American success story of Booker T. Washington and the European-derived existentialism of Ralph Ellison.

Perhaps the most crucial aspect of the new art, and its most innovative, was its emphasis on the performative nature of black culture, the basis of a radical aesthetic. Stephen Henderson argued for this position in his anthology *Understanding the New Black Poetry*, a point underlined in von Hallberg's linking of a number of contemporary avant-gardes, including Black Arts, to a performative aesthetic. As Baker notes, Henderson asserted a specifically black radical poetry, and he did so by shifting the definition of poetry from reified art object to shared performance: Regardless of whether the text exists on the page, poetry takes place when a black audience responds to a given "verbal performance" by a black artist.[21] Playing the dozens, rapping, signifying — these forms of word-play, which emerged from street life, cried out for embodiment in oral and written forms. Their embodiment would not only overturn prevailing literary assumptions but also revolutionize the African American populace. In similar fashion, Baraka seized on the concept of performance, as well as self-determination, to proclaim the need for a literature that would answer directly to the black community. The new art would advocate not private but communal experience — demonstration, performance. Following his participation in both Beat circles and in the 1950s experimental poetry group Umbra, Baraka moved uptown to found the Harlem Black Arts Repertory Theater/School, to further what he saw as "blues, jazz, holler, and other expressive forms of the 'lowest classes of Negroes.'"[22] As Aldon Nielsen has argued, such efforts furthered Umbra's assertion of black cultural issues through marked language experiments — poetry would necessarily be transformed, reconnected to its oral sources and to the music that represented for many the greatest achievement of African-American art.[23]

In fact, poetry — more than fiction — would become a privileged means of expressing black difference because of its inherent musicality, its links to both music and speech. Its forms could be molded away from European aesthetics through the inscription of a distinctly oral tradition, one that might be linked both to the black sermon as cultural performance and to more ancient African religious practices.[24] For Baker, this emphasis on the performative as an expression of a revolutionary black art also involved a fundamental shift in the relationship between artist and audience:

> Spokesmen for the Black Aesthetic seldom conceived of the "text" as a *closed* enterprise. Instead, they normally thought . . . of the text as an occasion for transactions between writer and readers, between performer and audience. . . . They called for the "destruction of the text"— for an open-endedness of performance and response that created conditions of possibility for the emergence of both new meanings and new strategies of verbal transaction. ("Generational Shifts" 17)

According to Baker, Black Arts theoreticians never restricted the literary to written form. Neal argued that in African-American poetry, "the text could be destroyed and no one would be hurt in the least by it."[25] Like jazz, black poetry would inscribe (and perform) a living tradition. European avant-garde artists experimented with syntax, typography, and performance to disrupt the rules of signification and destroy an overweening tradition, as in Marinetti's fantasy of destroying Italy's academies and museums. The experimentalism of Black Arts directed a similar challenge to standard English — attempting to break its rules and regulations, dislodge its cultural authority, and renovate the minds of those black Americans taught its ideology through a performance of difference. Rule-breaking bore witness not just to formal novelty but to a vibrant and generations-old culture, in a "rejection of the life-styles, social patterns, and thinking in general of the

Euro-American sensibility."[26] In black America, Smitherman argues, "verbal performance becomes . . . a teaching/socializing force" ("Power of the Rap" 263). Now teaching would affirm black speech and culture as an antidote to internalized racism. As Baraka noted, "Being told to 'speak proper,' meaning that you become fluent with the jargon of power, is also a part of not 'speaking proper.'"[27] The new poetry would overthrow the white man's "jargon of power," and ultimately his political machine as well.

Since its inception, the Black Arts movement has inspired the loyalty and venom typical of avant-garde groups,[28] but most controversial — and relevant to Sanchez as an emerging black feminist — was the extent to which, as I have mentioned, Black Arts served as the cultural arm to the politics of Black Power. At its most fundamental, Black Power implied unity (through opposition to a generalized "white America"), pride in black identity, and nationalist independence (psychological, political, and economic). Neal explained that the Black Power concept, the source of the new Black Arts, perceived "Black America" as a single unit:

> Black Art is the aesthetic and spiritual sister of the Black Power concept. As such, it envisions an art that speaks directly to the needs and aspirations of Black America. In order to perform this task, the Black Arts Movement proposes a radical reordering of the western cultural aesthetic. It proposes a separate symbolism, mythology, critique, and iconology.[29]

Karenga similarly links the artistic and political arms of Black Power: "The battle we are waging now is the battle for the minds of Black people, and . . . if we lose this battle, we cannot win the violent one." Black art *must* be "functional, collective, and committing" to be revolutionary. In the context of imminent violent conflict, "individualism is a luxury that we cannot afford, moreover, individualism is, in effect, non-existent."[30]

This bracketing of the personal put women in a precarious position, to say the least, because the collective, with its emphasis on battle, was both male-dominated and largely unconcerned with the situation of black women. As Nielsen points out, the Umbra group and other avant-garde coteries of the times "were largely operated as male enclaves" and that legacy was passed on to the Black Arts movement (*Black Chant* 161, 162). Nielsen cites one woman poet as asserting that women "were to dress 'African,' assume the persona of 'the Motherland,' and raise little revolutionaries,"[31] for the revolution would be fought by powerful black males and required women's subservience. Black Power emphatically reinscribed patriarchal relations within the new black order. Indeed, its united front was predicated on the subjugation of women. Many of the most celebrated twentieth-century African American leaders (Elijah Muhammad; Malcolm X; Martin Luther King, Jr.; Stokely Carmichael; and Baraka), bell hooks argues, participated in American patriarchy. Baraka "discussed the formation of a black, male-dominated household with its inherent anti-woman stance, as if it were a positive reaction against white racist values." Black activists' emphasis on black male power was "a move to gain recognition and support for an emerging black patriarchy." Baraka equated feminism with "devilish" whiteness, claiming that "we do not believe in the 'equality' of men and women. We cannot understand what the devils and the devilishly influenced mean when they say equality for women."[32]

Perhaps the most stinging account of the masculinist agenda of Black Power is Michele Wallace's *Black Macho and the Myth of the Superwoman* (New York: Verso, 1990) — controversial, she has argued, precisely because she named the blatant sexism that propelled what she calls the "Black Movement." According to Wallace, the "Black Movement" was predicated on the concept of black macho, which denigrated black women and excluded them from the revolution:

> Black Macho allowed for only the most primitive notion of women — women as possessions, women as the spoils of war. . . . As a possession, the black woman was a symbol of defeat, and therefore of little use to the revolution except as the performer of drudgery (not unlike her role in slavery). (*Black Macho* 68)

The prototype for the black activist appeared in LeRoi Jones's 1965 essay, "American Sexual Reference: Black Male" in *Home*. Here Wallace sees Jones pitting "the noble savage against the pervert bureaucrats, the super macho against the fags."[33] In blatantly homophobic rhetoric, Jones argues that "Most American white men are trained to be fags," dependent on technology, "soft." In the context of the taboo on "taking" the white woman so guarded by patriarchal white culture, "the most heinous crime against white society would be . . . the rape, the taking forcibly of one of whitie's treasures." For Wallace, "Jones had transformed [Norman] Mailer's 'sexual outlaw' into the role model for the black revolutionary — 'the black man as robber/rapist,'"[34] indebted to the same imperialism and sexism that propelled white American expansion. Predicated on this supermasculinity, black macho exploited homophobia and the desire to possess women as an index of black manhood.[35] bell hooks tempers her condemnation of Black

Power with an acknowledgment of its gains for African Americans. Still, like Wallace, she points to sexism and homophobia in the construction of virile black manhood, in that Baraka and others in the movement merely duplicated racist stereotypes of the strong, virile black man as revolutionary. As hooks points out, Baraka asserted that the ultimate battle would be waged between white men and black men. At the same time, two pernicious assumptions deeply connected black and white men: sexism and a fundamental acceptance of violence.[36] Clearly, then, the limits on the revolution appear both in its homophobia and in those gender concerns that Black Power — and Black Arts — wanted most to suppress.

How, then, does Sanchez negotiate the imperatives of Black Power, and the avant-garde agenda of the Black Arts movement, as a black woman writer? Like that of other women in the movement, Sanchez's work from the period is ambivalent. In *We a BaddDDD People*, even more dramatically than in her first book, *Home Coming*, Sanchez attempts a poetry whose purpose is to spur activism and fundamentally alter her hearers' sense of themselves as black Americans. In terms of her subject matter and her polemical statements, Sanchez makes full use of the concepts of black power and black unity, and, at times, engages in the same homophobic rhetoric that Jones and others exploited.[37] She makes it clear as well that revolution means cultural and physical warfare. In terms of form Sanchez follows Black Arts theory, using the field of the page as an expressive medium for the spoken experience of Black English; further, many of her idiosyncratic markings convey aspects of the performance her poems are meant to enact when they are read. Like others in the movement, Sanchez emphasized the performative nature of her work by making recordings, and in reading her work Sanchez breaks into chant at various points, sustaining notes for long periods and creating cadences. On the page, her then-novel uses of slashes, capitals, spaces, and repeated letters (more common among recent poets, such as Ntozake Shange) are visual disruptions that suggest the primacy of pitch, tone, and duration to the work. Although readers could hardly translate her notations so as to repeat the performance — in the way that Gerard Manley Hopkins's markings can be replicated to produce the accents of his verse — Sanchez's improvisational and idiosyncratic forms provide a way to *hear* her work through its visual signs, and they necessarily alter the reader's concept of poetry itself as a written form and anticipate more recent performance poetry. In this respect, and in accordance with the Black Arts project, they combine revolutionary rhetoric with avant-garde effects.

Frequently Sanchez makes use of this avant-garde surface to position her work against a European tradition, again in keeping with Black Arts tenets. Sanchez's poem "To CHucK," from *Home Coming*, is a wry ars poetica that appropriates an attention-getting avant-garde surface. At the same time, even as the poem is a sort of homage to e. e. cummings, the poem situates Sanchez's cultural politics against that of a white male predecessor. In this sense, it anticipates the dialogue Harryette Mullen engages in with Stein in the intertextual *Trimmings*. The opening of "To CHucK" unambiguously announces the repetition of the famous experimental style of a prominent white male modernist:

> i'm gonna write me
>   a poem like
>   e. e.
> cum
>   mings to
>   day. (*Home* 20)

Satiric and political poems by cummings may be in evidence here. But more specifically, Sanchez directs her attention in "To CHucK" to cummings's love poetry. Although "To CHucK" employs cummings's familiar textual disruptions, the poem adapts his love motifs, shelving idealism in favor of explicit sexuality ("you / mov / ing iNsIdE / me touc / hing my vis / cera"). Ultimately, Sanchez suggests political implications in her sexual imagery and puns:

>   i'
>   m
>   go
>   n n
>   a sc
>   rew
>   u on   pap   er
>   cuz u
>   3
>   o
>   o
>   o
>   mi
>   awayfromme

The visual whimsy locates the debt to cummings. Yet the transcription of black English ("gonna," "cuz," "mi") hints that, in distinction from cummings's visual poetics, Sanchez's purpose is not just to disrupt convention but to reach readers who speak *her* language. The experiment, then, is part of her expression of a shared culture, not just a break with traditional poetic form. This verbal/visual play as an assertion of black difference goes further, with the theme of love-making: the (hetero)sexual love between black man and black woman *is* revolutionary, if that man and woman abandon white standards of beauty and celebrate their bodies in all their parts, like the letters and phonemes of words ("ca /re / ss my br / ea / sts my / bl /ack / ass"). The liberating language of e. e. cummings is open for adaptation to a black aesthetic.

Sanchez pushes the issues of race, inheritance, and "white" avant-gardism further. As the poet "screws around" with words on the page, the whiteness of paper — in contrast to the erratic black text — is a racial matter:

        imgonnawritemea
    pOeM
                like
                    e.
    E. cu
            MmIn
        gS to
                    day   cuz
    heknewallabout
                scr
                    EW
    ing
    on   WH
                    ite pa per. (*Home* 20–21)

"Scr [/] EW [/] ing" obviously dismantles language, but cummings's experiments diverge from Sanchez's more oblique desire for "scr / EW / ing / on WH / ite pa per" as a symbolic attack on whiteness — including that of the page itself. Here, then, in a parodic love poem, is the origin for what has been called Sanchez's "linguistic war with America"[38] in a mock avant-garde form. In this appropriation of a spatialized poetics, sexual love emerges as the bond that unites black women and men against oppression by the white world, even as "screwing" or playing with language rearranges the hierarchy of poetic form — its traditional black-and-white conventions. In this way Sanchez signifies on cummings. Like Major's *Dictionary*, "to CHucK" stakes a claim: cummings's poetics emerges as an ironic but highly available usable past for black poets. Reversing the position of male poet and female love object, Sanchez exploits cummings's form to launch a critique of an Anglo-American avant-garde that failed to address fully the racial division symbolized by white paper and black ink. The result is a hybrid of visual and speech-based avant-garde modes.[39]

"To CHucK" anticipates Sanchez's later themes of a revolution based on sexual love, which I will return to. Yet more frequently in her early work, and particularly in *We a BaddDDD People*, Sanchez's avant-garde effects are shot through with invective against "wite Amurica." Sometimes overtly homophobic, the poems make full use of black nationalist thinking, from Frantz Fanon to Malcolm X and Black Power rhetoric. The nationalist revolution Sanchez supports involves a oneness of all black voices that silences opposition, including any from black women — this in contrast to the concern with black sexuality and gender in "to CHucK." In "right on: wite america," for example, "u & me" represent the audience, part of the poet's community and of the broader "we" of the book's title (*We a BaddDDD People*), unified by their shared social history:

> this country
> might have
> needed shoot /
> outs / daily /
> once.
> but there ain't
> no mo real / wite /   all american
> bad guys.
> just.
> u & me.
> blk / and un/armed.
> this country might have
> been a pion
> eer land.   once.
> and it still is.
> check out
> the falling
> gun/shells   on our blk/ tomorrows. (*Bad* 27)

The cowboy-and-Indian-style white masculinity "needed shoot / outs" not so much to support American expansion — the ostensible historical rationale — as to play out the culture's inner conflicts. By contrast, black targets of contemporary "gun/shells" have become the external objects for these "all american" men; the "u & me" are equally united in their status as victims, and they are in equal danger of extinction, of losing shared "tomorrows." Their oneness is based on white oppression and seemingly involves no divisions *within* black America.

In poems that rage against whiteness, the "we" repeatedly emerges united, an insistent voice that urges the solution of Black Power:

> WE NEED.
> WAR. DISCIPLINE. LEARNEN.
> LAND. PLANNEN. LOVE.   AND
>   POWER. POWER. blacker
> than the smell of death
>   we the hunters need
> to destroy
>   the BEAST
>   who enslaves us. (*Bad* 51)

This poem's title is a lengthy citation: "'To Fanon, culture meant only one thing — an environment shaped to help us & our children grow, shaped by ourselves in action against the system that enslaves us.'" And its polemical content relies on the black-and-white contrast between the white "BEAST" and the black "hunter." Poles are simply reversed. A unified front trumps the exploration of difference.

This nationalist promotion of racial unity typifies Black Arts avant-gardism. Indeed, women in the movement defended the rhetoric of the unified front, even long after the heyday of Black Power. In interviews published in 1983 — nearly a decade after the emergence of black feminism — Giovanni dismisses "this man-woman thing" as "boring," and Gwendolyn Brooks adheres to a heterosexist racial unity, asserting that "problems" between black men and women "are family matters," the result of a "divisive tactic": "women are not going to be winners on account of leaving their black men" (Tate, *Black Women Writers at Work* 67, 47). Such statements reveal often entrenched attitudes about racial unity. Still, even in the movement's early days, the party-line often masked subtle opposition. Without rejecting Black Power, women in the movement sought to define it not only more inclusively but differently, challenging the equation between revolution and male domination. Although less pointed than Loy's lampooning of Futurist bombast, Giovanni's "Seduction" (*No More Masks!* 1968) deflates masculine high seriousness and constructs female sexuality as the greater power. The male addressee will "go on — as you always do," spouting abstractions ("'What we really need . . .'" "'what about the situation . . .'"). The speaker meanwhile seizes control, slowly "taking your dashiki off," until the man can only query, "'Nikki, / isn't this counterrevolutionary . . . ?'" "Seduction" satirizes the rhetoric of revolution and implies that men miss the point: The *real* revolution is, as Audre Lorde would later put it, "the erotic as power." Still more direct is Kay Lindsey's "Poem": "now that the revolution needs numbers / Motherhood got a new position / Five steps behind manhood."[40] Not only is the "natural" black woman relegated to reproduction — she's supposed to be happy about the new attentions her oppression merits.

Such instances of women's vocal dissent provide early evidence of feminist consciousness within the Black Arts agenda. It was a new awareness, and one largely ignored by the growing movement of white, middle-class women advancing the idea that the personal is political.[41] By now well documented, the relatively narrow agenda of the new feminism eventually led black women to voice concerns different from those of their white "sisters." Writing in 1970, the same year *We a BaddDDD People* and *The Black Woman* were published, Pauli Murray notes the lack of attention to "the struggles of black women and their contributions to history," even in "books published on the Negro experience and the Black Revolution" (Pauli Murray, "The Liberation of Black Women" 91).

By the late 1970s, Audre Lorde, among others, had made it abundantly clear that "Black feminism is not white feminism in blackface,"[42] and Alice Walker had coined the term "womanism" to express her own and others' divergence from the Anglocentric feminist movement and to make black lesbianism visible; "womanist" described "A black feminist or feminist of color," as well as "a woman who loves other women, sexually and/or nonsexually" (Walker, *In Search of Our Mothers' Gardens* xi). Sanchez's efforts were earlier than these and certainly less formulated. At this time, she would never have concluded, with Murray, that "the Negro woman's fate in the United States, while inextricably bound with that of the Negro male in one sense, transcends the issue of Negro rights" ("Liberation of Black Women" 191). Instead, inserting the concerns of black women into the masculinist rhetoric of Black Power, Sanchez's work voices what one critic has called a "prefeminism" in Sanchez's plays of the same period.[43] Even before 1972, when Sanchez officially joined the Nation of Islam, she used her poetry to voice the need for — if not the realization of — black feminism, and she did so in a poetics committed to a conception of linguistic innovation and renovation of the black written word. In uneasy relation to her nationalism, her early poetry questions the masculinist rhetoric of Black Power. The result is a subtext that runs throughout *Home Coming* and *We a BaddDDD People*, a voicing of difference within the rhetoric of revolution, and of a black feminist consciousness in the context of Black Arts militance: an example of feminist "infiltration" of a masculinist avant-garde agenda.

Sanchez's hints that nationalism entails a high cost for black women are striking in *We a BaddDDD People*, since this volume is Sanchez's most dedicated pronouncement of Black Power. Yet one of the implied tenets of this revolutionary artistic practice also helped supply Sanchez with a means of resistance: a distrust not just of art-for-art's-sake but also of language isolated from revolutionary action. Since overthrowing white power was the purpose of this engaged art, action had to take precedence over words — even in the context of the politicized gesture of embracing the black vernacular. Ron Karenga put it simply: "all art must reflect and support the Black Revolution" (Ron Karenga, "Black Cultural Nationalism" 33). For Don L. Lee, the knowledge that "i ain't seen no poems stop a .38" and "no metaphors stop a tank" means that "until my similes can protect me from a night stick / i guess i'll [. . .] buy me some more bullets."[44] Baraka's "poet-assassin" (ironically derived from the European Apollinaire), with his murderous words, is perhaps the only ideal user of language.[45] Black Arts writers were trying to use their art to incite revolution so as to ensure that the poem never be an end in itself, a mere art object.

Often, then, a distrust of rhetoric reinforces the Black Power consciousness. Sanchez points out that the evils committed by white America "cannot be resolved / thru rhetoric" (*Bad* 50); even as she asserts the power of Black English, she also underlines its limits — a theme consistent with Black Power's call to arms. Indeed, poets themselves were put on the defensive by Black Power activists who denigrated "mere" writing when armed conflict seemed imminent.[46] But Sanchez also uses the motif of distrusting talk to attack the movement itself. Even in the nationalistic *We a BaddDDD People*, Sanchez critiques the rhetoric of revolution and calls, however hesitatingly, for an entirely *different* language from that of invective or what Baker calls the hermeneutics of overthrow: a language that might explore not just the economic and political interests but the spiritual and emotional needs of black women and men. Sanchez's implied criticisms of Black Power reveal the beginnings of an assertion of differences *within* "black America"; ultimately that sense of difference will lead Sanchez to a critique of gender politics and a resistance to any narrow view of black womanhood in a hybrid poetics incorporating elements from both Black Arts avant-garde theory and traditional poetic forms.

In "blk / rhetoric," the nature of language as revolutionary act paradoxically becomes the locus of both Black Power and a potentially feminist perspective in a poem that largely adheres to Black Arts precepts about the radical potential of Black English rendered in written form. The poem calls for leaders who will challenge the prevalence of a particular kind of rhetoric. The *idea* that "black is beautiful" is not at fault. But the focus on purely material factors — the drive to create black-owned businesses, for example — threatens to extinguish the real revolution that must take place through the realization of a new black consciousness, which Sanchez believes is urgently needed:

> who's gonna make all
> that beautiful blk / rhetoric
> mean something.
> > > > like
> i mean
> > who's gonna take
> the words
> > > blk / is / beautiful
> and make more of it
> than blk / capitalism.

The rhetoric may be beautiful, but there is an underlying inadequacy in its application: the Marxist-influenced analysis of capitalism narrows the field of activism to material well-being and defeats the very concept of "blk / is / beautiful." Calling for cultural renewal — the coup by which the beautiful in America is reclaimed for blackness — Sanchez redefines the revolution and takes Black Power to task. The young "brothers and sisters" need to move "in straight / revolutionary / lines," but under a different leadership:

> who's gonna give our young
> blk / people new heroes

        (instead of catch / phrases)
        (instead of cad / ill / acs)
        (instead of pimps)
        (instead of wite / whores)
        (instead of drugs)
        (instead of new dances)
        (instead of chit / ter / lings)
        (instead of 35¢ bottle of ripple)
        (instead of quick / fucks in the hall / way
            of wite / america's mind)
  like. this. is an S O S
     me. calling. . . . .
           calling. . . . .
                  some / one
  pleasereplysoon. (*Bad* 15–16)

The illusory "catch / phrases" of Black Power reveal more than a revolutionary's distrust of too much talk and not enough action. The political emphases of Black Power, particularly the movement's insistence on "blk / capitalism," mean that "cad / ill / acs" become the objects of desire; in Sanchez's emphasis on its syllables, the word itself is linked to the "illness" of materialism. It is an implicit condemnation of Black Power to mix the false solutions of "blk / capitalism" with those problems Sanchez and others saw as inflicted on black culture by "wite / america's mind": that through American capitalism, the black population is placated with "wite / whores," "drugs," and "new dances."[47] The forces of *both* Black Power and white capitalism are misleading black Americans; the real revolution is an "SOS" that is going unanswered. Sanchez's poem responds to Baraka's poem "SOS," which opens, "Calling black people / Calling all black people." In this respect, Sanchez critiques the nationalism of Black Arts' most prominent spokesman in the very poetic form he advocated.[48]

Sanchez's critiques of Black Power leave open a space for the analysis of gender relations within the movement. Yet Sanchez's resistance to the materialist thrust of much Black Power rhetoric is complicated by her allegiance at this time to the Nation of Islam. Those poems in *We a BaddDDD People* that portray black womanhood as a source of revolution — while they harbor the potential for a black feminist project — frequently echo the Nation of Islam's position that women should bolster black manhood and produce the children who will fight the next generation's struggle.[49] Sanchez joined the Nation in 1972, shortly after the publication of *We a BaddDDD People*. She explains that "the Nation was the one organization that was trying to deal with the concepts of nationhood, morality, businesses, schools." But its activism exacted a price from black women: "In the Nation at that time women were supposed to be in the background. . . . I fought against the stereotype of me as a black woman in the movement relegated to three steps behind. It was especially important for women in the Nation to see that" (Tate, *Black Women Writers* 139–40). Sometimes men at her readings would walk out. She tells the story of one man who suggested "that the solution for Sonia Sanchez was for her to have some babies, and I wrote a long satirical poem called 'Solution to Sonia Sanchez.'" Her own desire was for a recognition of difference: "I wanted them to understand, without causing schisms" (Tate, *Black Women Writers* 139).

At the time she wrote *We a BaddDDD People*, even as she sought to resist its sexism, Sanchez was exploring the Nation's redeeming possibilities for black women. The book is dedicated to "blk / wooomen: the only queens of this universe," and it opens with a dedicatory poem (followed by a page-long list of female friends and comrades) that proclaims, "i am a blk / wooOOOMAN."[50] Rather than violent confrontation, Sanchez implies, the ages-long history of black womanhood might serve as a means of renovation, if not revolution:

> my brown
>   bamboo / colored
> blk / berry / face
> will spread itself over
> this western hemisphere and
> be remembered.
>   be sunnnnnNNGG.
> for i will be called
>   QUEEN.

This proclamation of black female pride might be the source of change for the entire "western hemisphere," which will be reborn:

> and the world
>   shaken by
> my blkness

                    will channnNNGGGEEE
colors. and be

                                    reborn.

                                    blk. again. (*Bad* 6)

This song of change posits a return to a black (African) origin as against
the Western Hemisphere, a rebirth through the original vessel: the black
female body. The poem asserts the power of this black womanhood, a
strength that resides in an essentialist view of the black woman as
"QUEEN," as agent of birth, that in many ways supports, rather than ques-
tions, the complementary role of black virile manhood supported by the
Nation of Islam. The very spirituality that allowed Sanchez to articulate a
critique of Black Power's materialism thus led her to an equally problem-
atic, limiting representation of black women.

There is, however, still another sort of poem in *We a BaddDDD People*. A
number of poems here are concerned with the effects on women of a na-
tionalist agenda. Without directly criticizing either Black Power activists or
the Nation of Islam, Sanchez calls for an intimacy (based on exclusively het-
erosexual bonding) not addressed by these movements. There is an emer-
gence of a sexual politics in these poems, meant to be a corrective to the
militarism of Black Power and an assertion of black women's needs. The ab-
sence of intimacy, and its relation to black oppression and lack of selfhood,
is the subject of "for our lady," a reflection on Billie Holiday:

yeh.
    billie.   if someone
had loved u like u
shud have been loved
ain't no tellen what
kinds of songs

                        u wud have swung
gainst this country's wite mind. (*Bad* 41)

The truncated "u" of the poem is stripped of the selfhood necessary to fight
against "this country's wite mind." To have sung, or given voice, is indeed
to have "swung" a blow against one's oppressors, but Sanchez's Billie is
a tragically failed revolutionary woman precisely because, notoriously
abused, she lacked the saving power of love. The message here is ambigu-
ous: Sanchez makes black *female* power dependent on heterosexual bond-

ing. Nonetheless, she also implies that for Billie to have been loved "like u / shud have been loved" might have incited a revolution *between* black Americans as well as against the dominant white culture. In this way Sanchez begins to add a different agenda to the nationalist rhetoric of overthrow:

> yeh.   billie.
> if some blk / man
>   had reallee
> made u feel
>   permanentlee warm.
> ain't no tellen
>   where the jazz of yo / songs
>   wud have led us.

This kind of "leading" still involves the collective "us" of Sanchez's unified black community, and it might still involve violent revolutionary change. But to be "permanentlee warm," to be nurtured by a man who is capable not just of killing but of loving, also means revolutionizing conceptions of gender within the black community. Black self-love still awaits black women and men; "ain't no tellen" where such a road "wud have led us."

Even more overtly than "for our lady," "so this is our revolution" addresses the issue of sexual politics. Here Sanchez attacks both men and women for failing to uphold the ideals behind revolution, because of distorted attitudes toward sexuality and the body. Deluded black men are "shooten needles into they arms / for some yestuhday dreams," while

> sistuhs fucken other sistuh's
> husbands
>   cuz the rev o lu shun dun
> freed them to fight the
> enemy (they sistuhs) (*Bad* 63)

Competing for the attention of men means that "sisters" are divided. In the resulting mock "rev o lu shun," ironic meanings emerge from the word, as black men and women learn not to love but to "shun" one another. Sanchez's challenge is directed toward the whole community:

> how bout a fo /
>   real /   revolu/shun
> with a fo / real
>   battle to be fought

outside of bed /

       room / minds.

The "fo real" battle clearly contrasts with that of a manipulative sexuality. For Sanchez, this "fo real" revolution involves "blk/culture" and its children who need to be "taught to love they blk/ selves" (*Bad* 63). It is a movement toward birth and nurturance, a female (and male) culture of "taking care of business" by raising the next generation through healing, not violence; and it is a call for a community of mothers and fathers to give birth to a new black culture — as women do to children — and to take responsibility for its growth and well-being. In other words, it is a revolution in which the personal and the political cannot, must not, be divided.

"If you're going to say something, your house must be in order, because there's so much disorder outside," Sanchez has said of her political poems (Tate, *Black Women Writers at Work* 143). Despite the largely militaristic, public rhetoric of *We a BaddDDD People*, Sanchez maintains that "In the early Sixties I became aware that the personal was political" (*Parnassus* 364). In *We a BaddDDD People*, the racial politics that claimed the attention of those in both the Black Power and Black Arts movements is at times altered so as to address the as yet uncharted territory of male/female relations in "black America." This emphasis on difference appears throughout, in poems that attack the patriarchal assumptions of black men and of the movement: "a poem for my father," "indianapolis / summer / 1969 / poem," and "blk / wooooomen / chant," among others, all address the question, "blk/mennnnnNN [/] do u SEEEEEEE us? HEARRRRRR us? KNOWWWW us?" (*Bad* 45). Although only intermittent in this volume, such notes resonate with Sanchez's account of how a communal sensibility merged with personal issues in the work of black women writers in the 1960s, before the conceptual framework of black feminism was in place. On the one hand, she says, "I think there was a similar voice, almost a communal voice" in 1960s poetry. Yet,

> Many women understood that . . . a nation could not evolve from people talking about what should be without involving the two of them, without acknowledging that what will be comes from their working together. You can fully understand revolution if you can fully understand what it is to love a man. Because in order to be a true revolutionary, you must understand love. Love, sacrifice, and death.
>
> (Tate, *Black Women Writers* 143)

It is this trio, which poems like "so this is our revolution" begin to articulate through an angry reaction against self-deception and exploitation, that black activists must embrace.

The motif of a "fo real" revolution that might revolve around both gender and racial issues begins, then, to take shape in *We a BaddDDD People*. Still, Sanchez's endorsement of the politics of Black Power and the poetics espoused by Black Arts theorists remains apparent in the more declamatory poems in the volume, like "listenen to big black at s.f. state" or "life / poem," which baldly repeats, "shall i kill" (*Bad* 55), anticipating Nikki Giovanni's infamous "Nigger / Can you kill / Can you kill."[51] In the wake of this politicized language — its rhetoric of violent overthrow merged with an innovative textual politics — the publication of a book simply called *Love Poems* three years later hardly seems like a "revolutionary" event. Here Sanchez arranged, in loose chronological order, sixty-nine brief, apparently apolitical, "personal" poems and dated each one, as though to root them in a particular historical moment. The first four of these poems, written in 1964, predate by five years the publication of *Home Coming*. It would seem that, in contrast to the agenda of Black Power and the communal, performative voice that motivated Sanchez's linguistic experiments in the late 1960s, a largely lyrical and purely intimate group of poems had accumulated for nearly ten years.

The contrast between public and private, political and intimate, in these two collections surfaces even in the divergence of each volume's dedicatory pages. *We a BaddDDD People* opens, as I mentioned earlier, with a dedication to "blk/wooomen: the only queens of this universe," and that general dedication is followed by a page-long list of names, including "the sistuhs in THE NATION OF ISLAM and any other sistuhs i missed" (*Bad* 5). The book is intended to speak for and to a larger community than it at first seems to do — and particularly to women. *Love Poems* implies, from its first page, a preeminently private writing — poems we overhear, rather than hear performed. A page facing the book's first poem is empty except for a simple dedication to Sanchez's second husband: "This book is for my husband, John." The personal voice, speaking only for herself and to only one other, quietly announces an altogether different poetics.

The poems that follow bear out this initial divergence from the earlier two volumes. In place of the self-consciously disruptive, oral poetics of *We a BaddDDD People*, we find a series of free verse poems and haiku — all adhering largely to a sense of organic form, rather than disrupting syntax or orthography. For the most part, Sanchez is following the rules — providing the number of syllables required for haiku, generally using standard English — in a collection of meditative poems. She reflects on her life and relationship with a male lover, recording particulars about her surroundings, as in the tradition of rigorous observation that Sanchez encountered through her first creative writing teacher, Louise Bogan. In fact, for Sanchez, both Bogan and the formalism she coached her students in remain important, despite the Anglo-American tradition they represent. Citing Bogan as "a very important influence," Sanchez remembers her first experiments with form during her student days at New York University:

> Though some resisted form as too rigorous, I did not because I thought that my sprawling work needed form. To this day, I teach my students the villanelle, the sonnet; I preach all the exercises and discipline that Bogan gave to me. I began to move, to see how form can work, can demand a certain kind of response. (*Parnassus* 362–63)

Love Poems contains free verse and haiku, rather than villanelles and sonnets. But even in these forms, the contrast with the Black Arts avant-garde agenda could hardly be more pronounced.

The opening lines of "July" (dated 1964) exemplify this free verse mode and the individual consciousness that shapes it: "the old men and women / quilt their legs / in the shade / while tapestry pigeons / strut their necks. / as i walk, thinking / about you my love . . ." (*Love* 4). As in the style of any number of more mainstream poets whose free verse predominated during the 1960s (Robert Lowell, Anne Sexton, Robert Bly), Sanchez practices a poetry here that links external detail to state of mind and uses a first-person pronoun (however altered through the lack of capitalization) to signal the presence of a consciousness whose private musings become the stuff of poetry. Nowhere do we hear the militant — and communal — voice of *We a BaddDDD People*: the call to arms, the invective, the uses of Black English, the oratorical flourishes and allusions to figures from African American history and culture, from John Coltrane to Malcolm X, are all absent, if not repudiated. In its place is a confessional voice apparently in direct opposition to the avant-garde aesthetics of theorists like Karenga, who declared that "Black art, like everything else in the black community, must respond positively to the reality of revolution" ("Black Cultural Nationalism" 32).

Yet as I see it, Sanchez forges a complex personal poetics in *Love Poems*, once again voicing a subtle, if not militant, feminist perspective. In fact, the poetics of *Love Poems* challenges the notion that political writing must be spoken by a public, communal voice or take overtly disruptive form, that of a (masculine) avant-garde agenda that entails violent overthrow as the only means of social change. In the genre of the love poem, Sanchez calls for a new consciousness not just in relation to the white world, but in gender relations *between* black women and men. Sanchez was not alone among Black Arts poets in writing love poetry. But she explores an idea neglected in Black Arts theory: Intimate relationships reflect and can change political realities. Zora Neale Hurston voiced similar convictions nearly a half century earlier, for the very exclusion of the larger white culture from the communities described in novels like *Their Eyes Were Watching God* and *Jonah's Gourd Vine* constituted a radical assertion of racial difference. Condemned by the generation that followed, which (particularly in the work of Richard Wright) was preoccupied by describing the relations not within black communities but between blacks and whites in "protest" literature, Hurston was long seen as reactionary and escapist. Her rediscovery by Alice Walker bore witness to the flowering of a black feminist consciousness since the years of both Black Power and the white, middle-class feminism of the 1970s.[52] Sanchez's *Love Poems* belongs to this other tradition of black women's writing — writing devoted to the work of witnessing how a life might be freed from the political rhetoric (if not political action) that determines consciousness just as surely as racial or gender oppression does. It is a poetry that draws on the redemptive powers of intimacy as an instrument of political awareness, challenging Black Arts militance by calling on a combined racial and sexual politics to transform the world. It is revealing that she makes this case in far more traditional form than the speech-based, colloquial disruptions of the Black Arts style. In contrast to Neal and Karenga, Sanchez connects the Black Arts movement to precursors. Mentioning her admiration for the women poets of the Harlem Renaissance, Sanchez rejects the avant-gardist renunciation of predecessors and traditional form alike.[53]

As in the writing of Pablo Neruda, another influence on her work for its traversal of the personal/political divide,[54] Sanchez explains how her work crosses rhetorical and generic borders — the engaged and the lyrical, the political and the intimate — in ways that anticipate the hybridity of poets like Susan Howe and Mullen: "If you describe me, as some critics do, as a lyrical poet, I say yes, I am, but I'm also a hard-hitting poet and a political poet because this is a lyrical world and a terrible world, too, and I have

to talk about that" (*Parnassus* 365). Much of *Love Poems* consists of poems
that question assumptions about the public/private divide, as in "After the
fifth day":

> with you
> i pressed the
> rose you brought me
> into one of fanon's books.
> it has no odor now.
>   but
> i see you. handing me a red
> rose and i remember
> my birth. (*Love* 23)

Invoking the traditional love token, the rose, Sanchez links her poem to a
long European tradition. But, as in Loy's use of this emblem in "Anglo-
Mongrels and the Rose," Sanchez also challenges traditional versions of the
trope. Initially, the universe of the poem seems to prepare us for Donne's
solipsistic lovers for whom love "makes one little room, an every where"
(Donne 89): "with you / i pressed the / rose you brought me." Given this
opening, we might be surprised to come across the charged allusion to "one
of fanon's books," which suddenly (and far more quietly than in the poems
of *We a BaddDDD People*) breaches the intimate setting and invokes not just
the broader world — Donne's "Busie old foole, unruly Sunne" bothering
the two lovers — but community and *polis* (Donne 93). Fanon's enor-
mously influential writings on pan-African identity and the African dias-
pora suddenly particularize these two lovers as not European at all.[55]

Sanchez mentions that she avoided any allusions to race in her earliest
lyrical writings: "My early poetry was introspective, poetry that probably
denied or ignored I was black" (*Parnassus* 364). Here, even in this relatively
early poem (dated 1967), she takes the other road — making sure we see
that "if you write from a black experience, you're writing from a universal
experience as well" (Tate, *Black Women Writers* 142). Although the physical
token might decay ("it has no odor now"), its loss of vibrancy also marks the
passage of time, bearing witness to the speaker's understanding of her own
identity: "i remember / my birth." Reliving the moment, the speaker makes
a very different claim from that of a preeminently personal, Wordsworthian
recollection in tranquillity: The memory of intimate exchange marks a
birth not just into love but also into an awareness of a shared cultural iden-

tity that necessarily leads to a new political consciousness. The rose bonds with the pages of Fanon; the personal experience of "birth" through the bestowal of love is inextricable from a burgeoning social awareness.

Sanchez's haiku in *Love Poems* also conflate the speaker's awakening black cultural identity with awakening feelings of love:

> Was it yesterday
> love we shifted the air and
> made it blossom Black? (*Love* 25)

Once again, the poem opens with a subjective experience seemingly limited to the dynamic between two lovers; the "yesterday" of the first line seems to point either to love's fleetingness or to its less frequently sung longevity. It is not the "we" that shifts, but the "air": the lovers alter the world, making it theirs. But the final line transforms the reader's assumptions. Framed by two capitalized words — the initial "Was" and the final word "Black" — the poem testifies to what we would otherwise see as a different sort of blossoming. A proclamation of love from the past marks the advent of a new black consciousness; the union of the two lovers becomes a political act, indistinguishable from cultural politics, or from a historical moment supposedly anathema to the timeless genre of the love poem. Love, then, *is* the revolution — because it allows the two lovers to conceive of themselves *as* black, through their intimacy, their union.[56]

The issue of the conjoining of not just *any* two but of two black Americans — clearly, given Sanchez's orientation, heterosexual — sheds light on the subtle political purpose, and the limitations, of these love poems. Through anecdotes Wallace describes the frequency with which black men in the movement in the 1960s dated white women and still expected black women's allegiance to them, while, conversely, white feminists resistant to dealing with black women's concerns might demonstrate their liberalism by dating black men.[57] According to her, the conjunction of sexual and racial politics bred resentment among black women. Sanchez's love poems, in a context charged with interracial disharmony, as well as efforts to achieve unity, proclaim the necessity of black women's liberation. Just as significant, they offer narratives that make the rhetoric (particularly "black is beautiful") come to life: Sanchez's lovers are living proof that black women and men need only one another to satisfy their need for beauty. In this they offer a corrective to the misogynistic claim that the black woman's "aspirations and values are closely tied to those of the white power structure and not to those of her man." In the face of the black male's destruction by "his woman," Neal concludes that the "only way out" is "through revolution."[58] Sanchez's poems don't deny black men's "sense of powerlessness." But neither do they tolerate the suggestion that black women are responsible or that uprising is the only answer. She depicts instead an ideal partnership defined by both race activism and gender equity. Although such poems offer solely a heterosexual perspective, their portrayals of the politics of intimacy provide an early foray into the territory of sexual politics within black communities.[59]

In their focus on sexuality, these love poems also broach what Cornel West sees as a taboo subject in America. Even a generation after *Love Poems*, black sexuality, according to West, remains taboo within discourse, even as it fascinates white Americans. At the heart of this psychosexual issue is a political one — the control, the policing, of black bodies. For West, the first important step is to demystify the black body itself:

> This demythologizing of black sexuality is crucial for black America because much of black self-hatred and self-contempt has to do with the refusal of many black Americans to love their own black bodies — especially their black noses, hips, lips, and hair. . . . White supremacist ideology is based first and foremost on the degradation of black bodies in order to control them. (Cornel West, *Race Matters* 85)

This notion of self-love, and the proclamation that black is beautiful, motivated a very particular kind of political writing for Sanchez. In contrast to the more nationalistic, revolutionary rhetoric of *We a BaddDDD People*, the intimate *Love Poems* are both Sanchez's counter to "White supremacist ideology" and an early examination of the subject that concerns West today — the intersections of racial and sexual identities, inextricable from political realities. During this period, women writers established a body politics in poetic manifestos ranging from Anne Sexton's "In Celebration of My Uterus" to Giovanni's "Ego Tripping." Particularly for black women poets, it was of paramount importance to redefine the beautiful in a culture whose versions of sexual attraction were drawn in white lines.

Even here, however, Sanchez's commitment to portraying black America as unified and whole leads her to speak in the communal voice about the same theme of nationhood that predominates in *We a BaddDDD People*. "A Blk/Woman/Speaks," for example, with its rhetoric of "our emergen Blk Nation" could well have been included in the earlier volume. One of the only undated poems in the book, "A Blk / Woman / Speaks" attempts to give voice to all black women, like the dedicatory poem to *We a BaddDDD People*, in dialogic relation to Hughes's "The Negro Speaks of Rivers":

> i am deep/blk/soil
> they have tried to pollute me
> with a poison called America. (*Love* 68)

Hughes represents archetypal blackness as seminal river; Sanchez's response casts woman as earth. This representative speaker is entirely different from the more intimate voice of most of *Love Poems*; the invocation of "America" signals the communal sensibility of the earlier collection. By the poem's end, the claim of being "deeeeeEEEp [/] blue/blk/soil" is linked to the black woman's role of child-bearing — reflecting the Nation of Islam's gender divides, by which women were to bear and raise "black warriors." The speaker will "burn on our evening bed [/] of revolution":

> i, being blk
>   woooOOOMAN
> know only the way of the womb
> for i am deep/red/soil
>   for our emergen Blk Nation. (*Love* 68)

The love of this poem can be equated with an endorsement of the agenda of gender roles decreed by the Nation.

Nonetheless, many of the poems in the book, in contrast to "A Blk / Woman / Speaks," go further. They imply that the natures of "man" and "woman" have gone unexamined, and that before questions of gender identity are raised, as West suggests, there can *be* no revolution. In this respect Sanchez enacts an ambivalent dialogue with the essentialist rhetoric that elsewhere serves the Nation's agenda. In "Poem No. 12," for example, the speaker can only begin to imagine a new black womanhood:

> When i am woman, then i shall be wife of your eyes
> When i am woman, then i shall receive the sun
> When i am woman, then i shall be shy with pain
> When i am woman, then shall my laughter stop the wind (*Love* 70)

The poem closes with a transcription of chant typical of Sanchez's experiments in *We a BaddDDD People*: "When i am woman, ay-y-y, ay-y-y, ay-y-y, [/] When i am woman . . ." The final ellipsis may mark the richness of this new psyche. But paradoxically it also betrays the elusiveness of that same condition of "being woman"; just as the cry itself is a lament for what does not yet exist, the poem as a whole can define "woman" only through a list of mythlike gestures, longed-for but impossible to attain. Implicitly, the "I," as a black subject, cannot be included in the category "woman," synonymous with white femininity. Through faith alone, the poem strives to generate the reality of a black female identity for the speaker, yet the use of the future tense belies the possibility of "giv[ing] birth to myself." Although the African woman (the archetypal "queen of the universe" whose laughter will "stop the wind") might be celebrated in mythic terms, she remains elusive as a reality for the speaker.

If archetypal womanhood remains elusive, a cry of the future, the abuse black women have suffered at the hands of black men doesn't go unmentioned. Yet for Sanchez this behavior stems from the fact that black male subjectivity also remains virtually uninvented. To this extent, Sanchez resists essentialist constructions and calls for black male and female liberation; her work of this period needs to be seen in the context of the emerging awareness of the contemporary assault on black males. "To All Brothers: From All Sisters" takes for granted that black women have had to absorb the frustrations of black men's oppression, both acknowledging their distress and calling for a new respect. The poem echoes Cleaver's title, "To All Black Women, from All Black Men," in which he addresses the black woman as a "Queen" "bereft of her man" (205) for the four hundred years of black male enslavement and oppression that have made of him "a sniveling craven . . . a vile, groveling bootlicker" (*Soul on Ice* 209). He appeals to the black woman: "Let me drink from the river of your love at its source . . . and heal the wound of my Castration" (207). Sanchez's poem seems to create a dialogue with Cleaver's text. Its opening, like those of many of Sanchez's haiku, seems to isolate the poem in the realm of individual loss: "each nite without you. [//] and I give birth to myself. [//] who am i to be touched at random?" (*Love* 95). Yet it quickly moves to the shifting incarnations of black manhood that traverse the entire course of American history, through which black women retained the same role of long-suffering supporter:

to be alone so long. to see you move
in this varicose country
like silhouettes passing in apprenticeship,
from slave to slavery to pimp
to hustler to murderer to negro

to nigguhdom to militant to revolutionary
to Blackness to faggot with the same
shadings of disrespect covering your voice. (*Love* 95)

However blameworthy, such disrespect results from the frustrations of re-
strictive notions of masculinity, which have hardly changed during the
shifts from slavery to hustling, from the oppression of "nigguhdom" to the
false rhetoric of the militant, and from the proclamation of Blackness to
the homophobia and heterosexism apparent not just in others but uncriti-
cally in Sanchez's own language. In Sanchez's heterosexual (and hetero-
sexist) agenda, "All Brothers" need to learn how *not* to "touch at random";
they must learn how to define themselves — how to invent their masculin-
ity, based on something other than Wallace's view of the macho sensibil-
ity.[60] As Sanchez tersely puts it in "Prelude to Nothing," "i challenge the
mind to believe in man [/] in any man who loves without hating." Presum-
ably, this hatred is directed toward women, and the gaps in intimacy are
difficult to bridge: "NOW HEAR THIS. NOW HEAR THIS. [/] man hasn't
been invented yet" (*Love* 29). Sanchez's search to redefine the black male
was indeed controversial — a potential breaking of ranks. And yet the flaws
in this revolutionary agenda — the construction of love through the exclu-
sion of homosexuality — are also apparent. Sanchez excludes this poem
(as well as the more invective-studded poems from *We a BaddDDD People*)
from her selection, *I've Been a Woman*, first printed in 1978 and now the only
source for many of her earlier poems; the distance between this early work
and Sanchez's mature writing is apparent as well in her inclusiveness in re-
cent volumes, particularly of gay and lesbian identities, as I discuss below.

Sanchez has said that "My work, really, has always been motivated by
love": "In the Sixties, the country had to be shocked with the horror of how
it had raised Negroes who hated themselves, who were bent on wiping
themselves out, intent on not seeing themselves, on being invisible" (*Par-
nassus* 366). In *Love Poems*, Sanchez begins to explore gender difference
and the need for healing in order to understand and experience a revolu-
tion of self and society. The much-needed new state of mind is never fully
defined, but we do learn that simply "to be" is linked to being loved:

we have come to
believe that we are
not. to be we
must be loved or

touched and proved
to be. this earth
turns old
and rivers grow lunatic
with rain. how i wish
i could lean in your cave
and creak with the winds. (*Love* 49)

The movement from the communal to the intimate inverts the more violent aspects of Black Arts rhetoric that Sanchez herself promoted: "to be," to believe in one's own existence, to combat the experience of invisibility (described by writers from W. E. B. DuBois and Ellison to Wallace), means to "be loved or [/] touched and proved [/] to be."[61] The question of metaphysical being takes on new meaning in the context of racial and sexual politics; the intimacy of the final lines, the seclusion of the cave, is the point of departure for a new identity.

The "i" as black woman, a new subjectivity for a new political age, remains difficult for Sanchez to proclaim. With or without the rhetorical apparatus of *We a BaddDDD People*, Sanchez's writing in the early 1970s bears witness to the linguistic and political struggle to voice a black feminist politics as well as a feminist avant-garde poetics within a masculinist radical movement. In the midst of a feminist politics that had little interest in black women's issues and a Black Power movement that remained stridently patriarchal, Sanchez's struggle was marked with conflicts between unity and difference, between essentialist and more fluid conceptions of black female identity. Sanchez's poetics at this time, particularly the divide between *We A BaddDDD People* and *Love Poems*, reveals the difficulty of forging a feminist avant-garde sensibility that could wed a new conception of racial identity to the examination of repressive gender roles within the revolutionary black vanguard. Yet even in Sanchez's hesitance to express conflict within the black community, both of these early books represent experiments in a new terrain — the creation of a new poetics, a new set of images, that might begin to voice an oppositional consciousness of race and gender.

Both Sanchez's choices for her selected poems, *I've Been a Woman*, and her work since reveal that the two modes of her poetics — Black Arts avant-gardism and lyric intimacy — continue to play a role in her conception of black identity and politics. The question is how easily the two are reconciled. Sanchez's *A Blues Book for Blue-Black Magical Women* (1974), her only book devoted exclusively to black women's consciousness, still evidences the same tensions I have described between racial unity (explicitly, here, the platform of the Nation of Islam) and an expression of an emerging black feminist subjectivity. *A Blues Book* is a mythological exploration of black womanhood that in some ways resembles Loy's "Anglo-Mongrels." It is Sanchez's work that most clearly celebrates the spiritual, as opposed to political, tenets of the Nation of Islam. The book is dedicated to Sanchez's father and to "my spiritual FATHER, THE HONORABLE ELIJAH MUHAMMAD." Its sections trace a personal and communal history: "Queens of the Universe" introduces the volume, followed by "Past," "Present," "Rebirth," and "Future." Although this book is Sanchez's only one devoted exclusively to the psyche of black women, it is also her most patriarchal, advancing the Nation's view of women as the bearers of the next generation of black warriors and the supporters of the nation-building activities conducted by black men.

In recent years, however, Sanchez's poetics registers a new sense of the possibility of wedding a communal black voice to an explicit gender politics. This writing reveals as well that Sanchez rejects her earlier homophobic rhetoric and, rather than needing to articulate a black identity as essential and unified, perceives its oppositional status in terms of a new inclusiveness and sense of intersecting and overlapping elements of self. "Poem for Cornel West" includes one of Sanchez's characteristic catalogs that praises West's purposeful inclusiveness: "He acknowledges us all. The poor. Blacks and whites. Asians and Native Americans. Jews and Muslims. Latinos and Africans. Gays and Lesbians" (*Like the Singing Coming off the Drums* 131). The "us all" of Sanchez's new sensibility is clearly meant to heal wounds and assert connection over divisiveness. At the same time, Sanchez has less difficulty voicing an overtly black feminist perspective, one that need not be seen as subverting black unity. With the work of such writers as Barbara Smith, hooks, Wallace, Shange, and others in place, Sanchez builds on her earlier, more ambivalent attempts to assert the importance of feminist awareness. *Wounded in the House of a Friend* (1995; hereafter *Wounded*) contains a devastating account of the rape of a black woman ("Eyewitness: Case No. 3456") as well as a satiric commentary on the Clarence Thomas–Anita Hill sexual harassment hearings, with the explanatory title "Introduction of Toni Morrison, and Others, on the Occasion of the Publication of Her Book *Race-ing Justice, En-gendering Power: Essays on Anita Hill, Clarence Thomas, and the Construction of Social Reality*." With apparent ease, this piece satirizes the media's treatment of Thomas as a black male ("Of course it ain't strange for the *New York Times* [/] to delight in your accomplishment of weight lifting. [/] We all know that Black men's bodies are important [/] to them, to women, other men, Phil Donahue, academics, [/] voyeurs, scientists, journalists, oprawinfrey, undertakers" [*Wounded* 54]) and praises the work of Morrison's "wordsmiths" "who [forge] a place for us to [/] begin to understand the madness of this western psyche, [/] the madness of men bonding in public against all women" (55–56).

Perhaps equally telling, both *Wounded in the House of a Friend* and *Like the Singing Coming off the Drums: Love Poems* display the extent to which the earlier division between Sanchez's public, Black Arts rhetoric, and private lyric meditations is apparently no longer problematic. Each book combines in a single volume the political commentaries and the love poems that Sanchez earlier saw fit to divide into separate poetic statements. In particular, the recent collection of love poems, like the earlier volume of that title, contains intimate lyrics in the form of haiku, tanka, and sonku. But it also includes public tributes to Ella Fitzgerald, Sweet Honey in the Rock, Tupac Shakur, Bambara, and Brooks, as well as the mixed genre "Love Poem" [for Tupac] and "Love Conversation" [AIDS day 1994 in Philadelphia, for Essex Hemphill]. Such crossings of the communal and the intimate, as well as of poetic genres, mark Sanchez's comfort with a necessary meeting of public and private selves.

Sanchez's early work, though conflicted, broke ground: Drawing on Sanchez's earliest efforts, more recent black poets and critics furthered the rhetoric and the poetics that Sanchez began at a time when her explorations of gender conflicts within the movement were welcomed by neither white feminists nor Black Arts activists. Of her early experimentation Sanchez notes that "For many of us our change in style was synonymous with a change in content" (*Parnassus* 367). Of the more recent, less militant poems, she explains — referring to the title *Homegirls and Handgrenades* (1984) — that "hand grenades are the words I use to explode myths about people, about ourselves, about how we live and what we think" (*Parnassus* 364). This is the different sort of experiment that marks Sanchez's inquiry into the personal and political in *Love Poems*, where intimate connections are inextricable from the lives of whole communities.

Sanchez's position as a woman negotiating the masculine perspective of Black Arts resembles that of Anglo-American women poets of the modern period. More recent feminist avant-gardists, however, have the considerable advantage of access to a tradition of feminist experimentalism that Sanchez, as well as Stein and Loy, found unavailable. The final two chapters of this book shift from the examination of women poets' dialogues with the cultures of male-dominated avant-garde movements to the question of inheritance *among* feminist avant-gardists, an approach that reveals increasingly diverse influences and hybrid forms. A fundamental difference both to Susan Howe and to the younger Harryette Mullen has been the increased availability of works by — and examples of — feminist avant-garde predecessors, including Stein, others of the modernist generation, and the women poets of Black Arts. It is that layered and rich legacy of both continuity and innovation that informs the increasingly hybrid works of the poets to whom I now turn.

TRADITIONS OF MARGINALITY

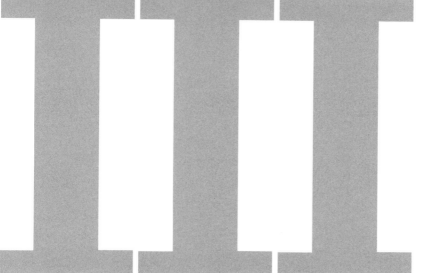

4

"UNSETTLING" AMERICA

Susan Howe and Antinomian Tradition

In 1983 Kathleen Fraser and a group of San Francisco poets, discouraged by the lack of visibility of contemporary women innovators in both avant-garde and feminist circles, founded *HOW(ever)*, the first journal in the United States devoted to feminist avant-garde writing. For the poets who edited *HOW(ever)*, recuperating a specifically feminist avant-garde lineage was of critical importance, for their work was committed to exploring not just linguistic experimentation but the relationship between the construction of gender and the structures of language. As editor, Fraser asserted several goals for the journal: to recuperate women avant-gardists of the modern period, to foster dialogue between contemporary women poets and feminist scholars, and to nurture a community of avant-garde writers caught between the divergent camps of a "mainstream" feminist poetics and the largely male circles of the literary avant-garde. It was a project dedicated to the notion "that aesthetics, form, language usage are intimately bound up in positions and constructions of gender and power" (Kinnahan, "Hybrid").

HOW(ever) marks an important juncture in the history of avant-garde women poets in America. There was little "usable past" of feminist innovation available to women writers of the modern and early postwar years. Feminist avant-garde poets from Stein to Sanchez occupied an anomalous position in American letters, struggling against the frequent masculinism of avant-garde rhetoric while attempting to voice feminist alternatives. By contrast, for more recent poets, dialogue with earlier feminist experimentalists often replaces the debates with contemporaneous male avant-garde groups. To be sure, belatedness is evident in the work of many contemporary poets, who acknowledge modernist precursors — often by way of a process Lynn Keller calls "the historical transmission and modification of modernist poetic techniques."[1] This sort of transmission has affected recent feminist avant-gardists in distinct ways. If women avant-gardists of the modern period positioned their work in ambivalent, even adversarial, relation to a largely masculine avant-garde agenda, contemporary feminist avant-gardists assert an increasingly hybrid set of lineages. As I will show in these final two chapters, feminist avant-gardists merge diverse sources to construct versions of a usable past, to claim a place in a continuing feminist history.

Among such writers working to articulate a feminist avant-garde tradition, Susan Howe establishes herself as the literary descendent of a number of lineages. My focus in this chapter will be her exploration of an alternative strain in American feminism. Howe is frequently associated with the Language group, whose disjunctive texts began to appear in the 1970s, focusing on what Marjorie Perloff has called "the word as such" in radical texts that powerfully oppose the personal lyric privileged in American letters. Like theorists of the Black Arts movement, Language writers challenge readers to address the workings of class and their relations to linguistic structures in contemporary mass culture.[2] Common ties with Howe are striking, including debts to crucial precursors like Stein, Pound, Charles Olson, and other anti-Eliotic American poets. Still, from her earliest publications, Howe has distinguished her poetics from the Marxist roots of such poet-theorists as Ron Silliman and Bruce Andrews. As Ann Vickery points out, despite parallel lines of inquiry into language practices, Howe stated early in her writing career that "the political genealogies of $L=A=N=G=U=A=G=E$ tend to exclude her, focusing as they do on theories that take little account of women's experience" (Vickery, *Leaving Lines of Gender* 83). Howe holds that she has "never followed an agenda or program," and she clarifies that her early inspirations were not those of Language writing:

> I wasn't reading the Russian formalist critics. I had no Marxist background, having never been to any university. . . . Most of the Language poets were in universities during the late sixties, and their work is fueled by the political rage and the courage of that period. I can understand it and identify with it, but at a remove. (Keller, "An Interview" 20)

Howe's writing certainly does show ties to the varied innovations and political commitments of the Language group. But her poetic practice is also noteworthy for its parallels with the project of *HOW(ever)*: the goal of recuperating and testifying to feminist avant-garde traditions in American poetry. For Howe, this tradition includes Stein, Loy, and H.D. But it merges as well with lineages defined in other ways, what Keller terms "a predominantly male iconoclastic tradition" in Howe's writing. Howe names Robert Duncan, Olson, William Carlos Williams, Wallace Stevens, and Hart Crane, among others.[3] I argue that, in grafting poetic and historical figures in hybrid fashion, Howe differs from her contemporaries in linking avant-gardism to a lineage rarely identified at all in American letters: that of women's spiritual and political dissent. In much of her engagement with the question of lineage, Howe reveals the association in U.S. history and literature between constructions of the feminine and the accusation of antinomianism, and she connects both to "avant-garde" activism from the period of Puritan settlement onward. Howe has been especially concerned with the textual violation and silencing of women writers, particularly the bowdlerizing of Emily Dickinson's texts. Merging traditions both literary and historical, aesthetic and sociological, Howe writes about figures ranging from Anne Hutchinson and Mary Rowlandson to Swift's Stella and Lear's Cordelia. In the process, Howe attests to — and her work actively creates — a feminist avant-garde usable past.[4]

In her recovery of textual resistance, Howe pursues both a historical and a theoretical project, and her writing, like H.D.'s, is emblematic of an avant-gardist's paradoxical pursuit of the past. Like Fraser, Howe privileges those who radically contest gender difference. As Keller points out, contesting difference leads Howe to identify a "feminine element" in Olson, for example, "despite his work's disturbing elision of women" (*Forms of Expansion* 192). In this complex set of retrievals, Howe clarifies that gender difference impinges on the visionary, rigidly constructing a dualistic sense of self that threatens individuals' creativity and the well-being of the body politic. Howe's poetics — her fragmented, displaced lines, nonce-words and visual constructions — represent a textual form of antinomian resistance. As in the subtitle of her critical book *The Birth-Mark: Unsettling the Wilderness in American Literary History* (Hanover, N. H.: Wesleyan U.P., 1991; hereafter *BM*), Howe's writing bears witness to feminist "unsettlement" that combats conventional language and explores ways to obliterate linguistic and social constraints, including rules of gender difference.[5] As she argues of Dickinson, "Poetry leads past possession of self to transfiguration beyond gender" (*My Emily Dickinson*, hereafter *MED*, 138).

In the discussion that follows, I chart the parallels between Howe's concern with the suppression of a feminized antinomian dissent in American history and the recuperative editorial project, begun just a few years after Howe began to publish, of the journal *HOW(ever)*. I demonstrate the awareness of what Fraser calls a "tradition of marginality" both in Howe's work and in the approach taken by Fraser and other poets associated with *HOW(ever)*. I also discuss the ways this shared antiessentialist avant-garde tradition contrasts with second wave feminist poetics during these years. I then focus on Howe's invocation of feminist traditions in one central text, *Articulation of Sound Forms in Time* (1987). Here, as in much of her writing, Howe invokes dissident feminist voices, from Anne Hutchinson to H.D. Howe describes the tale of a Puritan minister who embarks on an errand into the wilderness and gets lost in the "feminine" terrain he had set out to conquer. Having crossed geographic and psychic boundaries, he returns only to be rejected by his town and flock. In the Calvinist city on a hill, civic rejection, a sign of God's will, means either loss of spiritual election or an equally frightening challenge to faith itself. The minister's strange tale is the inception of Howe's disjunctive sequence. Discussing the poem's first section, I focus on Howe's treatment of gender-coding in language to demonstrate her deconstruction of "woman" and the feminine. In a further section I extend the discussion to Howe's treatment of metaphors of gender crossing in Puritan theology, and I illustrate the comparisons with Hutchinson, Dickinson, and H.D. that inform Howe's text. In the story Howe evokes, the minister's failure augurs the downfall of the Puritan errand. But for Howe it also signals the fundamental challenge of her own poetics — to acknowledge an avant-garde legacy that dismantles difference.

In 1992, in the final issue of *HOW(ever)*, editor Kathleen Fraser summed up the situation that had led to the journal's founding nine years earlier:

> we felt unfamilied, without a *place* in which to find or assert our own particular hybrids. Unpredictable by definition, "the new" seemed to have become quickly over-prescriptive in journals shaped by various male-dominant poetics or a feminist editorship whose tastes/politics did not acknowledge much of the poetry we felt to be central to our moment — the continuously indefinable, often "peculiar" writings being pieced together by women refusing the acceptable norms. We wanted to make a place for these writers. But we weren't fond of the grip of rules nor the territorial claims of the male manifesto tradition. . . . We were

interested in how works were freshly constructed and language reanimated within the experience of "female"-gendered lives.[6]

This statement — its desire for family and its inquiry into what constitutes the female in women's lives — reflects Fraser's sense of the marginalization of feminist avant-garde writing and theorizing in the circles of both second-wave feminism and a burgeoning radical poetics. As one example, elsewhere Fraser points to the exclusion of Barbara Guest from "a major anthology of the works of the New York School," an "erasure [that] was my first in-person encounter with this common historic practice."[7] As she notes, anthologies through the mid-1980s consistently ignored the work of women experimentalists, while representing a tradition that comfortably included "Joyce, Beckett, Olson, and Ashbery," and indeed Fraser's formal education had failed to introduce her to female modernists.[8] Fraser was not alone in observing such omissions. One critic argued in a 1984 article that the history of modernism still ignored the work of women innovators,[9] and Howe makes similar observations; she contends that the "American practice" of a poetics that "involves a fracturing of discourse, a breaking of boundaries of all sorts" has been largely excluded from the canon. The omission is further vexed by gender, for as Howe notes, even "when the history of this sub sub group gets written even *here* women get shut up or out" (Bernstein, *Politics* 192–93).

In the late 1970s, Fraser began to teach graduate seminars "in feminist poetics and modernist women writers." Increasingly, in these classes, "working methods [of young women poets] began to include collage, disruption, and sentence fragmentation. . . . Often these works were inspired by the poems and poetic prose of Woolf, Stein, Loy, H.D., Djuna Barnes, Moore, Richardson, Jean Rhys, and Lorine Niedecker, all of which investigated states of female mind and experience" (Boland and Fraser, "A Conversation" 388). Yet the texts of these precursors remained largely invisible to critics. As Fraser tells it, "Poetry scholarship seemed to be comfortable with Dickinson and then, with the exception of a minimal nod to Marianne Moore, Elizabeth Bishop, and H.D., to jump over the major innovations of modernist women writers" (Hogue, "Interview with Fraser" 16). Like Rachel Blau DuPlessis, Carolyn Burke, and other feminists interested in the avant-garde, Fraser began questioning why there was "no acknowledged tradition of modernist women's poetry continuing out of H.D., Stein, Dorothy Richardson, Woolf, Mina Loy, Djuna Barnes," among others ("Tradition" 61). At the same time that scholars engaged in "gynocriticism"—rediscovering and proffering readings of neglected women's texts, often fiction, by such writers as Kate Chopin, Charlotte Perkins Gilman, and others — the erasure of modernist women innovators was increasingly brought home to Fraser. At the same time, as Fraser recalls, even in the absence of a body of criticism about such writers, "We began to understand the links back to the innovative practice of modernist women whom we hadn't understood to be an important part of our family." [10]

As she noted in the above statement about the founding of *HOW(ever)*, in addition to facing the erasure of feminist avant-garde precursors, Fraser tackled an uncomfortable division between male-dominant avant-garde journals and an emerging feminist poetics that privileged what she calls a "common language" aesthetic. Fraser mentions the editorial limitations and frequent sexism of "both the mainstream and more avant-garde publications" of the 1970s and 1980s (Hogue, "Interview with Fraser" 17), yet she found problematic as well the feminist "call for the immediately accessible language of personal experience as a binding voice of women's strength" ("Tradition" 58). For many feminists, "the emphasis on finding a common language through poetry was crucial to forging community and establishing a shared identity. But there never seemed to be a comfortable place for experimental women poets" (Boland and Fraser, "Conversation" 398). As second-wave feminism gained momentum, "It was as if women were being told that we couldn't afford the 'luxury' of the more experimentalist texts, in a period urgently focused on female identity and its instatement in the mainstream culture. Some even equated innovative practice with 'elitism'" (Hogue, "Interview with Fraser" 16–17).

Michael Bibby and Kim Whitehead both show that the feminist emphasis on identity took the form of poetry written to be as accessible as possible, in transparent language. Poet-activists aimed to generate new awareness of female experience, often by exploring previously taboo subjects. As the title of the 1973 anthology *No More Masks!* suggests, this approach urged political awareness by means of the "naked" truth and an intensely personal voice. As the anthology's title also indicates, the central challenge in this poetic tradition can be encapsulated by Muriel Rukeyser's famous question, "What would happen if one woman told the truth about her life? / The world would split open." Rukeyser's varied and complex poetics is appropriated to the charge of a transparent truth-telling. Developing this confessional mode, feminist movement poetry emphasized open form and political message. According to Whitehead, feminist poets were driven by a need "to avoid alienating the rank and file of the women's movement through the use of the elite's poetic techniques,"[11] which, as Fraser argues, included any "inaccessible" or unrecognizable avant-garde experimentation with syntax, diction, or form. As Jan Clausen later noted of 1970s feminist poetry, "what had begun as an anti-traditional movement had to a certain extent developed its own dogmas, conventions, cautions, clichés, taboos," including a prevailing "obsession with accessibility" ("A Movement of Poets" 31, 23).

Unhappy with the predominant assumptions of "movement" poetry, Fraser strongly felt that "feminist and traditional critics [were] failing to develop any interest in contemporary women poets working to bring structural and syntactic innovation into current poetic practice," and she felt herself hungry for "a place where our issues could be aired and some new choices put forward in women's poetry — asserted and selected by women." In this spirit Fraser, with poets Beverly Dahlen and Frances Jaffer, founded in 1983 the first-ever journal devoted to feminist avant-garde writing, specifically with attention to recovering works by modernist women. The name *HOW(ever)*, alluding to a phrase from Marianne Moore's "Poetry," signified to Fraser "an addendum, a point of view from the margins" ("Tradition" 61–63), and, as Vickery points out, the publication was often abbreviated *H(er)*, suggesting ties to such predecessors as H.D. (*HERmione*, among other key texts), and stressing "process and method in foregrounding the word *how*."[12] Launching a "formal and intellectual critique which did feminist cultural work,"[13] *HOW(ever)* joined the ranks of the many feminist literary journals and publishing collectives that had thrived since the late 1960s, but with the specific purpose of voicing an alternative feminism largely ignored in scholarly, activist, and literary circles.[14]

Over the same years that Fraser was striving to bring feminist avant-garde poetics into greater prominence, Susan Howe was developing a body of innovative poetry and scholarship, as were such writers as Lyn Hejinian, Carla Harryman, Leslie Scalapino, and others. Howe was not part of the editorial network of *HOW(ever)*, yet her concerns at this time were markedly parallel to those of Fraser and her San Francisco colleagues. Howe hoped — like Fraser — to recover a past of suppressed women's voices. In a 1990 interview, Howe noted the absence of an acknowledged feminist avant-garde tradition:

> When I read books about American poetry and even current discussions among poets . . . I generally read about men. Yes, Dickinson is in the

canon. But she is treated as an isolated case, not as part of an on-going influence. . . . Stein is brought in but again as an isolated case, with influence, but somehow a break in the line. Marianne Moore the same, an isolated phenomenon. . . . [And] with H.D. we must always hear of her romantic connection to Pound, Lawrence, even the Williams friendship is presented not in terms of poetry but romance or rejection. And it's usually their influence on her, not her influence on them. (Foster, "Interview" 26)

Like Fraser, Howe hoped to illustrate the extent to which work such as hers was part of an ongoing feminist lineage.

Howe's poetry and scholarly work on this question appeared periodically in the pages of *HOW(ever)*. Howe published in *HOW(ever)* excerpts from *My Emily Dickinson*, "The Illogic of Sumptuary Values" (later collected in *Birth-Mark*), and "Women and Their Effect in the Distance,"[15] all of which emphasize the invisibility of feminist avant-garde lineage, even as Howe continued to engage with such crucial male antecedents as Pound, Olson, and Duncan. Howe reclaims Dickinson as a predecessor, lampooning the notion that a "male Muse-minister" was the real force behind her work; and she exposes the politics of textual control in the editing that regularized Dickinson's punctuation, spacing, and uses of variants. Howe analyzes a manuscript page: "These lines traced by pencil or in ink on paper were formed by an innovator. . . . There are political implications here," for Dickinson's texts necessitate "an end to passive consumerism" (*HOW(ever)* 3.4 [1986]: 12). Howe notes as well the patriarchal underpinnings of Dickinson's packaging and subsequent consumption, not just through Thomas Johnson's aggressive editing but also through later institutional control:

> One hundred years after her death if I quote from her poems or letters in a book, and I use either the Johnson edition of the *Complete Poems* or Franklin's edited *Manuscript Books* as the source, I must obtain permission from and pay a fee to The President and Fellows of Harvard College and the Trustees of Amherst College.
>
> . . . Poetry is never a personal possession. The text was a vision and gesture before it became sign and coded exchange in a political economy of value. (13)

Such commodification mitigates "vision." It is no coincidence that the original texts are female-authored, and its overseers are the President and Fellows of institutions entrenched in patriarchal tradition. Kin to the editorial project of *HOW(ever)*, Howe's contentions, as Linda Kinnahan points out, emphasize process, marginality, and the importance of the extratextual to the understanding of any published work ("Peculiar Hybrid").

Like Fraser, Howe has expended considerable effort both to recover radical female voices and to address the effects on contemporary writing of lost textual legacies. Howe opens *My Emily Dickinson* with the construction of two forebears erased or misrepresented all too often (especially as of 1985, when Howe was writing):

> In the college library I use there are two writers whose work refuses to conform to the Anglo-American literary traditions these institutions perpetuate. Emily Dickinson and Gertrude Stein are clearly among the most innovative precursors of modernist poetry and prose, yet to this day canonical criticism from Harold Bloom to Hugh Kenner persists in dropping their names and ignoring their work. Why these two path-finders were women, why American — are questions too often lost in the penchant for biographical detail that "lovingly" muffles their voices.[16]

Reminiscent of Woolf's Oxford halls in the opening of *A Room of One's Own*, Howe's evocation of the "college library," and the institutionally sanctioned books within it, points to a patriarchal control that effectively silences innovative women by lovingly suppressing their texts in favor of the more sensational biographical detail — a cult of personality. Howe's witness of this lost or trivialized avant-garde tradition connects the work of Dickinson and Stein to her own, for, like herself, both precursors "conducted a skillful and ironic investigation of patriarchal authority over literary history." Far from making the claims for novelty that preoccupied writers of the historical avant-gardes, both Howe and Fraser assert that even as the Pound tradition and its offshoots are central to their work, they follow as well in a long line of a politically defined and specifically feminist transgression — one too often unacknowledged, even by feminists themselves. Howe critiques Cixous, for example, for neglecting Stein, despite the fact that "All the elements that Cixous longs for in the writing women *will* do, can be found in Stein, who clearly broke the codes that negated" (*MED* 11–12).

For Howe, such textual innovation emerges from a neglected lineage of feminist spiritual and literary resistance. Hogue draws Fraser and Howe together: both write "against the grain of the dead father's Law," to forge a feminist "spiritual activism" ("Infectious Ecstasy" 62, 52). It is a spiritual inquiry that is also rigorously informed by the legacy of Puritan theocracy. Howe describes Dickinson in this light:

> The issue of editorial control is directly connected to the attempted erasure of antinomianism in our culture. . . . The excommunication and banishment of the early American female preacher and prophet Anne Hutchinson, and the comparison of her opinions to monstrous births, is not unrelated to the editorial apprehension and domestication of Emily Dickinson. . . . The antinomian controversy continues in the form, often called formlessness, of Dickinson's letters and poems. (*BM* 1)

Though finally rescued from accusations of formlessness, Dickinson's innovations sparked an initial reception kin to that of Anne Hutchinson's antinomian rebellion. Howe identifies "Dickinson's refusal during her teens to join the Congregational Church during the Great Awakening" as emblematic of a feminist genealogy: The poet's defiance of "great community pressure recalls the stubborn strength in isolation of Mary Rowlandson. Her intuitive spiritual apprehension links her with Anne Hutchinson and Mary Dyer" (*MED* 54). Dickinson's apprehension hearkens back to prior examples of female heterodoxy: Hutchinson's assertion of direct revelation and her resistance to enormous social pressure parallel the stalwart survival of Mary Rowlandson in captivity (the subject of an extended essay in *Birth-Mark*). Howe presents Rowlandson as exhibiting not just strength in isolation but also a literary daring kin to Hutchinson's un-feminine speech.

All three figures — Hutchinson, Rowlandson, and Dickinson — represent an unrecognized strain in American letters, one that paves the way for Howe's textual liberties.[17] As Howe tells it, writing poetry is for her "'an unruly, multisubjective activity,'"[18] a latter-day antinomianism: "Strange translucencies: letters, phonemes, syllables, rhymes, shorthand segments, alliteration, assonance, meter, form a ladder to an outside state outside of States" (*BM* 46). Howe locates in these women's dissidence, and their linguistic disruptions, a precedent for showing how gender operates as a limitation in language. In pursuit of this vision, Howe embraces the "feminine element" in a number of male writers central to her poetics, from Melville to Olson. Melding influences, Howe complicates the sense of lineage we are likely to glean from her writings; she constructs a hybrid of various sources, voices, and historical moments. Throughout, she combines archival research with ecstatic poetic utterance, and, I would argue, does so to craft a distinctly feminist avant-garde usable past. Accordingly, before discussing

Articulation of Sound Forms in Time, I would like to explore the examples of Anne Hutchinson, Mary Rowlandson, and Dickinson — three of Howe's most important antinomian, feminist forebears.

Howe's tale of origin begins with Hutchinson's unbecoming blasphemy. It was no lesser figure than the preeminent Thomas Shepard (whom Howe describes as the "earnest persecutor of Anne Hutchinson and repudiator of 'erroneous Antinomian doctrines'" [BM 56]) who, among others, saw to it that, following her court and church trials, "Mrs. Hutchinson was silenced" (BM 58), banished from the Massachusetts Bay Colony in 1638, for having criticized the colony's patriarchs for preaching what she held was a covenant of works rather than the New England Puritans' covenant of grace. "Incloser," the piece from which this description of Shepard is drawn, explores Shepard's strangely divided autobiography — a book whose unlined, marginless pages contain writing that begins at both ends and works inward from each extreme toward an empty center. Its reversibility figures a powerful self-division between public and private texts, but the ambiguity does not extend to the persecution of Hutchinson, which Howe returns to repeatedly — including comparison between the scandalously outspoken Hutchinson and Shepard's own wife, "a woman of 'incomparable meekness of spirit, toward my selfe especially.'" [19] The contrast could not be more pointed: indeed, Howe recounts that Hutchinson's story served as a terrifying object lesson to generations of women who risked "unwiving" themselves of powerful husbands by acquiring learning or — worse still — daring to preach the word. One example Howe points to was the wife of the governor of Hartford, who, as John Winthrop described it in his journal, "was fallen into a sad infirmity, the loss of her understanding and reason . . . by occasion of her giving herself wholly to reading and writing." [20]

As Amy Schrager Lang explains, the accusations of antinomianism leveled against Anne Hutchinson stemmed from gendered roles: "the gender-specific problem of the public woman figures the larger dilemma of maintaining the law" (*Prophetic Woman* 3). Lang argues, "the crime attributed to Hutchinson at her trial is the violation of her role. She is condemned for playing the part of teacher, minister, magistrate, husband." Hence the cautionary tales penned by Thomas Welde, Cotton Mather, and other chroniclers and preachers — representations of Anne Hutchinson as Eve ("both seduced and seductress"), Jezebel (sexual wanton), and even Hydra ("the archetypal mother of monsters") (Lang, *Prophetic Woman* 65). It was less her heresy than her trespass upon the male domain of theological speech that resulted in Anne Hutchinson's excommunication and banishment.

That Hutchinson's transgression was fundamentally gendered in Puritan imaginations is apparent in the comparison — raised by Howe — between the Hutchinsonians' misguided notions and "monstrous births," which came "out of their wombs, as . . . out of their braines," as Welde explained.[21] The still-born "issue" of Hutchinson's follower Mary Dyer was the literal progeny of Hutchinson's doctrines. According to Winthrop's journal, Dyer's infant was born with a headless body adorned by horns and scales, the visible sign of God's vengeance against Hutchinson and her defenders, and a vindication of the Church fathers who would see them duly punished. (Similarly, the murder of Hutchinson and her family in an Indian raid years later was read as the unequivocal sign of God's judgment [Lang, *Prophetic Woman* 58].) As Lang points out, in arguing "that the misconceptions were God's visible demonstration of the monstrousness of the women's ideas," the patriarchs both disempowered them in mind and body (identifying interpretation itself as the province of men) and "turned the very femaleness of the women against them to prove them wrong" (56–57). Howe identifies the antinomian controversy as the founding moment in the feminist American past she claims as poet and scholar. Mary Dyer's "monstrous birth" becomes a figure for Howe's own de-forming texts — a dissonance of words born from the discordant voice of the heretical Anne Hutchinson and from the outlawed feminine knowledge of the midwife (witch) who birthed the still-born child. Howe's texts, her own identity, become that child itself/ herself: "One has just been born. A monist conception. It is a daughter a monster the other" (*BM* 119).

Howe describes this tradition as deliberately transgressing *literary* mores — a feminist "avant-gardism" of particular risk. Howe calls Rowlandson's 1682 "A True History of the Captivity and Restoration of Mrs. Mary Rowlandson," her account of Indian capture and eventual release, "the first published narrative written by an Anglo-American woman ostensibly to serve as a reminder of God's Providence." Yet, as Howe points out, it is manifestly un-feminine, opening with gunfire, the murder of children, a burning home, and the cutting open of a slain settler's bowels. Writing against the grain of femininity, daringly confronting the violence inherent in her story, "Mary Rowlandson saw what she did not see said what she did not say" (*BM* 128). Such literary transgression sets Rowlandson apart from her more celebrated counterpart — the "tenth muse," Anne Bradstreet. With undisguised irony, Howe calls Rowlandson's textual violence a "far cry from Anne Bradstreet's polished pious verse" (*BM* 95); she distances herself not just from the piety but also from the *poetics* of the circumspect

Bradstreet, whose "correct" verse, like her piety, manifestly served to keep her safe. Howe notes that "Anne Bradstreet gained public acceptance as a writer" in the shadow of Anne Hutchinson and the hapless Mary Dyer:

> The excommunication and banishment of Anne Hutchinson; the banishment of Mary Dyer; published reports of their "monster" premature babies; the reprimands or silencing of other women who were midwives, had medical knowledge, or transgressed the male boundaries of theology by preaching . . . were ominous precedents. Anne Bradstreet was the daughter of a governor of Massachusetts and the wife of a leading magistrate, both of whom were virulent persecutors of Anne Hutchinson.
>
> (*BM* 113)

The object lesson was a powerful one. In Howe's account, Bradstreet adopts both polish and piety in a necessary bid for survival. As Howe points out, Bradstreet's sister was not so lucky. In a reprise of Anne Hutchinson's offenses, Sarah Dudley Keayne trespassed onto the male domain of theological learning, having "growne a great preacher"; her husband Thomas Dudley wrote to his father-in-law, "shee has unwived her selfe." As a result, she was disinherited, lost her husband and custody of her daughter (thus figuring the demise of female lineage), and was finally relegated to historical oblivion.[22]

Howe contrasts the circumspect tradition of Anne Bradstreet with that of feminist innovators, whose daring renders unthinkable the degree of public acceptability Bradstreet's "polished verse" permitted. It is oddly appropriate, then, that Bradstreet's poems were reclaimed in later years by an American woman writer who advances what Fraser calls the "common language" aesthetic of 1970s feminism: In 1967 Adrienne Rich wrote the foreword to Bradstreet's newly available selected poems.[23] By contrast, Howe locates her lineage in the terrain of a feminist Puritan dissent wherein "The violence of ambiguity" is voiced, and "Disorder is another order" (*BM* 122). In the dichotomy between the verse-piety of Bradstreet and the heterodoxical "enthusiasm" of Hutchinson, Howe unequivocally chooses the latter path.[24]

For Howe, this antinomian enthusiasm disrupts gendered typing, and yet consistently it has been gendered feminine. Howe rebels against such linkage, against the metaphoric construction of difference, whether it condemns an essentialist view of woman or exalts it. Both Howe and Fraser characterize their feminist avant-garde precursors as advancing an anti-essentialist strain in American feminism, in contrast to the preoccupations of "movement" poetry — the work of such poets as Robin Morgan, Susan Griffin, or Alta, who created a body politics in their activism and their writing alike.[25] Howe's feminism, as I will show, challenges both binarism and regulated linguistic structures. Like Fraser, who in HOW(ever) attempted to give voice to a feminist avant-garde tradition firmly "opposed to an essentialist position that was oriented toward subject — the subject being women as they are organized around their biology," Howe unearths a strain of women's dissent that unsettles the very rudiments of language, and in the process combats our culture's long history of difference.[26]

Steeped in the secrets of historical records, a "library cormorant,"[27] Howe explains that "If you are a woman, archives hold perpetual ironies. Because the gaps and silences are where you find yourself" (Foster, "Interview" 17). It is this archival absence, the silencing of women in the annals of history and criticism, that has concerned Howe since her earliest work.

If Howe struggles against the literary piety of an Anne Bradstreet, disordering the gendered self, she also strives to give voice to the silenced, to emend historical record. DuPlessis observes that "Howe appears to be on the cusp between two feminisms: the one analysing female difference, the other 'feminine' difference."[28] Howe dramatizes this split in the introduction to My Emily Dickinson by reproaching Cixous for valuing "the feminine" but ignoring the revolutionary work of actual women writers, and also lamenting the fact that Sandra Gilbert and Susan Gubar's The Madwoman in the Attic fails to mention that a "penchant for linguistic decreation [is] ushered in by their representative poet Emily Dickinson" (MED 12–13), once again marginalizing women's innovations in favor of a presumptive view of the "feminine." In the words of the materialist feminist Monique Wittig, Howe avers that gender is "a primitive ontological concept that enforces in language a division of beings into sexes." It is crucial to acknowledge that "language has a plastic action upon the real," and therefore that gender "must be destroyed." And, as Howe also believes, "the possibility of its destruction is given through the very exercise of language." Wittig's description of her own work applies as well to Howe's: "Words, their disposition, their arrangement, their relation to each other, the whole nebula of their constellations shift, are displaced, engulfed or reoriented, put sideways. . . . They are hit in their meaning and also in their form."[29] Howe opposes identifying symbolic language as patriarchal, thus legitimizing "the dichotomy between male rationality and female materiality, corporeality, and sexuality," while "the system of binary oppositions remains the same" (Domna C. Stanton, "Difference on Trial" 170). Explaining her position, Howe points to the stutter that symbolizes vulnerability and alterity in Melville's *Billy Budd*:

> I hear the stutter as a sounding of uncertainty. What is silenced or not quite silenced. . . . A return is necessary, a way for women to go. Because we are in the stutter. We were expelled from the Garden of the Mythology of the American frontier. The drama's done. We are the Wilderness. We have come on to the stage stammering. (Foster, "Interview" 37)

Howe's aesthetic explores that stutter; her texts reveal history's hidden gender codes. Like historian Joan Wallach Scott, Howe not only emphasizes that history is gendered but also seeks to dismantle the structures on which such gender differences are based.[30]

In *Articulation of Sound Forms in Time*, Howe demonstrates her debt to an avant-garde tradition that shatters conventional usage by breaking down gender valences. Adapting an obscure incident from forgotten annals of American history, Howe trains her sites on the Puritan mission. As Perry Miller described it in *Errand into the Wilderness*, the Puritan city on a hill envisioned by John Winthrop and others was defined through its opposition to a savage land, seen as feminine; the Puritans read the text of God's will by interpreting emblematically the natural and social events in this polarized landscape.[31] Howe blurs the categories lodged in these metaphors of difference, fracturing the discourse of Puritan theology. In the peculiar story she adapts, Howe finds an allegorical figure for the de-gendering her own text enacts — its disjunctive language and broken narratives. The year is 1676, shortly after the start of King Philip's (Metacom's) War, the most profound danger English settlers had yet encountered in the Connecticut River Valley, and the same year Mary Rowlandson was captured in Lancaster, Massachusetts, by Metacom's attackers.[32] From the town of Hatfield, an army crosses the river and marches into the woods to drive several Indian tribes from their encampments. The resulting battle in the wilderness comes to be called "The Falls Fight" because, in the slaughter and confusion, many of the few Indians who escape the Europeans' fire "be[take] themselves to their bark canoes" and are "hurried down the falls" to their deaths (Susan Howe, *Singularities* 3; hereafter *S*).

Despite this apparently straightforward outline, exactly what transpired on this mission remains elusive in any historical record. In the first section of Howe's sequence, written in prose, Howe cites a letter composed over one hundred years after the incident, which in turn summarizes another. As becomes apparent, events are filtered through so many sources, and are in any case based on such a dubious original, that the nature of this historical narrative is impossible to determine. The central issue for Howe is that one Puritan minister gets lost in the forest after the Falls Fight and wanders for several days. He later attests that he and several others tried to surrender to the Indians with hopes of having their lives spared. Instead, they are covered with thatch, lit on fire, and made to run — until most burn to death. Somehow, despite this "baptism by fire," the minister escapes, but the story this "gentleman of publick spirit" tells is never fully believed. According to the 1781 letter, "Many people were not willing to give credit to [his] account, suggesting he was beside himself." His story is riddled with ironies: He is a man of the cloth engaged on a military mission, an imperialist who loses his errand — and perhaps his sanity — in the wilderness he sets out to conquer.

But most provocative to Howe is the minister's epicene name: Hope Atherton. Hope represents both a male subject and a feminized hero, a poet/wanderer who inadvertently turns the Puritan errand into his own erroneous journey. Like Mary Rowlandson, Hope crosses into the feminine-coded wilderness, even as his Christian name signals a similar doubling that challenges difference: "In our culture Hope is a name we give women. Signifying desire, trust, promise, does her name prophetically engender pacification of the feminine?"[33] For DuPlessis, *Articulation of Sound Forms in Time* can be read as an "allegory of how the center, how major man . . . entering almost accidentally some marginal space, goes from the straight and narrow to sheer errancy, sheer wanderings" ("Whowe" 163). But Howe is equally interested in the potential for the "other" lodged in Hope's name *before* his emblematic wandering — the mark of the feminine already inscribed in major man. Rather than reinforcing the law of the father, language in this case is a means of feminization, and the body (generally troped as feminine) provides a male vessel to house the (now) feminine concept of hope. These linguistic alterations resonate with the other metaphorical and literal crossings that Howe culls. The representative of civilization crosses into a wilderness that dupes him; he crosses the river that separates Europeans from Indians, believers from heathens; and he transgresses the borders between madness and sanity. Even as Howe critiques the imperialist mission, she also envisions Hope's journey as that of the marginalized (feminized) poet, who blurs socially defined categories of gender. To the Puritan imagination, Hope is immersed in the forest, "a place of wild beasts and uncontrolled lusts, of disorder and disharmony . . . the meeting place for [Satan's] witches and black priests," a place that acts as "a metaphor for man's estrangement from God."[34] The male Hope wanders in a fearsome terrain where redemption goes uncharted.

In "Hope Atherton's Wanderings," Howe evokes the Puritan duality between the unredeemed wilderness and the rationality of the symbolic system upon which Hope's civilization is based:

> Prest try to set after grandmother
> revived by and laid down left ly
> little distant each other and fro
> Saw digression hobbling driftwood
> forage two rotted beans & etc.
> Redy to faint slaughter story so
> Gone and signal through deep water
> Mr. Atherton's story Hope Atherton (*S* 6)

As Peter Nicholls points out, much of Howe's diction in this passage is taken — out of context — from a history of Deerfield, not of Hatfield at all. Nicholls's account reveals that Howe composed her linguistic collage by a method of chance operations that seems precisely *not* to point us toward the historical relevance of any of Howe's original sources.[35] And yet this arbitrary mode of construction suits Hope's wanderings, which appear in ironic fragments suggesting the breakdown of the masculine order of the state. The phrase "little distant each other and fro" suggests wasted, circular motion, as "fro" is divorced from the "to" that normally secures its context. Hope's "digression" is, like that of his allegorical brother, Young Goodman Brown, evidence of God's displeasure, a loss of self to the anarchic forces of (moral) wilderness. Most significant to this Christian soldier, the "slaughter story" — the crusade against the Indian tribes that gave his journey meaning — is a distant scene from which Hope is disconnected, "hobbling" in decomposition (Thoreauvian "rotted beans & etc.") as randomly as driftwood in water. The final line in the following strophe reads, "'Deep water' he *must* have crossed over," and Hope has indeed already crossed when the poem begins. The very first strophe evokes his ambiguous position: "Mr. Atherton's story Hope Atherton." His "hope" for a coherent story is coupled with the minister's masculine appellation, "Mr." But Howe immediately strips his name of this social label, and the Christian name Hope even more clearly suggests the feminine — ironic double of the anarchic wilderness.[36]

Howe's language here suggests Puritan culture in a state of explosion; its debris inhabits the page. Liberated from the social contract, words rebel in antinomian defiance, in ironic counterpoint to Hope's search for visible sainthood. Bits of stray signifiers subvert meaning and challenge the gendering of language itself:

> rest chondriacal lunacy
> velc cello viable toil
> quench conch uncannunc
> drumm amonoosuck ythian (*S* 10)

Disconnected from syntactic structures, fragments of Old English, Latin, and Indian languages struggle for center stage. But although it can be argued that the result of this linguistic stew is nothing more than babble, a decoding of the sort *Tender Buttons* invites demystifies this passage. The word "uncannunc," for example, conceals "uncanny," the Latin *nunc* (now), "annunciation," and even "unconscious" — dense allusions to Hope's spiritual journey. Similarly, the Latinate "cello" and the Indian-sounding "amonoosuck" come from different cognitive worlds that meet in the hybrid cultures of colonial America. Despite the reference to Hope's putative lunacy, the threat in this passage is less madness than the possibility of a divorce between the symbolic and conventional systems of meaning and value. In the Puritan view, social realities embody divine will. Surely language, man's primary social tool, should reflect (or at least aspire to) the transparency of the word of God. In stark contrast to this conviction, an antinomian might hold that outward signs have little to do with spiritual or inward states — much as in Howe's anarchic composition.[37]

It was precisely the trespass onto the prerogative of theological speech that resulted in Anne Hutchinson's silencing. Howe connects this patriarchal rule over the word with the misguided position that symbolic language necessarily connotes the law of the father and thus suppresses the "feminine." The title *The Birth-Mark: Unsettling the Wilderness in American Literary History* indicates Howe's goal to unsettle not *just* the symbolic but the *wilderness* itself, where wilderness is understood as the force the symbolic opposes: Howe destabilizes the trope, unsettles the *already* unsettled, to question the identification of the natural world with the uncharted, the feminine.[38] Dislodging gender codes and altering language are part of the same project — one that Howe admires in Dickinson, particularly in "My Life had stood — a Loaded Gun," a central focus of *My Emily Dickinson*. For Howe, one of the meanings of the allegorical Life in the poem is

The American continent and its westward moving frontier. Two centuries of pioneer literature and myth had insistently compared the land to a virgin woman (bride and queen). Exploration and settlement were pictured in terms of masculine erotic discovery and domination of alluring/threatening feminine territory. (*MED* 76)

Dickinson destabilizes this governing trope. She "went further than Browning, coding and erasing — deciphering the idea of herself, dissimulation in revelation" (*MED* 76). This concept of virginity is the metaphor on which New England was based: Puritan thought required that the female subject contemplate "the idea of herself" in wilderness. Dickinson dismantled both lexical landscape and metaphoric geography; Howe positions herself as Dickinson's descendent, a disrupter of feminine codes. As Dickinson's progeny, she refutes the "belle of Amherst" image by demonstrating how deliberate — and revolutionary — were Dickinson's idiosyncrasies: "Codes are confounded and converted. 'Authoritative readings' confuse her nonconformity" (*BM* 139); "If we could perfectly restore each packet to its original order, her original impulse would be impossible to decipher. The manuscript books and sets preserve their insubordination" (*BM* 144).[39]

In *Articulation*, Howe takes up the Dickinsonian mission by showing how gendered meaning is allotted to natural phenomena, and labels become dangerously fixed:

Anarchy into named theory
Entangled obedience

muffled discourse from distance
mummy thread undertow slough

Eve of origin Embla the eve
soft origin vat and covert (*S* 32)

Theorizing makes sense of anarchy by containing the unruly through law — entangled obedience results, while whatever resists is shunted to the margins (muffled discourse from distance). In this theory, there is nothing inevitable about the encoding of gender onto the world's events — yet Howe evokes a series of feminine associations we are likely to take for granted. Thus, in "mummy thread undertow slough," "mummy" evokes mother as well as death and bodily decay. An "undertow," a powerful draw toward oceanic submersion and annihilation, is a primary force of the feminine sea.

"Thread" suggests women's sewing and the story of Ariadne's feminine stratagem; "slough" suggests that aspect of the wilderness most linked to the female body. Only "thread" brings us to consider an actual occupation practiced by early American women; all the rest refer to natural phenomena, whose relationship to the social order becomes explicit in lines that link the power of myth to discourse. "Eve of origin" points to the source in Western culture for the association between women and both literal and spiritual death, for Eve's transgression precipitated the entrance of sin (and the pain of childbirth) into human history. This origin crosses linguistic boundaries: "Embla" is Scandinavian for Eve. Language reproduces gender typing (lowercase "eve" still evokes feminine darkness, in contrast to the Platonic light of rationality). This feminine "soft" origin is indeed "covert"— its power relations hidden by a logic that sees difference as natural.[40]

Just as Howe dismantles naturalized gender metaphors, she also dismantles bifurcations between the corporeal and the cognitive. Toward the close of "Hope Atherton's Wanderings," one striking passage combines highly symbolic signification with subversive rule-breaking:

Body perception thought of perceiving (half-thought

chaotic architect repudiate line Q confine lie link realm
circle a euclidean curtail theme theme toll function coda
severity whey crayon so distant grain scalp gnat carol
omen Cur cornice zed primitive shad sac stone fur bray
tub epoch too fum alter rude recess emblem sixty key

Epithets young in a box told as you fly (*S* 13)

Howe's word-fragments question familiar divisions — body and thought, materiality and abstraction. "Body perception thought of perceiving": subject and object are impossible to label; it is not that body is the object of the perceiving mind, for the lack of syntax prevents such easy categorization. This writing considers the ways in which body *constitutes* thought. "Perception" is the link between cognition and sensation; language operates *through* the body.[41] Similarly, gender divisions are codes imposed on language, and they need to be unsettled; appropriately, the first line ends with a single, open parenthesis.

In the word-collage that follows this first line, the bodily — grain, scalp, gnat — is juxtaposed with words suggesting abstract forms, from music (theme, coda, key) and architecture (architect, line, cornice) to geometry (euclidean). As though released from Pandora's box, as the final line suggests (Epithets young in a box told as you fly), these words emerge as both ordered (in the symmetry of Howe's visual construction) and chaotic, released from strict relationship to one another. They shift between the disciplines: "stone" suggests material reality and mortality (as in gravestone), associated with the feminine; yet it also evokes the rational, masculine language of architecture.[42] The play with etymology, juxtaposition, and the form and function of these words is complicated further by the allusion to Pandora's box: Pandora is the woman responsible for unleashing the evils of the world, but she also lets fly humankind's one solace: hope. Hope, it seems, is as much born of language as of woman.

As in this passage, much of "Hope Atherton's Wanderings" teases out elaborate allusions to the colonial enterprise and its obsession with an apocalyptic narrative: "Impulsion of a myth of beginning / The figure of a far-off Wanderer" (*S* 12). Europeans envisioned their settlement of the new world as a sanctified myth of beginning, which would culminate in vindication in this world and salvation in the next, an errand through which they might "possess a land without ever being possessed by it" (Miller, *Errand into the Wilderness* 6). The "impulsion" (impulse, compulsion) to mythologize their own beginnings led the Puritans to imagine the American wilderness as a tabula rasa waiting for their definitive text to be inscribed on its surface; the continent appeared as "a bare land, devoid of already established (and corrupt) institutions . . . where they could start *de novo*" (Miller 12). In this terrain, wandering connotes error, loss of mission. The "far-off Wanderer" is, in the context of the Falls Fight, the now-distant figure of Hope, lost in a terrifyingly unwritten wilderness.[43]

In the final section of "Hope Atherton's Wanderings," Hope's own language becomes fodder for a meditation on his ill-fated errand and its gender valences. Because of Hope's indeterminate status as male/female speaker, the feminine becomes impossible to locate:

Loving Friends and Kindred: —
When I look back
So short in charity and good works
We are a small remnant
of signal escapes wonderful in themselves
We march from our camp a little
and come home

Lost the beaten track and so
River section dark all this time
We must not worry
how few we are and fall from each other
More than language can express
Hope for the artist in America & etc
This is my birthday
These are the old home trees (*S* 16)

Hope Atherton strives to win his congregation back in the Puritan plain-style; ironically, this task encompasses "More than language can express." In his guise as male subject, he suffers from civic unrest: his epic home-coming, bathetic and unheroic, provides no Odyssean return. The failed hero has indeed "Lost the beaten track"; his error — which first landed him in the Indian camp — caused him to lose his errand. As Howe points out, according to Noah Webster, "erroneous" is the linguistic meeting point of "error" and "wandering": its first meaning is "Wandering; roving; unset-tled" (*BM* 54). "The figure of a far-off Wanderer" from Howe's earlier sec-tion desperately combats unsettlement.

At the same time, Hope is already lost, fallen along with all his compan-ions: "how few we are and fall from each other." The pun is both on the Falls Fight and on the biblical fall that testifies, in Calvinist theology, to Adam's breach of the covenant of works, which (according to New England Puritan thinkers) leads God to replace it with the covenant of grace.[44] If Hope's journey is to be interpreted according to his own theology, his becoming lost in the forest signifies God's displeasure — for prosperity indicates di-vine sanction. One might see Hope as feminized — equated with the un-regenerate forest that is his downfall, even as his symbolic message is rele-gated to the errata of history. Yet the passage confuses such gender codes, because its speaker is neither solely a fallen (male) leader nor a disrup-tive (feminine) force. As a writer — like Hope, whose name is nearly her own — Howe sees herself as crossing over, outside the social world's en-gendering, and this poetic/spiritual experience may explain her attitudes toward gender: "Little by little sound grew to be meaning. I cross an invisi-ble line spoken in the first word 'Then'. . . . There and here I encounter one vagabond formula another pure Idea. To such a land. Yet has haunts. The heart of its falls must be crossed and re-crossed" (*BM* 47). Crossing from sound to sense, Howe unmasks the visionary lodged in the symbolic, blurring the gender coding of both Hope and his wilderness, offering her own possibility of reaching an antinomian "pure Idea."

The titles *Articulation of Sound Forms in Time* and *Singularities* reveal this desire to subvert gendered tropes. Howe recalls the phrase "articulation of sound forms in time" as "a definition Schoenberg gives of music." She argues that sound connotes being alive, as in a newborn's first cry: "it's the articulation that represents life" (Foster, "Interview" 30). That fundamental crossing is also evoked in the title *Singularities*, taken from a lecture by Rene Thom: "In algebra a singularity is the point where plus becomes minus . . . the point where there is a sudden change to something completely else. It's a chaotic point. It's the point chaos enters cosmos, the instant articulation. Then there is a leap into something else" (30–31). The "leap into something else": the Puritan crossing of the ocean, Hope's crossing into the wilderness, the crossing of language between sound and sense, chaos into cosmos — these junctures are at the root of Howe's linguistic articulations, and it is the experience of the unsettled state that promises a new consciousness. As Hogue points out, Howe's reflection is critical for understanding that her poetic process is transformative, not prescriptive. I would add that her crossings of sound and sense privilege neither masculine nor feminine, but rather a living and vibrant otherness.[45]

Throughout "Hope Atherton's Wanderings," Howe upsets linguistic systems and their codes of difference. In the last section of *Articulation*, "Taking the Forest," Howe further plays upon the connection between antinomianism and the rejection of gender divisions. She does so specifically by evoking a number of predecessors to demonstrate a feminist lineage that counters, through innovative language, the pernicious effects of gender metaphors. In this final section, Howe explores a trope central to Puritan theology — the soul as feminine bride. This potentially subversive metaphor of sexual crossing underlies Hope Atherton's story and helps Howe to trace her own antinomian descent.

Why is land always said to be feminine? Why is wilderness called "Virgin." I still have no idea. The answer must be deep in the structures of Language. And the mystery of that structure is a secret of poetry unsettled by history. (Tom Beckett, *The Difficulties* interview 26)

Howe's query about the assignation of gender tropes to the natural world, like the linguistic disruptions in "Hope Atherton's Wanderings," can be read as a resistance to difference.[46] If gender constructions make themselves felt deep in the structures of Language, then Howe critiques such constructions by returning to history, for its narratives (even as they privilege power) unsettle poetry, disrupt the disruption. If the poles of poetry and history correspond to metaphor and metonymy, and authoritative histories need to be dismantled to admit suppressed voices, metaphors of difference also need to be examined historically, through lenses trained on their social contexts and effects. Thus, paradoxically, history disrupts — and instructs — poetry.

In "Taking the Forest," the final section of *Articulation of Sound Forms in Time*, Howe explores the metaphor of crossing in Puritan history and theology, from Thomas Shepard's likening of his conversion to oceanic crossing to the new world, to repeated tropes of crossing into (and conquering) the virgin wilderness.[47] The most powerful, and the most significant to Howe's lineage, is the crossing implied in the "feminine" soul of the Puritan male. The seemingly disruptive trope of the male soul as bride ironically reveals the dangers of all metaphoric gender constructions. As Keller argues, Howe's iconoclastic lineage — which embraces rupture — includes "Duncan, Olson, Williams, Stevens, H.D., and Hart Crane."[48] In this respect, Howe testifies to a hybrid poetic tradition that diverts the streams of difference. As I will show, Howe evokes a specifically *feminist* strain of this disruption. In other words, even as she rejects difference, she unmasks its pernicious historical effects. For Howe, this specifically feminist line of American descent centers on Anne Hutchinson, whose fate demonstrates the gendering of transgression that Howe opposes, and whose heterodoxy informs the achievement of feminist dissident poets from Dickinson to H.D.

Unpacking the metaphor of the Puritan soul, Howe, like H.D., draws on a wealth of biblical and early Christian literature that genders the soul (and the Church) as feminine. Here man's spirit is destined to be coupled with the ultimate bridegroom — the Christ. In the Puritan offspring of these sources, gender tropes shift frequently. The Puritan saints were figured as infants suckling at the breasts of the Father — a series of images that originates in the Bible and is elaborated much earlier by St. John of the Cross in his meditations on Canticles.[49] Another dominant trope was divine marriage — not just contractual, but passionate union that would involve all the pleasures of conjugal attachment. Michael Colacurcio describes this image of the gendered soul: "Always female, the soul of 'man' is the subject of one adequate passion, whose sole object is the Divine Other that is Christ." What Colacurcio calls "the sexual sacred" was an integral part of Puritan theology.[50]

What makes the Puritan version of these tropes unique is that the rhetoric of gender subjugation took on a markedly collective quality in Puritan thought, in which the abject is connected to the feminine and in this respect linked to humanity at large — atypically universalizing a feminine stance.[51] And, as Colacurcio points out, the Puritans developed the *legal* aspect of this loving bond, wedding passionate desire to the more mundane need for good citizenship. For Colacurcio, Winthrop's "Modell of Christian Charity" is the most significant exponent of this concept of union. In this speech — delivered in the middle of the Atlantic ocean to seven hundred settlers to New England —Winthrop created an analogy between Adam's passionate attachment to Eve and the ideal union of citizen to state. As Colacurcio puts it, "Winthrop had implied that law was just like love, that civil combinations were but reflections of that more ideal union of man and woman" (124). Versions of this trope are often overtly sexual: "Thus the soul settles itself upon Christ, hoping, expecting, longing, desiring, loving, embracing," Thomas Hooker writes, and John Cotton, in his own lengthy explication of Canticles, dwells in detail on the "kisses of the mouth" offered by Christ to his bride.[52] This gendering of the spirit permits the Puritan male to acknowledge the feminine lodged in the vessel of the body. Indeed, there seems to be an openness about gender in Puritan thought that has been lost to the descendants of Winthrop's city on a hill. In this respect Howe is attracted to the gender crossing lurking in what has often been dismissed as a literal-minded Protestant tradition hostile to art and mystical experience.[53] But Howe's skepticism about any such metaphoric construction is evident throughout *Articulation*, fueled by allusions to a tradition of American feminist dissidence that has time and again crossed the lines of difference, and which provides Howe's own genealogy. It's a national mission constructed through a highly questionable rhetoric — of crossing oceans (as in Shepard's and others' conversion narratives), land masses, laws. The phrase "Geographical assertion" signals the Puritan mission, a "disputation in dominion beyond sovereign" (*S* 20); settlers claimed land by divine right. But such missions are subject to disruption, gradual movement toward another's dominance: "infinite miscalculation of history" (17) suggests the fall of the theocracy in the new world, a descent that began even during the second generation of Puritan sons, whose declension gave rise to an acute sense of crisis manifested in apocalyptic jeremiads.[54]

Hence Howe's phrases about the construction of history and geography: "Emblem of fictitious narrative," "Collision and impulsion," "Mountains pitched over to westward" (*S* 19). History is the story of shifts of power;

thus "Latin ends and French begins" (35). The "Visible surface of Discourse" (36) — both the Puritan reading of emblematical meaning in natural and historical events, and the surface of language itself — contributes to fearsomely unreliable narratives, no more than "windswept hickory," a linguistic near-miss to history (39), through which women cross into silence along "Alfather's path" (38). More markedly than "Hope Atherton's Wanderings," "Taking the Forest" resonates with phrases that attest to the omissions of the discourse of history. Under cultural pressure, Howe argues, "Silence becomes a Self." Yet "In such silence women were talking. Undifferentiated powerlessness swallowed them" (*BM* 50). Thus "centuries roam audible silence" (*S* 24), and a national "Father the law / Stamped hero-partner" stretches to the poet's present: "Destiny of calamitous silence" (25). There is only "Patriarchal prophesy at heels of hope" (22). The "Collision or collusion with history" (33) is, for women, a story of displacement.[55]

Howe's awareness of women's omission from historical narratives parallels her discomfort with gendered tropes. Howe describes the vilification implied by the label "feminine." The antinomian controversy — much as it involved the literal silencing of the historical figure Anne Hutchinson — also represents the gendering of transgression: "Lawlessness seen as negligence is at first feminized and then restricted or banished" (*BM* 1). For Howe, vision is also labeled feminine ("'Fancy' is an irredeemably feminine word for most Americans" [*BM* 12]); that maneuver provides ammunition for marginalization: "If antinomian vision in North America is gendered feminine, then what will save it from print misfortune?" (*BM* 4). Most significant, the position of women in language needs to be historicized, not rendered merely metaphoric. What is the status, for example, of the female narrator of a captivity narrative such as Mary Rowlandson's when the story is transcribed — literally written — by a man, and when extensive editing by powerful male church leaders mediates any reader's reception of the text? As Howe notes of this practice, "A woman, afraid of not speaking well, tells her story to a man who writes it down" (*BM* 50).[56]

This historical and theoretical context informs Howe's exploration of the crossing by which, in Puritan theology, the male subject becomes the feminine bride. As Howe notes concerning Mary Rowlandson's narrative, "Protestant sermons came to rely heavily on each captive woman's suffering and deliverance as a metaphor for the process of Conversion" (*BM* 89), by which the soul weds Christ. Such conversion metaphors are implicit in Hope's journey into the wilderness. One passage in "Taking the Forest" in-

troduces the bridegroom motif in lines that suggest the subversive poten-
tial of this Puritan gender-crossing:

Visible surface of Discourse

Runes or allusion to runes
Tasks and turning flock

Evening red enough for chivalry

Algorithms bravadoes jetsam
All Wisdom's plethora pattern

paper anacoluthon and naked chalk

Luggage of the prairie
Wagons pegged to earth

Tyrannical avatars of consciousness
emblazoned in tent-stitch

Five senses of syntax

Dear Unconscious scatter syntax
Scythe mower surrender hereafter

Dear Cold cast violet coronal

World weary flesh by Flesh bygone
Bridegroom (*S* 36)

The final lines play on the notion of the Word made Flesh, invoking the gen-
der specificity of the human soul meeting the divine. "The soul is a bride,"
Howe tersely reminds us in *My Emily Dickinson* (131); here, our own "world
weary flesh" (with lowercase "f") is indeed bygone or superseded, dramat-
ically rendered unnecessary, by the Flesh (uppercase "F") of God Incarnate.
The symbols of death earlier (Scythe mower surrender hereafter) under-
line the ultimate redemption from death — through incarnation. Yet this
encounter with the flesh also suggests the social code of gender. Howe
evokes the trope of Christ as bridegroom to indicate the position of the male
Puritan settler: bent on conquering the savage, feminine wilderness, he is
metaphorically transformed into the willing virgin bride.

This is apparently the disruption Howe strives for. Much of the rest of
this passage evokes unsettlement in a self-reflexive account of Howe's po-

etics. Howe's "Visible surface of Discourse" (and, as should be evident by now, her poetry is profoundly visual),[57] is all "Runes or allusions to runes." In the paper anacoluthon of Howe's text, in which the lack of grammatical sequence (the meaning of that dense word) is the most distinctive formal element that disrupts the surface of discourse, cultural reference is destabilized. The language of the frontier (Luggage of the prairie) is dismantled, in a *dérèglement de tous les sens*: "Five senses of syntax" allow us to feel — viscerally — the unhinging of language. The appeal to unsettlement is explicit, in a recipe for the Steinian poetics Howe alludes to at the opening of *My Emily Dickinson*: "Dear Unconscious scatter syntax." Howe links the trope of gender-crossing to the unsettling of language — and the Puritan mission, it turns out, seems revolutionary indeed.

In this reflexivity, Howe seems to embrace the metaphor of crossing, the more so because of the related passage in H.D.'s *Trilogy*. Written during the Blitzkrieg in World War II London, *Trilogy* epitomizes H.D.'s resistance to violent overthrow, and the allusion to H.D. signals Howe's dialogue with another forebear who, like Stein, challenged the feminization of alterity. The "Lady" who appears at the climax of "Tribute to the Angels" represents regeneration in a utopic process that obviates sexual difference: Circumventing gendered typologies, H.D. distances the Lady from Mary and re-genders the trope of the soul as bride of Christ:

> I grant you her face was innocent
>
> and immaculate and her veils
> like the Lamb's Bride,
>
> but the Lamb was not with her,
> either as Bridegroom or Child;
>
> her attention is undivided,
> we are her bridegroom and lamb (*CP* 571)

Figuring the Lady as the deity, the soul as bridegroom, this re-gendering of the familiar trope is culled from the same section of *Trilogy* that supplies Howe with an epigraph for *Singularities*. H.D.'s lines refer to the Lady: "she must have been pleased with us, / for she looked so kindly at us" (*CP* 568). Howe cites as a fragment the lines that follow — "under her drift of veils, / and she carried a book." In addition to alluding to traditional images of the annunciation, these phrases couple the book, symbol of knowledge, with veils that obscure the Lady's body, and with it her identity. As an opening for

Howe's collection, this epigraph signals both her debt to H.D. and a shared fascination with the linking of woman and word, in which sexual definition is blurred, and space is made for the revision of identity itself.

Nonetheless, for Howe there are problems with the Puritan trope of the soul as bride of Christ. This potentially liberating theological stance privileges the feminine *only* as metaphor: The trope of the feminized soul allows the Puritan male to appropriate what he codes as feminine in contemplating the next world while legitimizing women's subjugation in this one. This is the analysis of the bridegroom trope that Colacurcio proffers concerning *The Scarlet Letter*: The trope of the passive, expectant virgin becomes a means of legitimizing women's powerlessness — not in the inner world of soul, but in the social world ruled by law. Thus, as Colacurcio points out, the trope itself is gendered, for the crossing it enacts is available only to the male subject, who incorporates the feminine into his subjectivity while maintaining mastery in the theocracy. Elsewhere Howe similarly unveils this problem of one-sidedness in an allusion to Anne Hutchinson — also the topic of Colacurcio's meditations. Hutchinson was denounced for the same gender crossing practiced — metaphorically, of course — by the Puritan male: "You have stept out of your place, *you have rather bine a Husband than a Wife and a preacher than a Hearer*."[58] Howe reminds us of the contingencies of the metaphor: Gender crossing was a male prerogative.

In *Articulation*, Anne Hutchinson and the antinomian controversy are specifically called to mind through a reference to enthusiasm, to the language of ecstatic prophecy (what Hogue calls "infectious ecstasy") that represents what happens to women when they cross the lines and claim a role not their own — that of prophetic pronouncement:

Girl with forest shoulder
Girl stuttering out mask or trick

aria out of hearing

Sound through cult annunciation
sound through initiation Occult

Enunciate barbarous jargon
fluent language of fanaticism (*S* 31)

The language of enthusiasm smacks of a dangerous self-aggrandizement, of direct, personal revelation — an initiation into the Occult, in which pure sound (here the word is repeated twice) registers God's voice and will directly to the hearer. It is certainly not divine — rather, a "barbarous" fanaticism. This language, as well as the experience of direct revelation, is what got Anne Hutchinson into trouble, for its privacy threatens the entire Puritan errand — that of the loving community, the bond of individuals wed to the state. Yet it is also no coincidence that Hutchinson, ultimately expelled by the Massachusetts Bay Colony, was an infantilized woman: "Girl with forest shoulder // Girl stuttering out mask or trick." Howe points out that enthusiasm (and its threat to the state) is consistently gendered feminine. During the Great Awakening, Charles Chauncy even compared the dangerous excesses of Jonathan Edwards's religious revival to Anne Hutchinson's transgressions.[59] In light of this gendered history, Howe invokes the feminist tradition for which she seeks recognition — from Hutchinson and Rowlandson through Dickinson, Stein, and H.D. — and the tradition that includes Melville, Olson, and Duncan. She does so to critique Puritan theology because, despite its *seemingly* fluid gender constructions, it reinforces a difference that reveals male privilege and shackles women.

The second to last poem of this section (and of *Articulation* as a whole) takes women's absence from "Alfather's path" (38) as its subject:

Last line of blue hills

Lost fact dim outline

Little figure of mother

Moss pasture and wild trefoil
meadow-hay and timothy

She is and the way She was

Outline was a point chosen
Outskirts of ordinary

Weather in history and heaven

Skiff feather glide house

Face seen in a landscape once (*S* 37)

This feminine landscape of hills that take the Virgin's color is of little use in reconstructing the "Lost fact" of forgotten women's lives. We cannot recover "the way She was." But neither can we know for certain what that elusive "She" stands for. A symbolic figure like H.D.'s Lady in *Trilogy*, bringing new vision and prophetic insight to her (female) beholder, seems all but impossible to locate; she remains no more than a "Lost fact dim outline," "Face seen in a landscape once" (37). I would argue that we are meant to be suspicious of this abstract, unnamed entity — to resist *She* whose capital "S" signals a monolithic feminine. The punning "Weather in history and heaven" gives us to understand that for the Puritans human history leads seamlessly into the hereafter. The question is not what She might be, but where She might be located in such a grand narrative.

Given their latter-day antinomianism, Howe's linguistic innovations — her plea, "Dear Unconscious scatter syntax"— might seem to fit neatly into a system in which language is linked to the father, and the unconscious is the feminine terrain of the irrational, not unlike the Puritan wilderness. But this and similar phrases in *Articulation* in fact serve not as ahistorical, metaphorical versions of a theory of gender, but as allusions to Howe's feminist lineage, a means to give evidence of an avant-garde tradition that long preceded her own innovations. This usable past, as Howe sees it and as Fraser similarly asserts, in fact rejects any theory that privileges difference in the construction of language, cultural symbols, or political categories.

Howe closes *My Emily Dickinson* with a statement that reveals the rejection of difference that is at the core of this poet's feminist textual politics: "Poetry leads past possession of self to transfiguration beyond gender" (*MED* 22). This degendered space is where the *social* self (with its inescapable mark of gender) might be dissolved and language used as a vehicle toward a different consciousness, of the sort that Wittig hopes to generate by transforming the sign, and that Stein explored in a poetics that challenged gender binarism. Howe's "Indifference" appeals to crossings in which poetry is the vehicle of an entirely different consciousness: "Poetry is redemption from pessimism. Poetry is affirmation in negation" (*MED* 138). This conviction illuminates the specifically feminist lineage that stretches from the dissidence of Anne Hutchinson through the linguistic heterodoxies of Mary Rowlandson and Emily Dickinson, to the innovations of H.D. and Stein. As in the similarly recuperative editorial project of *HOW(ever)*, Howe's work bears witness to an unacknowledged feminist tradition, hybridized with the dissidence of avant-gardist rebellion. It is an ambition that appears in the work of other recent feminist avant-gardists as well — poets who testify to an increasingly complex and multiple sense of lineage, as my final chapter will show.

5
"BELATEDLY BELADIED BLUES"
Hybrid Traditions in the Poetry of Harryette Mullen

Over the years that have elapsed since the period of the historical avant-gardes, feminist avant-garde poets have increasingly attempted, like Kathleen Fraser, "to reconstruct [a] preexisting tradition" of precursors. Far from exercising the avant-gardist prerogative to expunge any possible belatedness, feminist innovators are hungry for a history of their own. Like Howe, who locates that feminist past in the daring efforts of such early American women as Anne Hutchinson and Mary Rowlandson, Harryette Mullen constructs an experimental poetics that deliberately calls up divergent lineages. Even more pointedly than Howe, Mullen mixes the influences of avant-garde modes usually considered only in isolation, forging a hybrid poetics to illustrate the "mongrel" nature of American culture, female identities, and avant-gardism itself.

In her six books of poetry, Mullen has increasingly drawn on the spirit of Stein's linguistic experiments, particularly those of *Tender Buttons*, a text that influences many contemporary avant-gardists and exerts a particular pull on feminists intrigued by everything from Stein's serial form to her playful eroticism.[1] Mullen's poems, like Stein's language games, work by association and eschew linear logic; in this they plumb the richness of the written word in a poetics bent on the pleasures of signifying in intricate forms. Like other poets either directly or indirectly connected to the "Stein tradition," Mullen shapes her cultural critique by sidestepping the rules of syntax and fashioning a distinctively allusive, punning play with language that makes her texts profoundly visual. Mullen even uses *Tender Buttons* as the template for a book-length series of Steinian prose poems. But Mullen also invokes a range of other sources in highly dialogic texts that don't limit themselves to Steinian inflections. Of particular importance to Mullen, the formal innovations of the Black Arts movement and other African American experimentalists appear in her stylistic riffs. Mullen's work, like Black Arts writing, is colloquial, topical, and it engages with issues of racial and identity politics. She explores ways to represent diverse idioms, both employing and questioning concepts of the so-called "black vernacular" in texts that straddle the supposed divides between visual and speech-based poetics. Mullen has also developed strategies to mark her texts with culturally specific references, to help construct a self-identified African-American readership for her work. In these respects, Mullen draws on poetics and a cultural politics made available by Black Arts activists and neglected African-American modernists. Combining such influences with Steinian play, Mullen diversifies her own inheritance, challenging poetic categories and canons to provoke awareness of the varied influences that have shaped — and continue to transform — American culture.[2]

Mullen makes abundant use of intertextuality and allusion — strategies that position her own poetics as the product of interconnected communities. Mullen's poetic mixtures are unquestionably a form of tribute to her diverse precursors. But her hybrids also foster the notion of cross-fertilization in a critique (like Loy's earlier "mongrel" poetics) of social and aesthetic purity. In the discussion that follows, I illustrate Mullen's construction of a hybrid avant-garde tradition, as well as her creation of a formal texture bearing witness to such mixed modes, in two texts. I first discuss Steinian poetics and black feminist perspectives in *Trimmings* (1991), a serial poem that immediately reveals its stylistic ties to varied inheritances. *Trimmings* is explicit in its borrowing of elements of Stein's domestic landscape; Mullen adapts Stein's prose poem form, replete with word-play, and she "tries on" Stein's fascination with the erotic charge of feminine objects — particularly clothing. Mullen uses *Trimmings* as a means to explore inter-textually her relationship with *Tender Buttons* as a precursor feminist avant-garde text: Mullen's markers of African-American culture in *Trimmings* bring Stein's 1914 poem in dialogue with contemporary motifs linked to black women's lives. I argue that Mullen employs this conjunction to complicate our sense of culturally specific languages and avant-garde traditions, in a gesture of both homage and critique. Employing *Tender Buttons* as a point of departure, Mullen pays tribute to Stein's view of the endless possibilities for constructing one's language and one's self; implicitly she distances herself from essentialist conceptions of language and identity — including those promulgated by Black Arts poets. At the same time, though,

Mullen also uses an idiomatic diction and a range of references to black culture that position her as the "descendent" of Black Arts activists and such early black feminists as Sonia Sanchez. The connections Mullen establishes between *Tender Buttons* and Black Arts poetics acknowledge her debt to both traditions, even as, from her contemporary perspective, she challenges elements of each.

In the second part of the chapter I discuss Mullen's recent volume *Muse & Drudge* (1995), which reveals Mullen's increasingly disjunctive uses of intertextuality and allusion. Even more strikingly than *Trimmings*, *Muse & Drudge* relies on an impressive spectrum of predecessors, from Sappho to Bessie Smith, from Callimachus to rap. In a pun-laden, playful poem of lyric fragments, Mullen allows her varied sources to resonate in indeterminate fashion; since no single reader is likely to "get" all of her far-ranging allusions, Mullen effectively short-circuits ideas of mastery and (particularly relevant to avant-garde poetics) originality; she constructs a diverse audience whose varying subject positions make their experiences of reading Mullen's text radically different. Mullen's allusions hold out the possibility of what I call "collective reading," through which shared knowledge constructs the text and integrates the reference points of its audience.[3] Combining classical lyric and blues lyric, syntactic fragment and epic scope, the aural and the visual, Mullen's work demonstrates new directions in feminist avant-garde poetics, fostering both cultural and formal hybridity to demonstrate the "mongrel" nature of contemporary culture and avant-gardism itself. Far from revealing concern about belatedness, or from proposing any *single* derivation for feminist avant-gardists today, Mullen bears witness to an alternative feminist poetics that seeks — and successfully constructs — a diverse lineage of its own.

A 1984 anthology of Language writing included a section in which a number of poets commented on their contemporaries. Rae Armantrout wrote about Susan Howe, Barrett Watten about Ron Silliman, Charles Bernstein about Hannah Weiner. There are fifty-six of these entries. At the head of this section, announcing what might be perceived as a principal source for the positions on aesthetics and politics in the various selections that follow, the editors chose a single text for several of the poets to respond to. Not surprisingly, that text was *Tender Buttons*.

The entries in *The L=A=N=G=U=A=G=E Book*'s "Readings" section — all appreciations of *Tender Buttons* and all written by men — bear witness to Stein's importance to this particular avant-garde movement.[4] Yet among feminist avant-garde poets — some of whom, like both Howe and Mullen, share common ground with Language writing — Stein's influence is just as potent, perhaps even inescapable. The very notion of avant-gardism as I have defined it is far more heterogeneous than a theory of simple influence would allow for, and, as the projects described throughout this book demonstrate, feminist avant-garde writing is diverse both in the specific beliefs that motivate its writing and in its means of poetic innovation. Yet Stein's body of work, and *Tender Buttons* in particular, remains a source to be reckoned with for a range of artists who, like Mullen, see Stein as among their most important, and sometimes problematic, predecessors.

In particular, Mullen's work reflects changes working their way through recent feminist discourse in America, for Mullen doesn't simply acknowledge Stein's language experiments, as *The L=A=N=G=U=A=G=E Book* did, but contests them — and her — as well. In recent years, such feminist thinkers as Luce Irigaray to Monique Wittig have focused on the social experiences of language, sexuality, and the body; despite often varying assumptions and theoretical stances, they tend to share a common concern: Unlike Stein, these theorists all stress the social implications of speech, the impossibility of separating the symbolic realm of language from the social realities language reflects — a conviction that surfaces in writing like Sanchez's and Howe's, and in that of feminist avant-garde artists working in a variety of media, from visual artists like Barbara Kruger and Cindy Sherman to performance artists like Karen Finley and Anna Deveare Smith.[5] To the contrary, part of the legacy of *Tender Buttons* is the extreme privacy, even hermeticism, of Stein's language — a textual opacity that can both delight and infuriate. Like other recent feminist avant-gardists, Mullen has taken Stein as a crucial but often problematic forebear. To introduce Mullen's thinking about feminism, tradition, and the avant-garde, I would therefore like to return to *Tender Buttons*, the text with which this book began and a central one to Mullen's work.

There are many ways to approach *Tender Buttons*, but two have emerged with particular prominence. The first advances the view that Stein's writing demonstrates a kind of hypersignification, akin to a form of encryption. As I discussed in my first chapter, scholars like William Gass and Lisa Ruddick have established that Stein's poem is in many respects a hermetic text, through which she creates a personal idiom of domestic and erotic life. Particular words function metonymically, as idiosyncratic "clues," like *alas*, *ail-less*, and *aid her*, which all suggest "Alice" and the nickname "Ada." Similarly, individual words signify sexual experience (the color "red" or the word "cow").[6] As I argued in Chapter 1, Stein's fetishization of the word both exalts language to the status of a material object and participates in encoding the erotic subtext of *Tender Buttons* as a whole. Such readings as my own decode the poem and in the process assume that meaning does, in fact, inhere in Stein's apparent non-sense — that there is a profoundly important symbolic process at work.

Yet the opposite approach has also been taken to Stein's difficult text — a focus on radical *non*-meaning. Bernstein argues that Stein's greatest achievement in *Tender Buttons* is that she abandoned the signifying function of language altogether, evoking instead the sounds, the *non*-referentiality, of words, "the pleasure/plenitude in the immersion in language, where language is not understood as a code for something else or a representation of somewhere else — a kind of eating or drinking or tasting, endowing an object status to language" (*Poetics* 143). Bernstein associates this attention to the object status of words with what he calls "impermeable" or "anti-absorptive" writing: "By *absorption* I mean engrossing, engulfing / completely," he argues, while by contrast the impermeable is "interruptive, transgressive, / undecorous, anticonventional, unintegrated, fractured, / fragmented, fanciful" (*Poetics* 29). As he sees it, Stein's lack of transparency — her impermeable style — is revolutionary precisely because it draws attention to language and its singular pleasures; the desire to decode Stein's writing merely reflects the reader's urge to "make sense" of the poetry, an impulse that counters the most significant aspects of Stein's experiment. Stein's nonreferentiality is her most important legacy, especially to poets (like those of the Language group) who attempt to bring the whole mechanism of reference to the foreground of writing and reading.

These approaches constitute the two ends of the Steinian critical spectrum — the desire to push her text toward sense, especially (in recent years) a feminist one, and the urge to embrace the radical nonmeaning of her experiments with language. Yet both of these interpretive positions, for very different reasons, ultimately support the view that the "rooms" of Stein's domestic domain just barely leave the door ajar to the world outside. Clearly, a private erotic language threatens to shut that door, and indeed, this significant aspect of Stein's text required a host of feminist critics, bolstered by the advent of theorists like Cixous, Irigaray, and Kristeva, to break the code.[7] On the other hand, in Bernstein's view of the radical nonsignifying in *Tender Buttons*, the reader is kept at a deliberate, perhaps infuriating, distance — prevented, in Bernstein's terms, from "absorbing" Stein's resistant words. Breaking the rules of syntax, denotation, and logic, *Tender*

Buttons, by either approach, surely qualifies as a subversive text, over-turning linguistic (and, by extension, social) conventions and forging a distinctly new poetic idiom from the seemingly intractable material of everyday words. Yet Stein's experiment remains relatively far removed from the social and political realms that other avant-garde artists of her day addressed. One need only compare *Tender Buttons* to Loy's socioeco-nomic themes in "Anglo-Mongrels and the Rose" or Pound's proselytizing throughout the *Cantos* to see the extent to which Stein insisted on the pri-vacy of her language.

In her own way Mullen has entered into this debate about and with Stein. In embracing a feminism that doesn't take recourse to polemics or to personal utterance — that is deeply interested in the kinds of subjectivity language creates — her work is deeply indebted to Stein. Yet Mullen pushes Stein's language in the opposite direction from the one Stein origi-nally chose — back to an awareness of the *social* meaning of identity, as well as the complex relationships in American culture among race, sexual-ity, and economic privilege. Unmasking the social nature of sexual experi-ence is at the core of *Trimmings,* and in this Stein is both one of the moth-ers of Mullen's inventions and a predecessor who needs to be taken to task in the interests of a feminist avant-garde practice that needs its precursors yet clearly cannot stand still. Mullen inherits Stein's fascination with plea-sure and reluctance to dissociate that pleasure from language. In the pro-cess, though, the burden of her poetry is precisely to situate this pleasure in a landscape that sometimes seems as bleak and violent as Howe's Puritan America. Adapted by Mullen, Stein's innocent eroticism and her pleasure in parody become more self-conscious and more attuned to the social forces that inevitably shape eroticism.

The best indication of Mullen's response to Steinian poetics lies in the other (often overlapping) influences on her poetry: black feminists (Mar-garet Walker, Gwendolyn Brooks, Lucille Clifton), underacknowledged African-American avant-gardists (Jean Toomer, Melvin Tolson, Nathaniel Mackey, Lorenzo Thomas), and Black Arts innovators (Sanchez, Amiri Baraka, and others). Well before Mullen entered into poetic dialogue with Stein she was preoccupied with the question of the traditions and canons of African-American poetics. Mullen describes searching for precursors, writ-ers "at the periphery" of the African-American canon, in a quest to recover a "tradition of innovation within African-American poetry." "We all try to connect to something," Mullen asserts, but in the case of African-American experimentalism, "people don't know that there is a tradition." As a result, "innovative black poets don't seem to have any black antecedents." To fill this gap, Mullen argues that she is "constructing retrospectively . . . a black tradition" (Hogue, "Interview with Mullen," n.p.).

Mullen notes that her first book, *Tree Tall Woman* (1981), "was definitely influenced by the Black Arts movement, the idea that . . . you could write from the position of being within a black culture." Further, while "that project [Black Arts] had created a space for me to write," Mullen recalls that "I wanted to write within the space that had been created without necessarily repeating exactly what those folks had done" (Hogue, "Interview with Mullen," n.p.). The traces of this formative movement are certainly evident in *Tree Tall Woman*. As I discussed in Chapter 3, Baraka, Larry Neal, and others devoted to a black criterion in the late 1960s argued that the culture of African Americans had yet to be given voice in literary form. Seeking to combat the aesthetic and political hegemony of "white America," Black Arts poets proudly asserted black identity; as Sonia Sanchez remembers of this period, "the main thing was the idea of someone saying you were Black — and that was beautiful, and that was good . . . and that was political" (*Catch the Fire*, ed. Derrick I. Gilbert 222). For Sanchez and others the goal was to create new poetic forms — writing that would assert powerfully the performative nature of black culture, particularly of black speech and idiom, and launch a powerful indictment of white supremacy in all spheres of contemporary life. This new means of expression would revolutionize poetry, particularly its written aspect. Modes of jest and word-play — playing the dozens, rapping, and signifying — would be transformed into writing that would strike home to black listeners and readers of all socioeconomic levels and regions. The assertion of a shared, even universal black identity was critical, and indeed the Pan-Africanism of Frantz Fanon was a crucial inspiration for the movement. In poetic terms, the invocation of "Black English" from spoken to written forms was intended both to promote black pride and to provide a recognizable marker of cultural difference and dissent.

Although *Tree Tall Woman* sidesteps the kind of direct political statement that characterizes much Black Arts poetry, it does include biting indictments of racism that are indebted to those of Black Arts activists who critiqued white dominance. "Bete Noire" is a satiric portrait of "the white minstrel man / who hums ragtime tunes / and whistles the buckdancer's choice / while he darkens his face / with boneblack / made of human charcoal" (*Tree Tall Woman* 22). The poem "For My Grandfather, Lowell Palter Mitchell" opens with a reminiscence of "Granddaddy," a preacher, "in shades of black and white." The man who preaches "a meat-and-gravy sermon" dons "a serious, scowling black suit," while his "shirts . . . fresh from the laundry, / [are] 'washed whiter than snow.'" Such polarized imagery pervades the poem: "a starched white handkerchief," "your black Chevy," "a hospital bed with white sheet / tucked up" against "your huge head . . . / like a heavy dark flower." This man, whose words were his "meat and gravy," "appeared a final time / in black and white, / in a newspaper clipping / I keep between the pages of a black-bound Bible" (14–15). The irony of his identity's being virtually overshadowed by this dichotomy — perceived everywhere in the poet's reminiscence — emerges sharply in a poem that has as much to say about the man as about the pervasiveness of racial division.

Tree Tall Woman also reveals formal elements profoundly influenced by Black Arts experimentation with the written and spoken word. Frequent uses of the black vernacular — often in the form of quotations from other speakers — reflect the Black Arts enthusiasm for culturally specific idiom, geared toward a black audience. A poem that opens "I'm your momma" includes an appreciation of a woman's sharp speech: "don't roll your eyes at me. / You can aim those bullets but / you can't shoot em. / I mean, your young eyes aint no / match for mine" (4). Delight in the black vernacular — its imagistic richness and musicality — is evident throughout *Tree Tall Woman*, in narrative as well as in epigrammatic form: "The Joy" advises, "Put some starch / in your chef's hat, honey, / and start cookin" (35). This is a poetics that courts the ear through its diction and its rhythms, as in the self-reflexive "Playing the Invisible Saxophone En El Combo De Las Estrellas": "One of these days I'm gonna write a real performance poem," the poem begins, in a tribute to Black Arts performativity and to the aesthetics of a poetry based on jazz innovation:

> Yeah, gonna have words turning into dance,
> bodymoving music,
> a get-down poem so kinetically energetic
> it sure put disco to shame.
> Make it a snazzy jazzy poem extravaganza, with pizzazz.
> Poem be going solo,
> flying high on improbable improvisational innovation.
> Poem be blowing hard! (49)

Mullen takes pleasure in the black vernacular and in importing the forms and textures of African-American music into her own "improvisatory" text. She affirms black identity as the source of black art: Mullen's joyful "bodymoving music," her "flying high on improbable improvisational innovation," recall the playful poetic flights of such black pride poems as Nikki Giovanni's "Ego Tripping": "I was born in the congo / I walked to the fertile crescent and built the sphinx," the poet asserts, in an allusion to Hughes's "The Negro Speaks of Rivers" (another poetic ancestor affirming black identity and culture); "I am so perfect so divine so ethereal so surreal / I cannot be comprehended / except by my permission" (*Women and the Men* n.p.). Signaling that her origins are in the battles of the Black Arts movement, Mullen pays homage to the voices that preceded her own.

Trimmings moves in a somewhat different direction. Rather than presuming a shared and valorized blackness, here Mullen invokes an inheritance that crosses racial, political, and aesthetic lines. Mullen merges the Steinian and Black Arts traditions in a manner that pays tribute to both and, at the same time, uses each dialogically to comment upon the other. Published — appropriately — by Tender Buttons Press, *Trimmings* assumes the syntax and even diction of *Tender Buttons* in pun-laden prose poems about the politics of women's clothing — "girdled loins" wrapped in Steinian "tender girders" (*Tr* 26). *Trimmings* is replete with Steinian word-play, as well as with the erotic charge of feminine objects — particularly clothing. In summoning Stein as intertextual companion, Mullen distances herself from the essentialist, nationalist politics of much Black Arts writing; she calls upon a feminism rejected by male Black Arts theorists. At the same time, however, markers of African-American culture remain in *Trimmings*, revealing Mullen's continued ties to the Black Arts legacy and its importance to her textual politics.

Dual tributes emerge in subject matter and form. There are belts, earrings, stockings, and purses, like the petticoats, umbrellas, and shoes of Stein's poem. As in *Tender Buttons*, Mullen plays with words to release the reader's associative powers. As Bernstein argues of Stein, Mullen highlights the materiality of the signifier. But compared to *Tender Buttons*, Mullen's writing in *Trimmings* is far less elusive — less impermeable — and more inclusive. Mullen notes the "secretive" and "idiosyncratic" quality of Stein's language (Hogue, "Interview with Mullen," n.p.). Although Stein pushed signification as far as possible toward opacity, Mullen's goal is more that of creating points of connection: Just as she cultivates the cross-fertilization of avant-garde traditions, she also combines conventional signification (absorption) with the materiality of language (impermeability). Mullen's stylistic links to Stein are readily apparent. Consider one of the brief prose poems in *Trimmings*: "Night moon star sun down gown. / Night moan stir sin dawn gown" (*Tr* 23). The method is paratactic, a Steinian means of composition that fosters a fruitful multiplicity of meaning. Mullen notes that Stein's use of the series or list can "create an alternate subjectivity," as well as "different levels of meaning" (Hogue, "Interview with Mullen," n.p.). In this instance, vowel shifts, rather than syntax, bear the burden of reference. The two lines mirror one another in the series of initial consonants, as well as in the movement in each from night to dawn. Certain clear associations and near-meanings emerge (sundown and evening gown can be easily teased out), and the allusion to a likely setting (the romantic moon and star). Yet the lines multiply rather than reduce possible readings; the lack of punctuation and syntax renders the whole indeterminate. Larger implications (for instance, that come "dawn," the "sin" will be "done") are hinted at, but the poem moves by generating relationships among sounds and creating localized meanings, rather than by linear logic.

These tactics that skew and defer meaning are overtly Steinian, resurrecting Stein's fascination with repetition and circularity — what she called "knowing and feeling a name" and "adoring [and] replacing the noun" in poetry (*LIA* 231). At the same time, Mullen's passage is more accessible than most of *Tender Buttons*, and her word usage is far less idiosyncratic. The movement from "night" to "dawn" implies the familiar narrative underlying any aubade, as does the Cinderella-like gown. In contrast to Stein's utterly unexpected juxtapositions, this passage presents the reader with a clearly definable family of words. Their relationships may proliferate into varying local meanings, but their connotations and associations all belong together. The result is a far more "absorptive" texture than that of *Tender Buttons*.

Perhaps more significant, Mullen's *Trimmings* is less elusive than *Tender Buttons* because its social context is so much more apparent. Like Stein, Mullen uses language as a source for polyvalent symbolic meanings. But she also pursues a course Stein never chose: She directly exposes the gender and race politics of attire. In these respects, Mullen's text offers an amalgam of Stein and Black Arts, as in the very shortest of Mullen's poems: "Shades, cool dark lasses. Ghost of a smile" (*Tr* 62). Mullen describes these "lasses" as "wearing their shades, maybe jazz divas, someone like a Billie Holiday" (Hogue, "Interview with Mullen," n.p.). Clearly there is an erotic and a social power that being "cool," hidden behind shades, evokes. Yet these minimalist sentence fragments also suggest a more political, less "chic" reading. Charged puns ("dark lasses" conjuring "glasses"; "shades" as sunglasses for the stylish, but also as a racist word denoting African Americans) render the final, simple phrase ("ghost of a smile") ambiguous. The smile might suggest a pleasurable memory or an invitation but it is also inseparable from the implication that "shades" — in the racial slur — are "ghosts," invisible presences in a culture bent on cover-ups, on hiding behind its own, often rose-colored, glasses.

Mullen uses Steinian linguistic play to address not just the *pleasures* of language and clothing but their social functions, the issue that Black Arts poets pursued relentlessly. In her own way, Mullen attends to the same questions that Sanchez addressed, with similar economy, in a poetic language at once multivalent and clearly marked by the awareness of racial difference, as in this haiku from *Love Poems*: "Was it yesterday / love we shifted the air and / made it blossom Black?" (*Love* 25). When Sanchez called for a "fo / real / revolu/shun" — a psychic transformation of *both* black men and black women — she was surely setting the stage for a poet like Mullen, whose musings explore the themes of race, gender, sexuality, power, and language. It is thus by way of principles drawn from the Black Arts movement that *Trimmings* removes *Tender Buttons* from its hermetically sealed locale and, so to speak, takes it out of the closet and into the street, using humor and linguistic play to underline the conjunctions between racial identity and gender in a semiotics of dress both playful and potent.

In choosing Stein as an intertextual companion, with Black Arts poetics as a complicating presence, Mullen uses in *Trimmings* what Henry Louis Gates identifies as a strategy frequently employed in African-American writing: the elaboration of repetition and difference. The process, in Gates's terms, involves a particular orientation toward language and the dialogic. "Signifying," Gates says, is the playing of various kinds of rhetorical games in black vernacular, and it can mean "to talk with great innuendo, to carp, cajole, needle, and lie," as well as "to talk around a subject, never quite coming to the point" (*Signifying Monkey* 54). Signifying contrasts with the "supposed transparency of normal speech"; it "turns upon the free play of language itself, upon the displacement of meanings" (53). In this sense it relates to Bernstein's description of "anti-absorptive" poetics, and to Gates it also involves "semantic appropriation," by which words can be "decolonized," given a new orientation. According to Gates, this double-voicedness is associative, and it employs puns and figurative substitutions to create indeterminacy (49, 22). In this respect, Mullen's "signifying" reveals the meeting points between Stein's linguistic "double-voicedness" and the political agenda of Black Arts poets.

In one such combination of Steinian and Black Arts–inspired strategies, Mullen addresses her motif of clothing in a riff on a television ad for laundry detergent: "Heartsleeve's dart bleeds whiter white, softened with wear. Among blowzy buxom bosomed, give us this — blowing, blissful, open. O most immaculate bleached blahs, bless any starched, loosening blossom" (*Tr* 31). In a language both lyrical and literary, heavy with alliteration, Mullen evokes the poetic tradition of the beauty of feminine clothing, as in the erotic gaze of Sappho or the elaborate enumeration of female adornments in the Petrarchan tradition, as well as in later poets, including Stein. This is a seemingly timeless literary pleasure — one Mullen clearly doesn't deny exists powerfully for any lyric poet. Yet this celebration of the beauty of words and dress acknowledges as well some very unlyrical truths — that the struggle to attain the "whiter white" (a redundant operation of either language or color) raises questions about America's obsession not just with cleanliness (the subject of TV ads) but with the valorization of what is as light as possible, in shirts or skin tone. Contemporary mass culture suffers from the "blahs" (a watered-down form of the blues); even the products offered us are geared toward the psychic comfort of the dominant: Each item is literally or symbolically "bleached" for a white consumer. This is a message advanced powerfully in the critique of the Black Arts period: The slogan "black is beautiful" challenged the rhetoric of white domination. In this mixture of elements Mullen thus creates a dialogue with her modernist and more recent predecessors, from Stein to Sanchez.

As in this example, Mullen alludes frequently to mass media in passages indebted to the critique of white capitalism articulated during the Black Arts period. But in Mullen's work, this predominantly Marxist analysis is altered, informed by more recent black feminist thought. References to television appear throughout *Trimmings*, and Mullen highlights in these passages the sense of urgency created by the experience of commodification, particularly its sexist and racist inflections. Of nylon stockings Mullen writes, "The color 'nude,' a flesh tone. Whose flesh unfolds barely, appealing tan [. . .] body cast in a sit calm" (16). Here the issue of what color "nude" is — the fact that the model for this skin tone is an Anglo one — is too often taken for granted by white women. Any woman "whose flesh unfolds barely" has become a commodity. Further, "glued" in front of sitcoms, the female body is static and passive, as though in a "body cast," under an injunction not to move. Other TV allusions, such as one to the evening news, suggest the potential for sheer banality in women's lives, regardless of social status: "Mild frump and downward drab. Slipshod drudge with chance of dingy morning slog" (49). Words, just barely altered from their "originals" in a TV or radio newscast, testify to women's representation in and by mass media, which often determine whether they see the morning, its weather report, or perhaps themselves as slipshod or drab. Beneath the diction of weather reports ("downward drab," "dingy morning slog") is the gendered nature of mood and appearance in contemporary mass culture, as in the words "frump" and "drudge" (hence the title for Mullen's meditation on that familiar bifurcation of female types: *Muse & Drudge*). In this recasting of pre-fab language, Mullen illuminates through a Steinian homophonic composition the gendered commodification of just about everything — even the weather.

Despite this surface of ubiquitous commodification, Mullen makes it clear that, however potentially controlling, mass media don't obliterate culturally specific language. Mullen marks her text with both mainstream speech and the black vernacular in what she calls a "splicing together of different lexicons."[8] Such a hybrid palate is crucial to Mullen's intertextual relation to both *Tender Buttons* and Black Arts influences. Mullen notes that her current view of the "idea of black voice" is "much more complicated" than when she first began to write, under the influence of Black Arts poetics. The conception of a nonstandard "black English" existing in opposition to "white" standard English is flawed: "I wouldn't say that standard American English is in any way a white language. It's a language that is the result of many people's contributions" (Hogue, "Interview with Mullen" n.p.). In this respect, like critic Aldon Nielsen, Mullen exposes the extent to which orality and textuality in poetic language are constructed categories; to Nielsen, Mullen's criticism and poetry reveal "the falsity of the assumed opposition between singing and signing in both Africa and America" (*Black Chant* 36). The linguistic splicing in *Trimmings* attests not just to such a poetic amalgam but also to the shared, hybrid tongue from which the poet draws.

This splicing allows Mullen to use her polyvalent language to question the categories "black" and "white" — to critique the construction of racial difference. Identity has become less stable, the self more complex than in the poetic world of *Tree Tall Woman*. Here the shaping force of language exerts its power with ambiguous results. Rather than assuming that "Black English" exists in polar opposition to standard or "white English," *Trim mings* offers up a linguistic collage that works toward the deconstruction of essentialist concepts: "Her red and white, white and blue banner manner. Her red and white all over black and blue. Hannah's bandanna flagging her down in the kitchen with Dinah, with Jemima. Someone in the kitchen I know" (*Tr* 11).

The bandanna and the Jemima figure suggest recognizable stereotypes of black women. Mullen notes that even though such images are most likely drawn from the white minstrel tradition, they constitute nonetheless a powerful "pseudo-black folklore" that has shaped views of blackness in America.[9] By refusing to exclude these representations from her text, Mullen implies that there is an important source for this language, one that needs to be traced: Such images are constructed both from red, white and blue nationalism and from a widely accepted culture of violence ("all over black and blue"), which takes its greatest toll on women and people of color (hence the racial overtones of "black and blue"). Similarly, the blues alluded to here conjures another type of folklore, one that may seem more genuine or authentic than that of Hannah and Jemima, particularly in the allusion to Louis Armstrong's "What did I do to get so black and blue?" (which points as well to Ralph Ellison's uses of the Armstrong song in *Invisible Man*).[10] Mullen's text refuses distinctions among the sources for what she calls her "recycled" language; in particular, suppositions that one kind of black culture is authentic and another inauthentic are highly problematic for Mullen. She notes that the pursuit of authenticity "is often nostalgic and often points to oppression," and that there is no "set of black behaviors that I must adhere to in order to be true to who I am."[11] In this respect her views diverge from the assumptions of Black Arts poets, who advanced the notion of an authentic, even universal, black identity, based on shared attributes — as in Johnetta Cole's elaboration of the meaning of black "soul." By contrast, Mullen's word-play claims all and any linguistic expressions in a critique of essentialism. Rather than insisting on racial purity, she demonstrates the interrelations evident in a hybrid culture.

One way Mullen gives voice to her "recycled" aesthetic is to signify specifically on Stein. There are several instances of intertextuality in *Trimmings* wherein Mullen infuses the very diction and syntax of *Tender Buttons* with elements of black language and culture. As I discussed in Chapter 1, Stein creates a dialogue between "distress" and "red." Mullen recasts this portion of *Tender Buttons* in the unexpected form of an excursion into the black vernacular with obvious Steinian intonations:

When a dress is red, is there a happy ending. Is there murmur and satis-
faction. Silence or a warning. It talks the talk, but who can walk the walk.
Distress is red. It sells, shouts, an urge turned inside out. Sight for sore
eyes. The better to see you. Out for a stroll, writing wolf-tickets. (*Tr* 34)

The most immediate Steinian source is the heading "THIS IS THIS DRESS,
AIDER," and the text of that "tender button" reads in its entirety:

Aider, why aider why whow, whow stop touch, aider whow, aider stop
the muncher, muncher, munchers.

A jack in kill her, a jack in, makes a meadowed king, makes a to let.
(*TB* 476)

One of the most frequently glossed sections in *Tender Buttons*, this passage
has often been read as punning on "distress," as well as on the notion of
"aid" and one of Stein's nicknames for Alice, "Ada." It is crucial to a number
of readings that emphasize the role of female sexuality in *Tender Buttons*.
For some, this involves a critique of the "meadowed king" who rises at the
expense of "her," as Ruddick suggests; among others, Gass sees an explicit
(and joyful) sexual scene; further, as I detailed in Chapter 1, I believe that
Stein provides a typically double perspective here — that of lesbian eroti-
cism and male heterosexual panic *about* that eroticism. For all of these read-
ings, sexuality provides the backdrop for Stein's polyvalent language.[12]

From the start of Mullen's appropriation, a revisionary dialogue emerges.
The short, uninflected questions ("Is there murmur and satisfaction," for
example) are reminiscent of *Tender Buttons*, and so is the diction — the mix-
ture of simple monosyllabic words ("dress," "red," "talk") with words de-
scribing states of consciousness ("happy," "satisfaction," "urge"). However,
in contrast to the original, Mullen's version alerts us to the ways in which
neither racial categories nor language use is ever pure. There is also a dou-
bleness at work in this passage that alters Stein's original — the experience
of psychic division among black Americans that W. E. B. DuBois called
"double consciousness." It was this sense of division *within* the self that
Black Arts writers sought most rigorously to overcome through a change in
black consciousness — converting the alienation of black Americans into
the concepts of pride and power, and invoking in their radically experimen-
tal texts the commitment to revolution.[13] That legacy is evident here:
Mullen's "talk," in contrast to Stein's, is culturally specific, and it affirms the
legitimacy, as well as the aesthetic pleasures, of Black English. "Dis" both al-

ludes to the sound of "this" in black English and to the verb "to dis," or dis-respect, someone, echoed in the overt competition of "talks the talk." A similar linguistic transformation occurs in the conjunction of European fairy tale (Red Riding Hood's "better to see you") and contemporary idiom ("writing," instead of "selling," "wolf-tickets," or hearing "wolf whistles").

A fundamental question that emerges is what happens when the seductive red dress is donned, perhaps by the Red Riding Hood figure. Is there "satisfaction" for flirtatious partners, a desire to shout with joy, or is there fear of violence — silence, warning? Evident in such passages, *Trimmings* does more than evoke feminine attire in all its ambiguously charged sensuality. The book also explores the extent to which that attire determines in large part how women are regarded, literally and figuratively, and even how they're treated: "is there a happy ending" for any woman's Cinderella-like transformation "when a dress is red" — when she puts on a piece of clothing that signifies passion and seduction, or availability and provocativeness? How is such a color "read" by male onlookers? How does race intersect with the erotic? Without providing any simple or polemical answers, Mullen links sexuality, clothing, violence, and desire, allowing the linguistic traditions of Stein and Black Arts to meet.

As this example makes clear, Mullen's text also addresses the exclusion of race from early feminist criticism, an issue that has been the subject of passionate revision by women of color for nearly two decades.[14] Adapting her poetic project to embrace the goals of an equally revisionist literary criticism, Mullen has described her original desire to "get a read on Stein and race." At the time she was writing *Trimmings* she was reading both *Tender Buttons* and "Melanctha," whose racist and classist images are the subject of reappraisals by critics as diverse as Sonia Saldívar-Hull and Bernstein.[15] Mullen's play on Stein's famous "rosy charm" passage is perhaps the most striking instance of her recasting of a passage from *Tender Buttons* to explore questions of race that rarely surfaced in Stein's poetry, but which were clear enough in "Melanctha." Mullen's revision pursues Stein's original connection between blackness and sexuality in *Three Lives* and inserts that perspective into her own recasting of *Tender Buttons*:

> a light white disgraceful sugar looks pink, wears an air, pale compared to shadow standing by. To plump recliner, naked truth lies. Behind her shadow wears her color, arms full of flowers. A rosy charm is pink. And she is ink. The mistress wears no petticoat or leaves. The other in shadow, a large, pink dress. (*Tr* 15)

The Stein text in question is "A PETTICOAT," and it reads in full: "A light white, a disgrace, an ink spot, a rosy charm" (*TB* 471). The passage is most likely about female creation, both on the page and of the body, and, as I have suggested, about Stein's invention of a subversive female fetishism. The white of a woman's undergarment is connected to the blank page, and the stain of blood to the writer's ink, a "rosy charm" whose power Stein asserts.[16]

Mullen has described this passage as her opening into *Tender Buttons* — perhaps even the point of departure for *Trimmings* as a whole. She sees Stein's text as an allusion to Manet's provocative (and scandalous) painting *Olympia* — the white woman staring boldly at the viewer, in a state of "disgraceful" sexual permissiveness, with the nearby "ink spot" (a black servant) waiting behind her. As Marianna Torgovnick points out in *Gone Primitive*, in Manet's painting, the black woman functions (like other primitive images in modern art) as the symbol for both exoticism and the white woman's "debased sexuality"; the impression is reinforced by an alert black cat (tail suggestively erect) at the edge of the canvas.[17] In response to both her predecessors, Mullen represents the nude white woman as "disgraceful sugar"; behind her the black woman in "a large, pink dress" has "arms full of flowers," in what is apparently a position of attentive servitude to her mistress. In Mullen's twice-removed version of Manet's original, the right to "wear an air" is completely dependent on a "shadow" version of the white woman's femininity — one that stands for sexuality itself.

Mullen's take on *Olympia*, and on "A PETTICOAT," concerns the otherness of black female sexuality in a culture in which femininity is equated with the naïveté of "pink" and the skin color "white."[18] This motif of the color-coded nature of femininity pervades the book as a whole. Mullen writes that in *Trimmings*

> The words pink and white kept appearing as I explored the ways that the English language conventionally represents femininity. As a black woman writing in this language, I suppose I already had an ironic relationship to this pink and white femininity. (*Tr* 69)

Throughout *Trimmings*, it is clear that evocations of the blues tradition and African-American speech confront the deficiencies of conventional language in representing blackness, most particularly black female subjectivity. In her "rewriting" of *Olympia*, the very ownership of sexuality is at stake: The transgressive eroticism of the sort Stein championed is clearly available only to the "light white" woman who "wears an air," but who is in fact clothed in what Mina Loy called "ideological pink," in this case nothing more than her own skin. By contrast, her "shadow standing by" is the symbol of such sexuality within the white mind, but the "ink" of blackness is literally "in shadow"; the word is repeated three times. A feminist reading of *Olympia* might suggest that Manet "owns" (or names) the white woman's sexuality as well, but Mullen's attention is drawn to the dynamic — both the social hierarchy and the necessary interplay — between black and white. In another section of *Trimmings*, girlhood and the color pink are also associated ("Girl, pinked, beribboned. Alternate virgin at first blush" [*Tr* 35]). This passage uses the same techniques of multiple meanings and the connotation of innocence conjured up by the color pink to point out the disturbing "naked truth": "Pink" is "a rosy charm" in the white world only when it's worn by someone "pale," "white," and "sugary." Mullen's portrait uses Stein to build on foundations laid by Black Arts poets in their critique of white dominance in American life.

Yet the wedding of Steinian and Black Arts techniques in this passage also challenges the frequently patriarchal rhetoric of Black Arts writing. Mullen focuses on black female subjectivity in a fashion that such poets as Sanchez, Audre Lorde, and June Jordan struggled toward and were often criticized for throughout the 1970s (as in the condemnation of Ntozake Shange's "For Colored Girls Who Have Considered Suicide / When the Rainbow is Enuf" as presenting negative depictions of black men). Stein is of assistance here: In this "ink spot" passage, Mullen revises the essentialist view of blackness invoked by Black Arts theorists. The one whose skin is "ink" is perceived by the dominant culture as inadequate, incomplete: The word "pink" minus the "p" gives us "ink." And yet the black woman harbors the power to signify, to contest through language the status of "other" — writing is produced with ink. Unlike Black Arts writers' assertions of essential blackness, this word-play calls on poststructuralist views of language to subvert the notion of fixed identity. As Mullen has pointed out, binary categories (black/white or ink/pink) are interdependent; in order to function as a sign, the signifier "pink" must be differentiated from its linguistic likeness, "ink." The construction of whiteness — of difference — is impossible without an oppositional other against which to define the self.[19] In this double-edged "signifying," Mullen casts her line back to Stein, black feminism, and Black Arts to reveal her debts to and her divergence from a richly evocative usable past.

Mullen has written that "Gender is a set of signs which we tend to forget are arbitrary. In these prose poems I thought about language as clothing and clothing as language" (*Tr* 69). The final poem of *Trimmings* reaffirms this link:

> Thinking thought to be a body wearing language as clothing or language a body of thought which is a soul or body the clothing of a soul, she is veiled in silence. A veiled, unavailable body makes an available space.
>
> (Tr 66)

Placed at the end of the book, this "trimming" serves as Mullen's ars poetica, the explanation for her use of the trope of clothing as language: The metaphor implies that one can *alter* one's language as easily as one can change an outfit, in the process altering identity. That shifting sense of identity is crucial to *Trimmings* — like language, the self is not fixed but malleable. At the same time, that which is "veiled" shows through language in Mullen's work, just as the often invisible body of the black woman finally makes its own space. Moving away from simply being "veiled in silence" is *Trimmings*' project. It is a goal that both acknowledges and diverges from Stein's subversive playfulness, for if *Tender Buttons* is daring because it eroticizes domestic space, Mullen's semiotics of clothing/language reflects women's position in the culture at large and black women's concerns in particular. Mullen creates a dialogic text, infusing Stein's hermetic diction with dissonant perspectives, bringing together divergent influences in hybrid form. For Mullen, as for any contemporary poet glancing back at what Fraser calls "preexisting traditions," recalling predecessors necessarily also means revising their approaches. Nonetheless, *Trimmings* is a homage to those writers whose lineage Mullen evokes.

If *Trimmings* takes as subject the erotics of attire in intertextual relation to *Tender Buttons* and Black Arts cultural critique, Mullen's more recent book, *Muse & Drudge*, shifts toward even greater hybridity.[20] Here Mullen bears witness not just to the legacy of twentieth-century avant-gardism but also to the tradition of lyric itself. If, as Albert Murray argues, the blues musician "turns disjunction into continuities" (*Omni-Americans* 59), then in *Muse & Drudge* Mullen has composed a long poem as blues: fragmented and improvisational, disjunctive in its continuities, bearing witness to a legacy of female song from Sappho to Bessie Smith.

As this study has made apparent, such friendly commerce with lyric is rare among avant-garde poets, who tend to reject both the prevalent subjectivity of the lyric "I" and the conventions of what Rachel Blau DuPlessis calls "the short poem and its epiphanies" ("Manifests" 49). But Mullen, like

DuPlessis, constructs lyric "otherhow" as an experiment in forging a performative text that can evoke the complexities of community, language, and poetic voice. Mullen's kaleidoscopic surfaces in *Muse & Drudge* reflect themes of identity and kinship, selfhood and origins. Elsewhere, Mullen argues that racial passing in the United States is a metaphor for assimilation, "a national mechanism for forgetting a history that links African Americans with other Americans in kinship.[21] Exposing such suppressed histories, *Muse & Drudge*, even more profoundly than *Trimmings*, explores the diverse influences and languages of a miscegenated culture. *Muse & Drudge* is not just a hybrid of avant-garde influences. It is also a *poetic* hybrid — a lyric long poem, a text that asserts hybridity in its attention to overlapping identities and voices, and in its very form. In a language borrowed in part from Stein's density of word-play, Mullen splices together competing lexicons into a highly allusive long poem that challenges the notion of any individual reader's mastery and assumes instead a diverse readership. As Murray points out, the blues — also a lyric form easily extended in length — is itself a hybrid, the offspring of European and African influences (*Stomping the Blues* 63). Mullen fosters her own version of this linguistic multiplicity — one that displays, often revels in, the varied lexicons of contemporary American culture[22] and reveals that such language is a locus of connected subjectivities. As Mullen asserts, *Muse & Drudge* "is deliberately a multi-voiced text"; she goes on to associate this quality with the hybridity of American culture: "'Mongrel' comes from 'among.' . . . We are among; we are not alone. We are all mongrels" (Bedient 652).[23]

The epigraph to *Muse & Drudge* reveals Mullen's interest in both cultural and formal hybridity. Two lines from Callimachus read, "Fatten your animal for sacrifice, poet / but keep your muse slender." A first response might be to register the race and gender valences that the lines, however unwittingly, encode to a contemporary reader. The fattened animal is the body denied subjectivity — a possible metaphor for the slave body — while the "slender muse" is an ideal of *dis*embodiment, a deified feminine soul that supplies the traditionally male poet with the means of androgynous creativity. By merging the Greek poet Callimachus with an implicit racial and gender politics relevant to nineteenth- and twentieth-century America, Mullen initiates a strategy of creating cultural hybrids: Classical and contemporary sources meet throughout the poem, and the unexpected mixture destabilizes both sets of allusions in a "mongrelization" of cultural reference points. As in Mullen's title, which also plays with the dichotomy between feminine inspiration (muse) and bodily female labor (drudge), this epigraph intervenes into the ideology of lyric production, its reliance on both a feminine ideal and an easily sacrificed other.[24]

But Callimachus's poem is also a defense of lyric, and in this respect its presence prefigures Mullen's play not just with cultural hybridity but with a specific form of poetic hybridity as well. Callimachus asserts in the poem from which these lines are drawn that he is denigrated for not producing a "continuous epic / of thousands of lines on heroes and lords," preferring to "turn out minor texts." Answering this challenge, Callimachus counters, "a long-eared gray for others, for me delicate wings" (Diane J. Rayor and William W. Batstone, eds., *Latin Lyric and Elegiac Poetry* 341–42). Calli-machus's advice to "keep your muse slender," attributed in the poem to Apollo and offered up directly to the poet, is a vindication of lyric. *Muse & Drudge* may critique the ideology that deifies the inspiring muse at the expense of her sister drudge, but Mullen nonetheless sides with Callimachus in at least one respect — in his defense of so-called "minor" forms — including lyric.[25] This stance is apparent in *Trimmings* and in *S*PeRM**K*T* (Mullen's third book), each of which is written in what Mullen advisedly calls the "minor" form of the prose poem, and each of which is, similarly, hybrid in nature — a sort of serial lyric. In this instance, splicing together lyric fragments into a discontinuous whole, Mullen critiques the hierarchy that elevates epic over lyric.[26] Thus, the presence of Callimachus at the start of the long poem *Muse & Drudge* signals Mullen's concern with a formal hybrid that will destabilize systems of poetic value.

If *Muse & Drudge* is a hybrid, a serial long poem that comes to the defense of lyric — a work to trouble the waters of established categories — its range of references has an equally destabilizing effect, for Mullen's continual allusions rule out the possibility of any single reader's mastery over her text. Mullen says she wants to "work in the interstices, where I occupy the gap that separates one from the other; or where there might be overlapping boundaries." She points out that the poem "addresses a diverse audience of readers, with the expectation that no single reader will comprehend every line or will catch every allusion" (Henning, "Interview" 9). As an example, one might peg Mullen's symmetrical visual form — four quatrains per page — as a nod toward the Sapphic stanza or, because of its complex rhythms, as an allusion to twelve-bar blues (or even to the Kansas City Four/Four beat).[27] Similarly, there are no easily identifiable sections in this eighty-page poem, and because the stanzas disobey syntax and supply no titles, little punctuation, and less closure, the poem invites its own construction in any number of ways — most significantly by means of a given reader's awareness of Mullen's varied references.

This poetic sampling undermines the notions of originality and mastery, challenging an overly conventionalized repertoire of avant-garde novelty. Drawn from widely divergent sources, Mullen's quotations assert hybridity as an aesthetic and political act. The very first stanza of the poem, for example, is dense with allusive word-play: "Sapphire's lyre styles / plucked eyebrows / bow lips and legs / whose lives are lonely too" (*Muse & Drudge* 1). Mullen embodies her "Sappho" — her woman artist — as "Sapphire," the popular name (derived from the "Amos 'n Andy" character) for an abrasive black woman. This derogatory term has been appropriated by black feminists to denote strength and defiance, notably by the poet and novelist who has taken the name "Sapphire."[28] Here, then, is Sappho singing the blues as well as Sapphire as lyric poet, a hybrid of lyric modes and cultural moments. Mullen has her take recourse to a more available tool than those of high art: Her "lyre" is her body. Thus Sapphire, the poet as muse's instrument, plucks not just strings but "eyebrows."[29] And her lyre (suggesting too a partner in crime, a "liar") "styles" not a literary production (as in lyr-ic) but the body as canvas. Her creation redefines the parameters of art. A Sappho fragment comes to mind: "I took my lyre and said: / Come now, my heavenly / tortoise shell: become / a speaking instrument" (Sappho, *A New Translation* 8).

This hybrid tribute to art culled from the odds and ends of contemporary culture is nonetheless shot through with ambivalence. Sapphire's art entails a violence to the body, as the given female form is altered to fit conventions of femininity: The "slender" body (recalling Callimachus's "slender muse") is the woman's *sole* work of art, and this work is most often denigrated, not unlike women's literal creation (in childbirth), traditionally devalued in favor of men's figurative creation (in high art).[30] This female creativity, then, is at once sorely undervalued and possibly misguided — a sacrifice to a false idol. The ambivalence toward this form of feminine creativity extends to the stanza's list of body parts (brows, legs, lips), through which Mullen mimics the tradition of Petrarchan encomiums devoted to individual, often disembodied, parts of the female form.[31] Mullen's lines at once parody such litanies (in the humorous "bow legs") and offer the possibility of reclaiming the tradition for a female-authored creation — as the love poems of Sappho, adoring the beautiful feet of a bride, or a young girl's gown, attest to a powerful self-fashioning.

But the female body is not the exclusive subject of this quatrain. There are also allusions to the blues in the lines "plucked eyebrows / bow lips and legs," suggesting the plucking and bowing that is done to a bass. Mullen's Sapphire is linked both to blues and to the written tradition of lyric and epic — the latter through the allusion to the crucial battle scene of *The Odyssey*, in which Odysseus "plays" his deadly bow with the delicacy of a lyre:

> the man skilled in all ways of contending,
> satisfied by the great bow's look and heft,
> like a musician, like a harper, when
> with quiet hand upon his instrument
> he draws between his thumb and forefinger
> a sweet new string upon a peg: so effortlessly
> Odysseus in one motion strung the bow.
> Then slid his right hand down the cord and plucked it,
> so the taut gut vibrating hummed and sang
> a swallow's note. (Homer, *The Odyssey* 404)

This epic moment of celebratory, aestheticized battle is clearly revamped in Sapphire's feminine self-fashioning, exalting her activity to the level of Odysseus's mastery. Yet a different lyric voice is also reasserted in the stanza's final line, "whose lives are lonely too," taken from Billy Strayhorn's poignant 1938 song "Lush Life," about the bereft speaker's loss of a lover. In one stanza, then, the references range from Sappho and Homer to Amos 'n Andy and Ella Fitzgerald. Such allusion creates a surface that reveals the shifting and limited nature of our own knowledge, for indeed no single reader is likely to catch all of Mullen's references. Similarly, on a formal level, there is indeterminacy in the doubling of parts of speech; "styles," "plucked," and "bow" are all verb forms that also work as nouns or adjectives. This open-endedness evokes a multiple sense of the word as an ambiguous juncture of subjectivities. Mullen's text reveals a poetics of multiplicity — of both repetition and renovation. By extension, and as the poem bears out, we are in a realm not of fixed identity (or of identity politics) but of language in flux, a coming together of linguistic registers that expands the possibilities of lyric voice.

In the next stanza, Mullen continues to evoke the musical origins of lyric, playing classical reference against the blues and mixing idioms to forge hybrid sets of phrases: "my last nerve's lucid music / sure chewed up the juicy fruit / you must don't like my peaches / there's some left on the tree"

(*Muse & Drudge* 1). There is a pun on "strung-out" nerves (which, plucked, make a perverse music). "Juicy Fruit" is testament to the way early blues double entendre (Rudy Greene sang the lubricious song of that title) filtered in innocuous forms into mainstream idiom (in the brand of chewing gum). These phrases pick up on the loneliness in the previous stanza, but, once again, in contrast to Petrarchan conventions (in which the female figure remains voiceless), here the rejected woman laments out loud, as in the blues tradition, pioneering an art of salvific metaphor and sheer wit. "You must don't like my peaches" alludes to Bessie Smith's lines, "If you don't like my peaches, don't shake my tree," a variant of Ma Rainey's "If you don't like my ocean, don't fish in my sea, / Stay out of my valley, and let my mountain be."[32] Sappho is present as well: "She was like that sweetest apple / That ripened highest on the tree, / That the harvesters couldn't reach" (Davenport trans. 40). The result is a lyric that splices together cultural sources and attitudes — the dissatisfied desire of Sappho meets the defiance of Bessie Smith.

Mullen notes — and the observation holds true in her own work — that "African American women writers have often used their texts to 'talk back' to texts by white men, white women, and black men in which representations of black women are absent or subordinated to other aims" ("Runaway Tongue" 259). Theirs is "a dialogic writing practice that operates against the tendency of the literate to view the illiterate and the oppressed as 'voiceless'" (263). A similar observation is made of Black Arts poetics. Lorenzo Thomas notes that the Black Arts project was "an attempt to recreate in modern modes the ancestral role of the African *griots* who are poets, musicians, and dancers whose songs record genealogies and . . . cosmologies." He quotes Ugo Rubeo's reading of Etheridge Knight's poetry as creating both a "'double dialogue with past and present'" and a "'mutual, dialogical pattern of oral communication' with the audience present."[33]

In her own poetics, acknowledgment of the potency of oral expression is crucial, but, as in *Trimmings*, it is coupled with textual, visual play. Mullen says that, particularly in *Muse & Drudge*, "I am writing for the eye and the ear at once, at that intersection of orality and literacy . . . so that [the poem] is never just a 'speakerly' or a 'writerly' text" (Elisabeth A. Frost, "An Interview" 401). Nielsen notes that despite the emphasis on the speakerly in African-American writing, this sort of textual innovation was present a decade before the Black Arts movement in such avant-garde groups as the Society of Umbra, which appropriated modernist experiments with language as the basis of a new black art, and he credits Mullen in helping to "reconfigure our understanding of African American cultural productions" by challenging this emphasis on the "vernacular."[34] In *Muse & Drudge*, the black female voice is appealed to (as in, "go on sister sing your song" [50]), but such evocations coexist with the experience of what Mullen calls "overlapping boundaries," through a mixing of registers of language and of the cultural politics that such hybridity reflects. Typically her stanzas draw on a number of discourses: "massa had a yeller / macaroon a fetter [. . .] / outside MOMA / on the sidewalk / Brancusi's blonde / sells ersatz Benin bronzes // Joe Moore never / worked for me" (58). Multiple perspectives are established through word-play, as in the shifting idiom from "massa" and "yeller" to "ersatz Benin bronzes." The world of high art (the acronym MOMA, with its inescapable echoes of "mama") incorporates the commercialization of African art (Benin bronzes), fittingly juxtaposed with the language of slavery: "Macaroon" has overtones of "Maroon" (defiant West Indian escaped slaves), but also of "quadroon" and "octoroon" (mathematical signals of hybridity or racial "impurity").[35] In the final line, "Joe Moore," a variant of "mojo," similarly juxtaposes root work with official high culture. In this mix of references, Mullen critiques the exploitation of black bodies and black art, as the Black Arts poets did; yet rather than "legitimizing an 'authentic' African American vernacular speech" (Thomas "Neon Griot" 310), Mullen evokes a play with a range of voices, sources, and associations that are necessarily "mongrel."

A particular concern for Mullen is how lyric, in all its diversity, has been continually reinvented by black women artists. She comments that the poem "is reclaiming the black woman's body, so that the body is hers. . . . The idea is that she can be in charge: she can play her own instrument, and she can play the tune that she wants" (Bedient, "Solo Mysterioso Blues" 660). Mullen's innovations play variations on this theme, familiar from such black feminist celebrations of beauty as Gwendolyn Brooks's "To Those of My Sisters Who Kept Their Naturals" or Sanchez's convergence of the proud black female body with the dream of nationalism: "my brown [/] bamboo/colored [/] blk/berry/face [/] will spread itself over [/] this western hemisphere and [/] be remembered" (*Bad* 6). Yet rather than reinforcing an essentialist view of black identity, Mullen is concerned with the way beauty is tied to a language that constructs that identity; her poetics, continually testifying to the hybridity of American culture, uses word-play to disrupt rigid conceptions of the body. One example of this rethinking of the body occurs through plays on the word "honey": "honey jars of hair / skin and nail conjuration / a racy make-up artist collects herself / in time

for a major retrospection" (*Muse & Drudge* 21). Women's self-transforma-
tions — body parts bought in "honey jars" that offer new skin and nail
types — may indeed be an art of conjuration worthy of "a major retrospec-
tion," but beauty is not just racy but raced or racially bound (honey as an
ideal hair color, for example). An overtone from Sappho raises another as-
sociation: "For me neither honey nor bee . . ." (Rayor, trans., 63). The ref-
erence to Sappho claims one strand of meaning in the word "honey" for a
woman-authored desire. At the same time, Mullen notes that honey served
as an offering to Oshun, an African loa, or Orisha, and in this respect she
destabilizes the references to beauty and suggests a more traditional form
of "conjuration."[36] Mullen's spliced-together phrases subvert dominant
meanings to interrogate words themselves, suggesting that the body, too, is
ultimately an instrument of language.

Such strategies of punning and multiple allusion recall the mixtures
of linguistic registers and cultural stances Melvin B. Tolson evoked in
The Harlem Gallery (1965), another of Mullen's antecedents. Tolson's tight
structures of rhyme (often punningly bilingual) combine a playful ap-
proach to the spoken word with the poem's visual presence on the page. In
his introduction to the book Karl Shapiro wrote that "Instead of purifying
the tongue, which is the business of the Academy, [Tolson] is complicating
it, giving it the gift of tongues" (13). Free of the "pernicious nostalgia" that
marred the innovations of such modernists as Pound and Eliot, Tolson
"complicates" both poetic language and accepted notions of black identity
through allusive word-play that anticipates that of *Muse & Drudge*. His was
not an approach welcomed by the Black Arts poets emerging just a few
years after the publication of *Harlem Gallery*. But for Tolson, as for Mullen,
language and identity are in flux, and poetry of note must acknowledge the
complex results: "Sometimes a Roscius as tragedian, / sometimes a Kean as
clown, / without Sir Henry's flap to shield my neck, / I travel, from oasis to
oasis, man's Saharic up-and-down" (Tolson, *Harlem Gallery* 19).

In the spirit of Murray, who notes that the blues is a hybrid of European
and African influences, and of Houston Baker, who points to rap as a formal
mix, a collage of styles, Mullen borrows strategies from musical modes to
posit a locus of linked subjectivities and poetic idioms. She notes that her
"improvisational approach to rhythm and rhyme" was influenced by the
"tight distichs of female rappers."[37] In one such instance, a collective "you"
is playfully taken to task: "If you turned down the media / so I could write
a book / then you could look me up / in your voluminous recyclopedia"
(*Muse & Drudge* 68). The ambiguous "you" reflects a strategy in which

women rappers play the dozens by addressing unnamed competitors. Creating humor in the juxtaposition between the simple, monosyllabic opening and the heavily Latinate close — with its punning nonce word "recyclopedia" — Mullen questions the hierarchy that elevates "high" art at the expense of "rappin" and bears witness to the genre's rhythmic and linguistic shifts and turns.

Further, though, Mullen hints throughout this and other passages at a kinship between the language games of rap and those of Stein — as in a line two quatrains earlier ("cross color ochre with stalk of okra"), or the glossolalia of another passage that suggests both the free-wheeling prose of *Tender Buttons* and scat singing: "mutter patter simper blubber / murmur prattle smatter blather / mumble chatter whisper bubble / mumbo-jumbo palaver gibber blunder" (57). In such linguistically layered lines, Mullen resumes Baraka's call for "an art that is identifiably African-American . . . an art that is a mass art" (*Catch* 58–59) with a complex response more akin to Tolson's allusive "gallery": the "recyclopedia" is an emblem of cultural hybridity — the impossibility of isolation or purity. Mullen notes that what she calls "black codes" continually enter "the mainstream" and are subsequently altered; "that," she says, "is partly what I am thinking about with *Muse & Drudge*" (Hogue, "Interview with Mullen" n.p.). The "recyclopedia" is testament to the way aspects of black — or other nonmainstream — cultural elements take new form and acquire new definitions when they are recycled, like a jazz artist's musical quotation or a rapper's sampling of spoken words and musical phrases. Given such continual cultural reinvention, one's language and positionality become, like the rapper's art, a constant remixing.

Nonetheless, despite this hybrid revamping of lyric, Mullen pointedly criticizes a different kind of "mongrelization" from the one her text seeks to epitomize. By contrast with the mixing of lexicons and cultural norms, there is the exploitation of black culture by a white mainstream. Like Black Arts theorists before her, Mullen is aware that some forms of hybridity render blackness invisible: in popular music there are "white covers of black material" and "unfurling sheets of bluish music" (32). Particularly pernicious is the denial of black creativity and authorship: "spin the mix fast forward / mutant taint of blood / mongrel cyborg / mute and dubbed" (42). A mass art like television that dubs black voices onto white bodies creates a "mongrel cyborg," rendering the black body itself mute; the mix is made to appeal to an audience that craves black "soul" but is deeply uncomfortable with the "mutant taint of blood," or with any experience of blackness. Elsewhere Mullen tersely describes "the invention of rock music" as "Whites covering black material" ("Optic White" 87) — a "mongrel" creation that, instead of acknowledging its origins, erases them. In *Muse & Drudge* Mullen similarly links to mass culture's productions racist definitions of white identity as the only "pure" strain of blood.

It is in this context that Mullen addresses passing as a denial of blackness and of kinship; she shapes her poetics against what she calls elsewhere an "aesthetics of assimilation."[38] Mullen's view here owes a debt to the Black Arts political agenda, since the very notion of passing implies opportunism, a rejection of blackness — all of which the program of "black pride" intended to subvert. Mullen doesn't endorse the implied separatism — even racial "purity" — of the Black Arts agenda. Yet her thinking does reflect the influence of Black Arts theory that asserted, in the words of Ron Karenga, "the battle we are waging now is the battle for the minds of Black people, and . . . if we lose this battle, we cannot win the violent one" (Karenga, "Black Cultural Nationalism" 32). In *Muse & Drudge*, passing is treated scathingly: "my skin but not my kin / my race but not my taste" (10). Rejection of kin by way of passing (changing one's "fate") is also "kin" to another rejection of blackness hinted at: "my race but not my taste" suggests the stereotypical preference for light-skinned over dark-skinned women. Questions of racial identity and privilege are inseparable from those of gender; both passing and oppressive standards of beauty threaten to erase the black body. At the same time, however, such insights need not lead to essentialist politics but, instead, can be realized on the level of the word — in a poetics that recharges language.

In distinction from the euphonious language commonly thought of as lyrical, Mullen pays homage to a blues aesthetic as a means to reach this linguistic ideal: "muse of the world picks / out stark melodies / her raspy fabric / tickling the ebonies" (*Muse & Drudge* 17). Adapted from Zora Neale Hurston's phrase "mule of the world" (referring to black women, and thus evoking the muse/drudge of Mullen's title),[39] this muse "picks out" tunes, refusing polish in favor of the stark and raspy voice that represents a rough-hewn art. As Mackey points out, Baraka emphasizes a "willfully harsh, *anti-assimilationist* sound" in describing a blues aesthetic.[40] Similarly, Mullen's muse tickles not the ivories but the ebonies, forging an aesthetics that reflects a celebration of the diversity of black experience, that refuses to "pass," even as it refuses to limit its linguistic range, or its cultural reference points, to one register alone. This "raspy fabric" is that of a lengthy jazz improvisation — analogous to this lyric long poem of linked fragments. As

Mullen asserts, it is an aesthetic that embraces reappropriation as well: "you can sing their songs / with words your way / put it over to the people / know what you doing" (17). Or, as Sappho has it, "I will now sing this beautifully / to delight my companions."[41]

Mullen's strategies in *Muse & Drudge* show the meeting of an oppositional cultural politics with formal innovation. With her hybrid sources Mullen demonstrates, through poetic form itself, the "mongrel" nature of American experience. I'd like to close by returning to the phrase from *Muse & Drudge* in my title, "belatedly beladied blues," which occurs in one of Mullen's four-stanzas series: "tragic yellow mattress / belatedly beladied blues / shines staggerly avid diva / ruses of the lunatic muse" (21). In this complex passage, puns, allusions, and word-play form an intricate maze. The palindromic "avid diva" suggests a way of "singing" the performance of words themselves, reimagining the domain of lyric not as that solely of personal utterance but of the play of language. This appropriation diva might redefine the literary trope of the "tragic mulatto" (deflated to "mattress") or the "yellow gal." She might reclaim the folkloric roots of the pejorative term "shines."[42] This diva is "shining" through her own "mastery" (suggested by "mattress") of form and idiom. She might, like her male counterpart Stag o' Lee ("staggerly"), be a force to be reckoned with, a vengeful female hero. Such a "beladied" singer (the Billie Holiday or Lady of written lyric) might reengender the familiar "ruses of the lunatic muse" to construct her own verse to a feminine ("lun-atic") moon — overcoming the split between idealized muse and mundane drudge, serving as her own inspiration.

The phrase "belatedly beladied blues" reflexively suggests Mullen's craft, a feminist blues, but one hardly concerned with its own belatedness. Mullen's work, from *Tree Tall Woman* to *Muse & Drudge*, reveals that innovation need not rely on a narrow view of how to make it new — by opposing, even seeking to destroy, existing traditions, as much avant-garde rhetoric has claimed. Like Howe's, Mullen's work reminds us of the complexity of origin, poetic and otherwise; its power lies in its *re*-invention, its hybridizing of divergent traditions. For Mullen, as for many feminist avant-garde writers today, the concern is not about arriving at the "belated" end of a lengthy tradition. It is, rather, in tracing a "beladied" version of that poetic history.

EPILOGUE

In 1982, the future editors of *HOW(ever)* engaged in the "collective labor" of finding a name for their new journal. They considered *Parts of Speech, Feminine Endings, Text/ure,* and other phrases that would evoke their "different perspective" on literature, language, and gender. They nearly settled on *I (too),* from "Poetry," with its famous opening, "I, too, dislike it" — the reference to Marianne Moore serving as a signal of their chosen poetic lineage. Eventually, though, they turned to the poem's next line: "Reading, it, however. . . ." "First," Kathleen Fraser remembers, "*However* was one word; then we broke it into its typographical and parenthetical components. The name represented for us an addendum, a point of view from the margins, meant to flesh out what had thus far been proposed in poetry and poetics" ("Tradition of Marginality" 62–63). Minus the "I" of *I (too),* the name they selected not only evoked an often invisible feminist avant-garde tradition in American letters but also de-emphasized the personal lyric voice so prevalent in other feminist poetry of the day. The focus was not on a shared or uniform political vision but rather on the question of positionality — as Fraser puts it, "a point of view from the margins" that would interrogate linguistic alternatives, researching the "how" of poetics, language, and gender.

As this book has shown, and as Fraser's publication helped to document, that marginal viewpoint has persisted in varying forms for a century in American poetry, the latter end of which saw what Fraser calls "the 'dig' for a female tradition of language inventiveness" ("Tradition of Marginality" 65). Yet Fraser's comments about the journal's "view from the margins" also reveal the distance that feminist avant-garde poetics has traveled in recent years. The list of contributors to *HOW(ever)* comprises a virtual index of significant experimental women poets: Barbara Guest, Beverly Dahlen, Susan Howe, Fanny Howe, Rachel Blau DuPlessis, Rae Armantrout, Norma Cole, Hannah Weiner, Mei-mei Berssenbrugge, Rosmarie Waldrop, Alice Notley, and others. Almost all of these writers are still underrecognized. Nonetheless, a new openness to experimental writing, as well as increasing attention to more varied forms of feminist poetics, may foretell a far different future.

Several volumes of a new journal, expanding the mission of *HOW(ever)*, are now available. *HOW2*, again founded by Fraser, is published on-line — a suitable medium for innovative writing — and promises to continue to publish a range of avant-garde women's writing and to create a bridge between feminist theory and feminist poetics, including new questions about gender and technology. Vickery points out not only that the new technology has fostered a broader, international dialogue (the editorial advisory board has members from the United States, the United Kingdom, Australia, New Zealand, and Germany), but also that "as an electronic journal, it invites multiple, nonlinear reading strategies" (*Leaving Lines of Gender* 100). As the founding of *HOW2* suggests, the ranks of the feminist avant-garde continue to grow, partly in response to new directions in feminist thought. Writers like Howe and Mullen, responding to currents in poststructuralist theory, exemplify a keen interest in language as a site of feminist politics. Such theorists (and poets or novelists) as Monique Wittig have inspired feminist examinations of the long-held avant-gardist assumption that cultural "revolution" must be realized in the radical form of a work of art; adapting this notion to specifically feminist ends, Wittig and others have helped create a literary climate more congenial to feminist innovators. Equally significant, emerging women writers now have an extremely diverse, and more accessible, past to draw on. As a young writer in the 1950s, Fraser had received little or no exposure to Moore, Stein, H.D., Loy, Laura Riding, and other poets she now sees as precursors — a situation unlikely today. As is the case with the belated critical acknowledgment of Language poetry, feminist experimentalists are at last receiving attention. New anthologies of innovative writing by women have appeared in the United States and Great Britain, and the work of experimental women poets is increasingly considered in studies of modern or contemporary American poetry, and of feminist poetics.[1] Carolyn Burke's biography of Loy and an edition of Loy's selected poems accompany new works on Stein and other feminist avant-gardists — scholarship that has helped revise views of modernist poetics.[2] Similarly, experimental writing by such poets as Howe, Fraser, and others is being published by more mainstream houses than ever before. Today the tradition of feminist avant-garde poetics includes the second generation discussed in this book, from Sanchez to Mullen, as well as many other women writers, some loosely associated with the Language group or other innovative approaches.

As is apparent from the preceding chapters, uses of language among these and other feminist avant-garde poets have varied widely, from a highly visual poetics to performance-oriented texts/readings, and mixtures of these and other modes informing the work of younger women, like Tracie Morris. Such poets as Ntozake Shange have built on the Black Arts tradition, incorporating both typographical experiments and a commitment to a performative aesthetic. By contrast, writers like Theresa Hak Kyung Cha and Erica Hunt have incorporated the signs and syntax of multiple languages, as well as photographs, charts, and letters, to form a collage of cultural identity. Exploring gender, race, and language, poets like Claudia Rankine, Jeanne-Marie Beaumont, Jena Osman, and Juliana Spahr promise myriad new directions for women avant-gardists. Perhaps just as significant, the influence of this radical writing is felt in the increasing daring of already-established women poets. Although the danger of dilution or appropriation of feminist avant-garde poetics is real, this stylistic expansiveness reflects greater acceptance of and interest in experimental women's poetry by a broad range of poets and readers — perhaps even a move from margin to center.[3]

Among feminist poets like Mullen, revision of antecedents is a testament to both continuity and change. Clearly no avant-garde practice can stand still. As this book has shown, feminist avant-garde poetics has reinvented itself again and again, over the course of a century. This study has sought to reveal that continuing richness and initiate a broader conversation among scholars concerning innovative feminist writing. Fraser pondered in the opening pages of *HOW(ever)*, "what about the women poets who were writing experimentally?" Although that question now seems easier to begin to answer than two decades ago when it was posed, recognition for avant-garde women writers is still lacking. This book is an initial step in the continuing scholarly examination of the traditions of women poets whose innovative writing has, for a century, sought to change through an altered tongue fundamental conceptions of gender, race, and history.

NOTES

INTRODUCTION

1. *HOW(ever)* 1.1 (1983): 1.
2. In the 1980s, for example, the radical theories of French feminism garnered much more critical debate than the work of contemporaneous avant-garde women writing in English. Such collections as Toril Moi's *French Feminist Thought: A Reader* (New York: Basil Blackwell, 1987), among other collections of theoretical writings, has no counterpart devoted to feminist avant-garde poets writing in English.
3. Simpson's *Poetic Epistemologies: Gender and Knowing in Women's Language-Oriented Writing* (Albany, N.Y.: SUNY P., 2000) and Vickery's recent *Leaving Lines of Gender: A Feminist Genealogy of Language Writing* (Hanover, N.H.: Wesleyan U. P., 2000) are the most important studies to date on experimental writing by American women. Simpson's term "language-oriented" reflects her epistemological focus, while Vickery's emphasis on "genealogy" does not engage directly with notions of the avant-garde. Mary Margaret Sloan, Maggie O'Sullivan, and Fraser all opt for "innovative," minimizing associations with either the theory or history of the avant-garde, despite their concern with feminist lineage.
4. See Perloff's *The Futurist Moment: Avant-Garde, Avant Guerre, and the Language of Rupture* (Chicago: U. of Chicago P., 1986), chapter 5.
5. Guest describes the evolution of the journal *The New Freewoman*, which ultimately became one of the outlets for Imagism and Vorticism, *The Egoist*. *The New Freewoman*, which arose from a feminist group called the Freewoman Discussion Circle, was founded by Harriet Weaver to promote the ideas of the feminist philosopher Dora Marsden. The name was changed to *The Egoist* to emphasize Marsden's idea that improvement for workers must come from what we would today call self-esteem. When Pound offered his services as editor, the journal became a venue for his circle of writers, and feminist politics gave way to an avant-garde agenda (although H.D. was briefly assistant editor, replaced by T. S. Eliot). The division between feminist politics and a largely male avant-garde is revealing. More recently, feminist avant-gardism has enjoyed a vocal presence in some journals. See Chapter 4 for a discussion of *HOW(ever)*.
6. Defining the avant-garde, Renato Poggioli focuses on "a common psychological condition," that of the alienation of the artist, and reaches as far back as Romanticism; under the rubric of alienation, avant-garde becomes an umbrella term, covering symbolism, modernism, and more radical movements (*The Theory of the Avant-Garde*, trans. Gerald Fitzgerald [Cambridge, Mass.: Har-

vard U. P., 1968], 4, 108–11). Differentiating modernism from avant-gardism, Charles Russell attributes "alienation" by contrast only to modernist writers, who try to recuperate the traditions of high art and recapture the dominant culture from which they feel alienated; avant-gardism, by contrast, challenges existing political and artistic institutions head-on. In my view, the idiosyncrasy of these poets' visions does not disqualify them from being called avant-gardists: in fact, their works embody the prevalent tension between political agendas and artistic liberation that has plagued virtually all avant-garde movements. The fate of Surrealism and other early twentieth-century movements reveals how uneasily political and aesthetic activism have coexisted. Poggioli even went so far as to assert the existence of *two* avant-gardes — the political and the artistic — an approach pursued by more recent critics as well. Although far from dividing activism and aesthetics in this fashion, feminist avant-garde poets have indeed tended to lean toward the antinomian end of the spectrum, avoiding the programmatic.

7. Adrienne Rich, Elaine Showalter, Alicia Ostriker, Alice Walker, Susan Stanford Friedman, and numerous other critics inspired by (and/or contesting elements of) second-wave feminism have established the importance of a range of traditions to women's literary production (Betsy Erkkila, Linda Kinnahan, Kim Whitehead, and others). See also *Where We Stand: Women Poets on Literary Tradition*, ed. Sharon Bryan (New York: Norton, 1993).

8. Von Hallberg notes that since the Futurists, avant-garde groups have been preoccupied with the continuity of avant-gardism (86), with its origins most often in the period Marjorie Perloff has called the "Futurist Moment." Von Hallberg does not, however, presume the death of the avant-garde, despite his emphasis on a sense of belatedness in the four post–World War II groups he considers poetic avant-gardes in America (see 83ff). Like von Hallberg, I assume that avant-gardism need not be limited to one historical moment; I disagree with Peter Bürger, who argues that because the avant-garde destroys tradition, there can be no tradition of avant-garde practice. The argument is one that Marinetti anticipated by prophesying his own irrelevance: "When we are forty, other younger and stronger men will probably throw us in the wastebasket like useless manuscripts — we want it to happen!" (51). Bürger implies that culture is static. Concerning neo-avant-gardes and the question of novelty, Rosalind Krauss demonstrates that the avant-garde's claims to originality are in fact based on notions of repetition, even of the fraudulent original, which she illustrates through the prevalence of the grid figure in visual art. Among other discussions see also Leslie Fiedler, Roland Barthes's "Whose Theater? Whose *Avant-Garde*?" in *Critical Essays*, trans. Richard Howard (Evanston, Ill.: Northwestern U. P., 1972), Matei Calinescu, John Lowney, David Lehman, and Hal Foster's "What's Neo about the Neo-Avant-Garde?" (*October* 70 [1994]).

9. Von Hallberg, *American Poetry and Culture 1945–1980* (Cambridge, Mass.: Harvard U. P., 1985), 13–14. It is interesting to note that in his more recent treatment of avant-garde poetry in America in the Cambridge series, von Hallberg takes a different position; as I have noted above, he remains skeptical about the

nature and effectiveness of neo-avant-garde groups, but he clearly labels both Black Arts and Beat poetry, among others, as poetic avant-gardes.

10. See Simpson's introduction, as well as Fraser's approach in *Translating*. I should note that readings of the intersections among male and female avant-gardists (in works by Susan Suleiman, Perloff, Bob Perelman, Kinnahan, DuPlessis, and Juliana Spahr, among others) have yielded important insights into modern and contemporary poetics. Those questions are, however, outside the scope of this book.

11. For Suleiman, such a position nonetheless provides advantages: "In a system in which the marginal, the avant-garde, the subversive, all that disturbs and 'undoes the whole' is endowed with positive value, a woman artist who can identify those concepts with her own practice and metaphorically with her own femininity can find in them a source of strength and self-legitimation" (17). The essays in Caws et al., *Surrealism and Women* (Cambridge, Mass.: MIT P., 1991) reveal both little-recognized women Surrealists and the misogyny that colored that movement, especially in its early days.

12. Marianne DeKoven, "Male Signature, Female Aesthetic: The Gender Politics of Experimental Writing," in *Breaking the Sequence: Women's Experimental Fiction*, 76, ed. Ellen G. Friedman and Miriam Fuchs (Princeton: Princeton U. P., 1989).

13. DeKoven noted that "Many women *are* writing experimentally but receiving little or no recognition for it; women writers who are successful and recognized write in traditional, conservative forms" (78). Recent books are strong indicators of long-overdue attention to and publication of avant-garde women writers: DuPlessis, Fraser *(Translating)*, Nancy Gray, Simpson, Vickery, and collections edited by Sloan, O'Sullivan, and Laura Hinton and Cynthia Hogue. For earlier anthologies of experimental women writers, see Friedman and Fuchs *(Breaking the Sequence)*, and Lou Robinson and Camille Norton, eds., *Resurgent: New Writing by Women* (Chicago: U. of Illinois P., 1992).

14. Analysis of feminist poetics retains a focus on the personal, the self, and the body. Jan Montefiore traces a poetics of experience that goes back to the Romantics (8ff), mentioning Irigaray, language experiments, and the female body, but never mentions recent avant-garde women poets (135ff): The prominent figures in *Feminism and Poetry: Language, Experience, Identity in Women's Writing* (San Francisco: HarperCollins, 1994) are Phillis Wheatley, Anne Bradstreet, Dickinson, Stevie Smith, Rich, Irena Klepfisz, Sylvia Plath, Judy Grahn, Audre Lorde, and Eavan Boland. Michael Bibby emphasizes "ways that feminist poetry of the Vietnam era articulated a politics of corporeality that situates the female body as the principal subject of historical struggle" (Michael Bibby, *Hearts and Minds: Bodies, Poetry, and Resistance in the Vietnam Era* [New Brunswick, N.J.: Rutgers U. P., 1996], 89). Whitehead argues that "feminists wanted a poetry in which they could name the experiences that societal and poetic taboos had previously kept them from expressing. . . . As a result, they turned to more open poetic modes" and accessible forms (xix). By contrast, focusing on women rather than *feminist* poets, Erkkila positions *The Wicked Sisters: Women Poets, Literary History, and Discord* (New York: Oxford U. P., 1992) as an

account of "the difficulty and complexity of sisterhood as an affirming model of women's literary history" and "seeks to study the category 'woman poet' as itself the subject of historical struggle" (8). As Carolyn Burke points out, "Because as readers, we are accustomed to the confessional mode in contemporary poetry, we may have difficulty hearing differently pitched poetic speech when produced by an author known to be female. Our expectations about what constitutes a 'woman's voice' may even put earmuffs on our capacity to hear more impersonal or nonpersonal voices" ("Supposed Persons," 132). Jan Clausen also points to the limitations of perceived criteria for feminist poetry, including an "obsession with accessibility" ("A Movement of Poets: Thoughts on Poetry and Feminism," in *Books and Life*, 23 [Columbus, Ohio: Ohio State U. P., 1989]).

15. Rich, "Transcendental Etude," in *The Dream of a Common Language: Poems 1974–1977* (New York: Norton, 1978), 73 and 76.

16. See Owens, "The Discourse of Others: Feminists and Postmodernism," in *The Anti-Aesthetic: Essays on Postmodern Culture*, ed. Hal Foster (Port Townsend, Wash.: Bay P., 1983), 57–83.

17. "When he flees the symbolic paternal order . . . a man can laugh. But the daughter, on the other hand, is rewarded by the symbolic order when she identifies with the father: only here is she recognized not as herself but in opposition to her rival, the mother with a vagina who experiences *jouissance*. . . . Therefore the invasion of her speech by these unphrased, nonsensical, maternal rhythms, far from soothing her, or making her laugh, destroys her symbolic armour and makes her ecstatic, nostalgic or mad" ("About Chinese Women," in *The Kristeva Reader*, ed. Toril Moi [New York: Columbia U. P., 1986], 150). Kristeva refers to Virginia Woolf and Sylvia Plath as examples of female artists who answered "the call of the mother" and subsequently went mad, for "if no paternal legitimation comes along to dam up the inexhaustible non-symbolized drive, [the woman] collapses into psychosis or suicide" (156, 158).

18. The omission of gender from considerations of avant-gardism continues among some critics who explore resurgences of avant-garde poetry in America. Simpson's and Vickery's studies are particularly welcome for this reason. One earlier exception is Quartermain, who emphasizes Howe's feminist vision and does not limit discussion of her poetics to its relation to Language writing. Walter Kalaidjian, who has made connections between the historical avant-gardes and the Language poets (see "Transpersonal Poetics: Language Writing and the Historical Avant-Gardes in Postmodern Culture," *American Literary History* 3 [1991]: 319–36), acknowledges "a distinctively feminist body of Language writing" (326), in part revolving around the journal *HOW(ever)*. But Kalaidjian's primary concern is with the "populist styles of leftist agitprop" combined with "modernist experimentalism" (328). Applying a limited definition of the avant-garde — and politics — to Language poetry, George Hartley selects several male poets (including Ron Silliman, Barrett Watten, and Charles Bernstein) whose Marxist orientation allows him to define them within an avant-

garde tradition through which he can replay the Lukács-Frankfurt School debate in the new guise of a Jameson-Language debate. DuPlessis, Lynn Keller, Perelman, and Linda Reinfeld all offer broader theoretical frameworks.

19. Cixous, "The Laugh of the Medusa," in *New French Feminisms: An Anthology*, trans. Keith Cohen and Paula Cohen and ed. Elaine Marks and Isabelle de Courtivron (New York: Schocken Books, 1981), 250. "[Woman's] liberation will do more than modify power relations . . . she will bring about a mutation in human relations, in thought, in all praxis: hers is not simply a class struggle" (253).

20. See DeKoven's "Male Signature" among numerous other discussions. Fuss's notion of "strategic" essentialism is one of many responses to such arguments.

21. See, for example, Fuss, *Essentially Speaking: Feminism, Nature and Difference* (New York: Routledge, 1989), xii, 40, and 98 for discussions of strategic essentialism.

22. Irigaray also "models" feminine writing in "The Looking Glass, from the Other Side" in *This Sex Which Is Not One*, trans. Catherine Porter (Ithaca, N.Y.: Cornell U. P., 1985), with its radical fragmentation of subjectivity, its profusion and confusion of pronouns, and its alteration of syntax and typeface. Such efforts are belied by Irigaray's stance in her more discursive writings. See Fuss 26 and 63 for particularly relevant discussions of Irigaray and discourse.

23. Aldon Nielsen has addressed this issue in the field of African-American poetics, tracing the work of the experimental Umbra group, which anticipated Black Arts activism, as well as drawing attention to earlier, neglected innovators like Melvin Tolson. See *Black Chant: Languages of African-American Postmodernism* (New York: Cambridge U. P., 1997), chap. 3 and 5. Also see Nathaniel Mackey, *Discrepant Engagement: Dissonance, Cross-Culturality, and Experimental Writing* (New York: Cambridge U. P., 1993), 17.

24. In *Forms of Expansion: Recent Long Poems by Women* (Chicago: U. of Chicago P., 1997), Keller notes that long poems by writers of color remain virtually invisible in recent studies of that genre. Along with Nielsen and DuPlessis (*Genders, Races and Religious Cultures in Modern American Poetries, 1908–1934* [New York: Cambridge U. P., 2001]), Mullen, Spahr, and Lorenzo Thomas explore the relationships among language, race, and identity.

CHAPTER 1

1. See Jacqueline Brogan's anthology, *Part of the Climate: American Cubist Poetry* (Los Angeles: U. of California P., 1991). For criticism on Stein and Cubism, see Randa Dubnick, *The Structure of Obscurity: Gertrude Stein, Language, and Cubism* (Chicago: U. of Chicago P., 1984), 28–44, and Stephen Scobie, "The Allure of Multiplicity: Metaphor and Metonymy in Cubism and Gertrude Stein," in *Gertrude Stein and the Making of Literature*, ed. Shirley Neuman and Ira B. Nadel (Boston: Northeastern U. P., 1988), 98–118. Gray also discusses Stein and portraiture.

2. As Ellen Berry points out, "Stein situated the contemporary composition — her term for the avant-garde text — within the everyday" (*Curved Thought and*

Textual Wandering: Gertrude Stein's Postmodernism (Ann Arbor: U. of Michigan P., 1992, 137). Berry makes distinctions between Stein's textual radicalism and the more programmatic politics of the historical avant-gardes (192 n. 12).

3. Louise J. Kaplan, *Female Perversions: The Temptations of Emma Bovary* (New York: Doubleday, 1991), 9. For discussion of this question, see also Susan Suleiman, *Subversive Intent: Gender, Politics, and the Avant-Garde* (Cambridge, Mass.: Harvard U. P., 1990), 149. In particular, Suleiman mentions Janine Chasseguet-Smirgel's "Perversion and the Universal Law," *International Review of Psychoanalysis* 10 (1983): 293–301.

4. DuPlessis, "'Seismic Orgasm': Sexual Intercourse, Gender Narratives, and Lyric Ideology in Mina Loy," in *Studies in Historical Change*, ed. Ralph Cohen, 264–91 (Charlottesville: U. of Virginia P., 1992). DuPlessis also draws on DuBois's and Gordon's "Seeking Ecstasy" in her account (see 16–18).

5. By the 1860s sexologists such as Karl Westphal, Richard von Krafft-Ebing, and Havelock Ellis began defining female inverts in terms of "their masculine behavior and their conception of themselves as male" (Lillian Faderman, *Odd Girls and Twilight Lovers: A History of Lesbian Life in Twentieth-Century America* [New York: Penguin, 1991], 41). This identity was hereditary, and it was swiftly equated by many with the woman movement. The result was a conception of an abnormal, "freakish" woman (see Faderman, 41–48). In *Three Essays on the Theory of Sexuality* (1905; English translation 1910), Freud refuses the labels "degenerate" and "innate" as absolute characteristics of inversion. Yet as Faderman points out in *Odd Girls* (130), in "The Psychogenesis of a Case of Homosexuality in a Woman" (1920 in *The Standard Edition of the Complete Psychological Works of Sigmund Freud*, vol. 18, ed. James Strachey [London: Hogarth P., 1955], 147–72), Freud identifies feminism as an indication of abnormality in women.

6. Linda Gordon, *Woman's Body, Woman's Right: A Social History of Birth Control in America* (New York: Penguin, 1996), 94. What Mort identifies as "the libertarian and utopian discourse of new moralists and sex reformers" was influenced by sexology and Freudian analysis (*Dangerous Sexualities* 146). Hence the emphasis on a normative heterosexual model. As DuBois and Gordon put it, "Both [feminist positions] were thoroughly heterosexist in their assumptions of what sex is. . . . They condemned those whose sexual behavior deviated from their standards, not only sexually exploitive men but also women who did not conform" ("Seeking Ecstasy on the Battlefield" 7–8). Woodhull's and Claflin's essays "Virtue: What It Is, and What It Is Not" and "Which Is to Blame?" and Woodhull's speech "The Elixir of Life" in *Feminism: The Essential Historical Writings*, ed. Miriam Schneir (New York: Random House, 1992) presented radical positions concerning "the problem of sexual love," often anticipating later arguments, including Loy's: "Sexual intercourse that is in accordance with nature, and therefore proper, is that which is based upon mutual love and desire, and that ultimates in reciprocal benefit" (Miriam Schneir, ed., *Feminism: The Essential Historical Writings* [New York: Random House, 1992], 152). The

assertion of free love is often, as in this passage, conflated with "natural" and "proper" sexuality.

7. See Mort 136ff: "Purity became hegemonic in the early women's movement" in England, though the sexual radicals emerged as a significant minority. Cott notes that the term "feminism" only began to emerge around 1913, in debt to but distinct from the older "woman movement" and Suffrage movement. The invention of the term "feminism" marked both a self-conscious modernism on the part of its users and "an explicit and semantic effort to exceed the bounds of — to insist on goals more profound than — the rising advocacy of woman suffrage": in particular, an embrace of radicalism that included advocacy of women's self-expression and economic independence, and opposition to double standards concerning sexuality (Nancy Cott, *The Grounding of Modern Feminism* [New Haven, Conn.: Yale U. P., 1987], 15).

8. Gordon, *Woman's Body* 129–30.

9. Frank Mort, *Dangerous Sexualities: Medico-Moral Politics in England Since 1830* (New York: Routledge, 1987), 148. On Stein and Toklas's relationship, see Catherine R. Stimpson, "Gertrice/Altrude: Stein, Toklas, and the Paradox of the Happy Marriage," in *Mothering the Mind: Twelve Studies of Writers and Their Silent Partners*, ed. Ruth Perry and Martine Watson Brownley, 122–39 (New York: Holmes and Meier, 1984), 129.

10. Ruddick has argued that Stein's bodily poetics parallels an interest in the mother as the repressed in Western culture, while DeKoven links Stein's experiments to the Kristevan semiotic. For more recent readings, see also Simpson, *Poetic Epistemologies*, and Spahr, *Everybody's Autonomy: Connective Reading and Collective Identity* (Tuscaloosa: U. of Alabama P., 2000). Despite Stein's inscription of role-play in the poem, she attempts to avoid "the trap of placing anything or anybody in a class, such as 'The Feminine' or 'The Masculine'" (Stimpson, "Gertrude Stein and the Transposition of Gender," in *The Poetics of Gender*, ed. Nancy K. Miller, 1–18 [New York: Columbia U. P., 1986], 2, 14–15).

11. Ernest Fenollosa, "The Chinese Written Character as a Medium for Poetry," ed. Ezra Pound, in *Prose Keys to Modern Poetry*, ed. Karl Shapiro (New York: Harper and Row, 1962), 142–44, as cited by Perloff, *Futurist Moment* 183. Perloff also cites the following: "We might come to believe that the thing that matters in art is a sort of energy, something more or less like electricity or radioactivity, a force transfusing, welding, and unifying" (*Literary Essays of Ezra Pound*, 49).

12. There are, however, profound challenges to conventional gender roles in Dada, both in the work of women artists such as Beatrice Wood and Juliette Roche, and in Man Ray's gender-bending photographs of Duchamp in the persona Rose Sélavy. Further, affinities exist between the motif of domesticity and Cubist still-life. See, for example, Gris's mixed-media collage "Breakfast" (1914), which could serve as a remarkably apt visual companion to *Tender Buttons*.

13. Yet however easy it may seem to label Pound's rhetoric as an appropriation of the female privilege of giving birth (Picasso and Wassily Kandinski are called "father and mother, classicism and romanticism of the movement" [*BLAST*

14. See *Futurist Moment*, "Ezra Pound and 'The Prose Tradition in Verse.'" Perloff notes Pound's reliance on Marinetti's rhetoric (including his focus on technology), despite Pound's assertions to the contrary.

15. *The Autobiography of Alice B. Toklas*, in *Selected Writings of Gertrude Stein*, ed. Carl Van Vechten (New York: Random House, 1962), 153, quoted in Perloff, *Wittgenstein's Ladder: Poetic Language and the Strangeness of the Ordinary* (Chicago: U. of Chicago P., 1996), 99. As Perloff points out, Stein evidences a certain amount of disdain toward the Futurist leader. One passage in *Autobiography* reveals Stein's dismissal of Marinetti following the 1912 Futurist exhibit in Paris: "everybody found the futurists very dull," Stein observes.

16. *Wittgenstein's Ladder* 110–12, 100–101. Perloff notes that Stein alludes to "A Negress. / Nurse"— the Sudanese nurse who appears prominently in the speaker's memories of childhood when, in the founding Futurist manifesto, he's thrust into the "Maternal ditch" after a motorcar accident (*Wittgenstein's Ladder* 103). Perloff reads an image of a fan, described as "electric," which the women in the poem take away from a man—figuring, in Perloff's view, the women's appropriation of "masculine" technology and a deliberate slight to Marinetti (108).

17. Kristeva's "chora" is relevant here; see Harriet Chessman, *The Public Is Invited to Dance: Representation, the Body, and Dialogue in Gertrude Stein* (Stanford, Calif.: Stanford U. P., 1989), 4. In *Reading Gertrude Stein* 241, Ruddick uses the word "oscillation" to describe movements between "the newly unearthed maternal dimension" and "the paternal/symbolic." DeKoven makes a similar point about what she calls Stein's "lively words" style but stresses the "presymbolic *jouissance*" of *Tender Buttons* (*A Different Language* 68, 76).

18. Chessman, *Public Is Invited to Dance* 91, citing an interview of Stein in Robert B. Haas, ed., *A Primer for the Gradual Understanding of Gertrude Stein* (Santa Barbara, Calif., Black Sparrow, 1971), 18.

19. DeKoven distinguishes Stein's early style of repetition and "insistence" from that of the "lively words" of *Tender Buttons* (in *Selected Writings of Gertrude Stein*, ed. Carl Van Vechten [New York: Random House, 1962]; hereafter *TB*). See *A Different Language: Gertrude Stein's Experimental Writing* (Madison: U. of Wisconsin P., 1983), 63ff.

20. Barthes's concept of textual "pleasure" is relevant (in *The Pleasure of the Text*, trans. Richard Miller [New York: Farrar, Straus and Giroux, 1973]): Significance "is meaning, *insofar as it is sensually produced*" (61) — and "the text of pleasure is a sanctioned Babel" (4). In addition, perversion is "the realm of textual pleasure" (9–10): "language in pieces. . . . Such texts are perverse in that they are outside any imaginable finality" (51–52). Barthes also addresses fetishism: Reading is "perverse" in that "the reader can keep saying: *I know these are only words, but all the same*" (47). Barthes, however, associates both "bliss" (*jouissance*) and fetishism with loss, not plenitude: Although he "perversely" reverses sexual polarities ("The text is a fetish object, and *this fetish desires me*"

[27]), he posits the "text of bliss" as one "that imposes a state of loss" (14): "it is the abrupt loss of sociality . . . *everything* is lost" (39).

21. I will call these capitalized phrases "headings" because I think it is misleading to use the word "title." Among other possibilities, each of the sections of *Tender Buttons* is itself a "button" in Stein's box, but each is not an independent poem that begins with an extratextual title. As *Tender Buttons* is sui generis, its divisions are parts of a larger, serialized whole. Each heading provides a focus of attention, a moment — a "title" would have more pretensions. DeKoven uses the term "subtitles" (*A Different Language* 77).

22. My focus will be on the "Objects" section, because it is here that the material world and the fetishistic strategy are most apparent.

23. Chessman elaborates on "the 'tenderness' of these 'buttons' [as] a human and bodily one." She also observes that, as words, "these buttons call our attention to the value they hold outside of their capacity to represent: their sound, their shape, their rhythm and length" (91).

24. William Gass describes how Stein "exposed the arbitrary conventionality" of title and chapter headings in *Four in America*. See *The World within the Word* (New York: Knopf, 1978), 67–68.

25. What Barthes calls an *"éclat du mot"* ("an explosion of words" [46]) in such writers as Mallarmé is relevant, as it provides a vocabulary with which to describe the nonreferential uses of language. The difference, as I see it, between an awareness of the materiality of language and Stein's practice is that Stein evokes "doubleness" in language, rather than subverting signification. See "Is There Any Poetic Writing?" in *Writing Degree Zero*, trans. Annette Lavers and Colin Smith (New York: Farrar, Straus and Giroux, 1968), 41–52.

26. DeKoven (*A Different Language*) argues that Stein's process is consonant with Kristeva's view that poetic language involves interplay between the semiotic and the symbolic; "musicalization" occurs *with* signification (see *Revolution* 65). But in Kristeva's view, return to the semiotic risks hysteria or psychosis in the female subject. My view of Stein diverges as well from Jacques Lacan's opposition between pre-Oedipal glossolalia and entry into the symbolic. Lacan asserts that the symbolic substitutes for the fantasized phallus of the mother; the very materiality of language is predicated on loss and unsatisfiable desire. On fetishism and language, see Lacan, "The Agency of the Letter in the Unconscious or Reason Since Freud," in *Ecrits*, trans. Alan Sheridan, 146–78 (New York: W. W. Norton, 1977).

27. Unpublished notebook D, p. 11, Yale Collection of American Literature, cited by Ruddick, *Reading Gertrude Stein* 93, 95, 96.

28. See, especially, Gass's "Gertrude Stein and the Geography of the Sentence" in *World within the Word* 63–123; Stimpson's "The Somagrams of Gertrude Stein" in *Critical Essays on Gertrude Stein*, ed. Michael J. Hoffman (Boston: G. K. Hall, 1986) 183–96; Fifer, "Is Flesh Advisable?" 472–83; and Ruddick's "A Rosy Charm" 225–40. See also Margueritte Murphy, "'Familiar Strangers': The Household Words of Gertrude Stein's *Tender Buttons*," *Contemporary Literature* 32 (1991): 383–402, for an exploration of Stein's desire to "reinvest

domestic labor with value, to make household tasks into code words for stability in her new domestic arrangement and for erotic lesbian love" (388).

29. In *Odd Girls*, Faderman argues that "lesbianism" is a twentieth-century phenomenon, a replacement for the "female friendship" that sanctioned woman-to-woman intimacy in nineteenth-century America.

30. See "Leonardo da Vinci and a Memory of His Childhood" in *The Standard Edition of The Complete Psychological Works of Sigmund Freud*, trans. and ed. James Strachey, vol. 11, 59ff (London: Hogarth P., 1961). Here Freud provides the same explanation of the castration complex and the possibility of emergent fetishism: "The fixation on the object that was once strongly desired, the woman's penis, leaves indelible traces on the mental life of the child. . . . Fetishistic reverence for a woman's foot and shoe appears to take the foot merely as a substitutive symbol for the woman's penis which was once revered and later missed" (96).

31. "Fetishism," in *The Standard Edition of the Complete Psychological Works of Sigmund Freud*, trans. and ed. James Strachey, vol. 21 (London: Hogarth P., 1961), 152–53; "Splitting of the Ego in the Process of Defence" in *The Standard Edition of the Complete Psychological Works of Sigmund Freud*, trans. and ed. James Strachey, vol. 23 (London: Hogarth P., 1961), 275. John Matlock shows that cases of female fetishism were in fact documented in the 1880s in France, but that the emerging discourse of "perversion" ultimately gendered fetishism as a male phenomenon. He speculates that the suppression of female fetishism kept alive a crucial "story of primal difference" (58) along gender lines. See his "Masquerading Women, Pathologized Men: Cross-Dressing, Fetishism, and the Theory of Perversion, 1882–1935" in *Fetishism as Cultural Discourse*, ed. Emily Apter and William Pietz, 31–61 (Ithaca, N.Y.: Cornell U. P., 1993). In *Feminizing the Fetish: Psychoanalysis and Narrative Obsession in Turn-of-the-Century France* (Ithaca, N.Y.: Cornell U. P., 1991), 102–4, Apter summarizes Schor's assembling of such case histories in her "Female Fetishism: The Case of George Sand" in *The Female Body in Western Culture: Contemporary Perspectives*, ed. Susan Rubin Suleiman, 363–72 (Cambridge, Harvard U. P., 1985).

32. See Butler, *Gender Trouble*: "The deconstruction of identity is not the deconstruction of politics; rather, it establishes as political the very terms through which identity is articulated" (148). Suleiman (142–43) summarizes recent efforts to theorize feminist parody. Ostriker discusses women's parodic uses of myth in poetry, and Yaeger describes how women remake and "play" with old texts. Suleiman mentions some of the sources for such assessments of feminist parody: Bakhtin's writings on carnival (*The Dialogic Imagination: Four Essays*, ed. Michael Holquist and trans. Caryl Emerson and Michael Holquist [Austin: U. of Texas P., 1981]) and Kristeva's theory of intertextuality.

33. Suleiman traces many parodic strategies to Surrealism and Dada, among other sources and makes the point that feminists need not deny (or bemoan) formal similarities between male avant-garde texts and feminist avant-garde revisions. Whether in Duchamp or in women novelists like Leonora Carrington or Jeanette Winterson (who figure in Suleiman's chapter on "Feminist Intertextu-

ality"), parody is a means of attacking patriarchal attitudes. It is worth noting similarities between Suleiman's ideas of parody and Gates's "signifyin(g)" (see chapter 5).

34. In the masquerade, "the woman loses herself . . . by playing on her femininity." One response to this compulsory practice is mimicry — a willed, self-conscious, and ironic version of masquerade (see Luce Irigaray, *This Sex Which Is Not One*, trans. Catherine Porter [Ithaca, N.Y.: Cornell U. P., 1985], 133–34). Riviere describes masquerade as an exaggerated femininity that helps women compensate for their intellectual capacities by placating the father for her theft of phallic power. See also Mary Ann Doane's "Film and the Masquerade: Theorizing the Female Spectator," *Screen* 23.3–4 (1982): 74–87; "Masquerade Reconsidered: Further Thoughts on the Female Spectator," *Discourse* 11.1 (1988–1989): 42–54; Matlock's "Masquerading Women, Pathologized Man"; and Apter's chapter "Unmasking the Masquerade" in *Feminizing the Fetish*.

35. The speculum "disturb[s] the staging of representation according to too-exclusively masculine parameters" (*This Sex* 155). Chessman (*The Public Is Invited* 94–95), makes a similar point about the speculum, applied to Stein's resistance to conventional vision in *Tender Buttons*. See also Wittig's *Lesbian Body*.

36. See Gass, *World within the Word* 101–4. For other explications of this passage, see Ruddick, *Reading Gertrude Stein*, who identifies the "Aider" section with "a scene of sacrifice and communion" (215); Neil Schmitz, "Gertrude Stein as Post-Modernist: The Rhetoric of *Tender Buttons*" in *Critical Essays on Gertrude Stein*, ed. Michael Hoffman (Boston: G. K. Hall, 1986), 123–24; Richard Bridgman, *Gertrude Stein in Pieces* (New York: Oxford U. P., 1970), 129–30, who interprets the passage more broadly; and Stimpson, "Gertrude Stein and the Transposition of Gender" 15–16, who sees a Jack the Ripper figure in the final section.

37. Gass argues for a pun on "kill" as "dying" (achieving orgasm) and a dildo image (103).

38. In "A Rosy Charm" 226, Ruddick points to the uses of "red" to suggest the female body, the motif of "boxes" or enclosures as figures for female sexuality, and the encoding of what is "dirty" as a parodic naming of lesbian "perversion."

39. Kaplan mentions Robert Stoller, *Observing the Erotic Imagination* (New Haven, Conn.: Yale U. P., 1985), 16–17, because he details "the infinite variability of the fetishistic objects or erotic preferences" (36n).

40. See "Leonardo da Vinci" 96. Kaplan explains that voyeurism or intensive looking is part of the sexual "performance" of fetishism. Kaja Silverman's *The Acoustic Mirror: The Female Voice in Psychoanalysis and Cinema* (Bloomington: Indiana U. P., 1988) provides a fascinating account of fetishism and the visual in film.

41. Although I believe Stein would reject Cixous's essentialist body-writing, her poetic practice anticipates Cixous's satiric account of Freudian-style anxiety: "Castration? Let others toy with it. What's a desire originating from a lack? A pretty meager desire" ("Laugh of the Medusa" 262).

42. See "A Rosy Charm."

43. For Elizabeth Grosz, such an object choice might itself represent a form of lesbian fetishism to counter the masculinity complex posited by Freud: The lesbian "displaces phallic value onto an object outside the mother's (or her own) phallus, but in contrast to the fetishist's, her love object is not an inanimate or partial object but another subject. Her 'fetish' is the result of not a fear of femininity but a love of it" ("Lesbian Fetishism?" in *Fetishism as Cultural Discourse*, ed. Emily Apter and William Pietz [Ithaca, N.Y.: Cornell U. P., 1993], 114).

44. "Femininity," *The Standard Edition* 22:134, quoted by Apter, *Feminizing the Fetish* 105.

45. Schor, "Female Fetishism" 368–69 (she cites Sarah Kofman's "Ca Cloche" in *Les Fins de l'homme: A partir de Jacques Derrida*, ed. Philippe Lacoue-Labarthe and Jean-Luc Nancy [Paris: Gallilée, 1981], 83–116); see also Grosz ("Lesbian Fetishism?"). In *Feminizing the Fetish*, Apter uses female fetishism to stress gender flexibility, masquerade as a "sartorial female fetishism" (98). But Schor points out that appropriating fetishism might reinstate a phallic norm in feminist discourse — a "subtle form of 'penis envy'" (371). In a later article, Schor proposes "a feminist irony that would divorce the uncertainty of the ironist from the oscillations of the fetishist" ("Fetishism and Its Ironies" in Fetishism as Cultural Discourse, ed. Emily Apter and William Pietz [Ithaca, N.Y.: Cornell U. P., 1991], 98). Also see Marjorie Garber's "Fetish Envy," *October* 54 (1990): 45–56.

CHAPTER 2

1. See Lucia Re, "Futurism and Feminism," *Annali d'Italianistica* 7 (1989): "Futurism from its inception had the merit of raising issues regarding the representation and regimentation of sexuality, the political roots and ramifications of sexual behavior, and the ideological over-determination of gender divisions and gender roles in contemporary society" (256).

2. Arnold gives an excellent account of Loy's embrace and rejection of Futurism, particularly because of its misogyny and investment in what Loy saw as the "war fever" of the 1910s (Elizabeth Arnold, "Mina Loy and the Futurists," *Sagetrieb: A Journal Devoted to Poets in the Imagist/Objectivist Tradition* 8.1–2 [1989], 86). Arnold explains Loy's marked ambivalence, including Loy's declaration that "Futurism is dead," in the very same letter in which she praises Marinetti's exuberance (85).

3. The so-called Sapir-Whorf hypothesis (which held that, as Deborah Cameron puts it, "linguistic differences determined differences in world view" [*Feminism and Linguistic Theory* (New York: St. Martin's, 1985), 97]) is most relevant as an analog to Loy's focus on the possibility of linguistic determinism. Cameron notes that the work of Sapir and Whorf "is both relativistic (asserts that reality is perceived differently) and deterministic (asserts that language is responsible)" (22–23). For feminist interpretations of linguistic determinism, see *Feminism and Linguistic Theory* (especially 96–100), and Cameron's *The Feminist Critique of Language: A Reader* (New York: Routledge, 1990), 12–13.

4. Loy's prose piece "Gertrude Stein" (*LLB* 289–99) complements a poetic tribute (*Lost* 94). Loy describes Stein as "Curie / of the laboratory / of vocabulary," releasing "a radium of the word." See Burke's "Getting Spliced: Modernism and Sexual Difference," *American Quarterly* 39 (1987) and *Becoming Modern* concerning Loy's and Stein's friendship.

5. In this Loy may fit Baker's notion of the "deformation of mastery," a strategy Baker links to African-American texts — the appropriation, and subtle reformation, of expected tropes or figures. Irigaray's term "mimicry" — a willed, ironic version of the "masquerade of femininity" — captures Loy's parody of the forms of a masculine literary tradition.

6. See Friedman's "Gender and Genre Anxiety: Elizabeth Barrett Browning and H. D. as Epic Poets," *Tulsa Studies in Women's Literature* 5.2 (1986) for a mapping of "the interface between genre norms and gender codes" (203), in particular the dualism between (feminine) lyric and (masculine) epic. Friedman summarizes William Rose Benet, *The Reader's Encyclopedia* (New York: Thomas Y. Crowell, 1965): "As a narrative of brave men's deeds, the epic often centers on the 'destiny' or 'formation of a race or nation,' reflecting a comprehensive sweep of history . . . and an elevated discourse of public ceremony" (204). She argues that Elizabeth Barrett Browning and H.D. revise epic conventions by fusing elements of the novel and the lyric with those of epic. Their position is both outside of, and within, the genre — a positionality similar to Loy's.

7. Loy knew about Margaret Sanger's controversial publication of *The Woman Rebel* through her friends Mabel Dodge and Frances Stevens. Although she expressed interest in Sanger, in a letter to Dodge Loy implies that policy changes offer only limited potential, and she rejected current feminist activism because "slaves will believe that chains are protectors" (Burke, *Becoming Modern: The Life of Mina Loy* [New York: Farrar, Straus and Giroux, 1996], 179).

8. Kouidis points out (see chapter 4) that Loy's later poetry is remarkable for its focus on the dispossessed and notes (*Mina Loy* 67–9, 83–4) themes of an ambivalent "evolutionary progress" and accompanying regression in Loy's "Love Songs." Loy's most progressive tendencies are apparent, too, in her other manifestos including much of her "Feminist Manifesto."

9. Burke describes Loy's involvements with both Marinetti and Papini in chapters 8 and 9 of *Becoming Modern*. See also Linda Kinnahan's discussion of this poem in *Poetics of the Feminine: Authority and Literary Tradition in William Carlos Williams, Mina Loy, Denise Levertov, and Kathleen Fraser* (New York: Cambridge U. P., 1994), 60–61.

10. See Kinnahan's discussion of Loy's satirical treatment of Futurism (60) and her helpful account of the rise of feminist thinking that Loy and others absorbed around 1913–1914 (43–45), fully described in DuBois and Gordon. Burke points out that the outlandishness of Futurism — especially its policy of free love — would have left women "members" open to accusations of immorality (161). She also describes the difficulty Loy later had positioning herself in relation to Duchamp's comical attacks on prudery, which often took the form of embarrassing women in their circle (218–19). Although Futurism's "scorn" played

no part in New York Dada, which was far more open to women artists and writers, Duchamp's "performances" were often enacted at women's expense.

11. It has not been possible to duplicate the variety of font sizes Loy originally used in her work. We have, however, used boldface wherever a large-type word appeared in the original.

12. In "The New Poetry and the New Woman: Mina Loy," in *Coming to Light: American Women Poets in the Twentieth Century*, ed. Diane Wood Middlebrook and Marilyn Talom (Ann Arbor: U. of Michigan P., 1985), Burke points to these same passages, but to Burke, Loy's rejection of "bread and butter" issues reflects her belief in "the differences between the sexes" (41). Yet that position was in fact being espoused by many feminists involved in the Suffrage movement, whom Loy apparently opposed.

13. The result was the "epic ambition" that inspired *The Waste Land*, the *Cantos*, and *Spring and All*. See James Longenbach, *Wallace Stevens: The Plain Sense of Things* (New York: Oxford U. P., 1991), especially chapters 4 and 5.

14. Considering the epic form more broadly, H.D. is clearly also a central figure, and Stein — with her pioneering of what Joseph Conte, Leslie Scalapino, and others have more recently called "serial form," is at the forefront of an alternative female tradition of one kind of "long poem." See Burke's "Getting Spliced" for an account of women poets' divergences from male models of poetic form.

15. "While at home in large areas of life, the epic writer must be centred in the normal, he must measure the crooked by the straight, he must exemplify that sanity which has been claimed for true genius. No pronounced homosexual, for instance, could succeed in the epic, not so much for being one as for what his being one cuts him off from" (E. M. W. Tillyard, *The English Epic and Its Background* [London: Chatto and Windus, 1954], 8). In addition to this alarming theory, Tillyard also discusses epic "seriousness" (5).

16. Simpson, *Poetic Epistemologies* 50, 52.

17. Despite the many changes that appear in various printings of "Anglo-Mongrels," the title remained constant. In *LLB*, "Anglo-Mongrels" is "collected" in a complete version of the poem's many separate sections, unfortunately not included in *Lost*. Although *LLB* contains many regularizations of Loy's punctuation and line breaks, thus misrepresenting crucial aspects of her linguistic idiosyncrasies, it still seems the "truest" version of the complete poem, and for this reason I will use it here. Other sources are the 1923 *Contact* edition, in which many sections are omitted, and the first appearance of the poem in *The Little Review* in 1923.

18. Burke also describes the unpublished story "Hush Money," in which Loy depicts herself as David in a father-son narrative (*Becoming Modern* 27, 248).

19. Loy's identification with her father must also have emerged in reaction to her highly punitive mother (see Burke's first chapter).

20. *LR* 16, 14, 18. Some advocates of eugenics supported war as the social equivalent of the Darwinian survival of the fittest. Arthur Keith, for one, articulated an evolutionary theory in the 1920s in which "evolution required racial-national rivalry: namely, war." The theory was subsequently "exploited . . . by

war-mongers and racists alike" (Barkan, *Retreat of Scientific Racism* 47). Yet there was also some affiliation between pacifism and eugenics as early as the 1890s, especially in the work of David Starr Jordan, a leader of the American peace movement. Jordan argued against war on biological terms, asserting that carnage would kill off the most "fit" of any given nation (Mark Haller, *Eugenics: Hereditarian Attitudes in American Thought* [New Brunswick, N.J.: Rutgers U. P., 1984], 87–88). Kevles summarizes the two approaches (war as "eugenic" or "dysgenic") as well; among other views was the possibility that "the remaining men would choose only the ablest and most beautiful women" and that "women would be reduced to scrambling after even unworthy men" (58). It is possible that Loy was influenced by the more pacifist version of eugenical thinking. In *Becoming Modern* Burke argues that Loy may have been influenced by "Wilson's idealism" (270).

21. *LR* 18. Kouidis explores Loy's engagement with self-creation in her chapter "The Female Self."

22. William James's "The Moral Equivalent of War," in *William James: The Essential Writings*, ed. Bruce W. Wilshire (Albany: SUNY P., 1984) presents a similar argument, yet without Loy's feminist agenda: James fears the inability "to envisage a future in which army-life, with its many elements of charm, shall be forever impossible, and in which the destinies of peoples shall nevermore be decided quickly, thrillingly, and tragically, by force, but only gradually and insipidly by 'evolution'" (355). James, like Loy, revises pacifist strategies: "So long as anti-militarists propose no substitute for war's disciplinary function, no *moral equivalent* of war . . . so long they fail to realize the full inwardness of the situation" (356).

23. Madison Grant, prominent racist in the eugenics movement in the 1910s and 1920s, complained that New York would soon produce "racial hybrids" and "ethnic horrors that will be beyond the powers of future anthropologists to unravel." In New York, the "native" Americans were "being literally driven off the streets of New York City by the swarms of Polish Jews." See Madison Grant, *The Passing of the Great Race* (New York: Charles Scribner's Sons, 1916), 5, 80–81, cited by Haller 149. Loy reacted to the war as many of her male compatriots in the arts did, moving to New York in 1916.

24. Charles B. Davenport, *Heredity in Relation to Eugenics* (New York: Henry Holt, 1911) 1, cited by Haller 3.

25. See Haller 76 and 86–87 for accounts of eugenics in the Progressive Era. Kevles explores the connection between eugenics and "the woman question" among liberals and those concerned with sexual liberation, including G.B. Shaw and Havelock Ellis (87).

26. Haller 6–7. See also Barkan 71, on the "war against immigration."

27. Galton, who published *Hereditary Genius* and concluded that inheritance was the basis for ability (see Haller 8–10), hoped to see eugenics become a national creed, through which legislation would better the "race" by promoting marriages among those of "good stock," preventing the unfit from reproducing, and prohibiting matches between good and lesser stock. The number of organ-

izations and publications created to promote this "creed" — including courses at Harvard, Columbia, Berkeley, and other universities — testifies to its influence, as well as a legitimation of racism (see Kevles 69; Haller 72). Haller cites the creation of groups like the Eugenics Record Office, Eugenics Research Association, and the American Breeders' Association (17–18, 59, 73, 62), as well as publications like *Eugenical News* and the *Eugenics Review* (73, 18): "By 1915 no one could write about eugenics without mentioning the remarkable growth of the movement in the previous five to ten years" (58). Kevles gives numerous examples of the prevalence of eugenical thinking and the frequent use of the word "eugenics," originally coined by Galton (57–58). Barkan describes scientific discourses and the ideology of racism in the early part of the century.

28. In *The Retreat of Scientific Racism: Changing Concepts of Race in Britain and the United States between the World Wars* (New York: Cambridge U. P., 1992), Elazar Barkan observes that "the topics of population and birth control attracted liberal intellectuals because in addition to their scientific merit, they gave cultural legitimacy to a sexual revolution" (185). See also Daniel J. Kevles, *In the Name of Eugenics: Genetics and the Uses of Human Heredity* (New York: Knopf, 1985), 87. Further: "Victoria Woodhull repeatedly invoked before lecture audiences 'the scientific propagation of the human race' as reason for sexual education and the emancipation of women" (Victoria Woodhull, *The Scientific Propagation of the Human Race* [pamphlet, 1893], cited by Kevles 21). Of the merging of sexual radicalism and "Fabian-socialist leanings," Kevles notes that "the eugenic ideas of George Bernard Shaw and Havelock Ellis" held that "since barriers of class and wealth kept people from eugenically optimal marriages, remove class distinctions and many more biologically desirable unions would be assured." Perhaps ironically, "eugenic enthusiasm was highest among social radicals"; this included issues of sex education ("eugenics took up subjects that had formerly been outside the bounds of respectable discussion" [66]). A now-prominent literary example appears in Charlotte Perkins Gilman's *Herland* (New York: Pantheon Books, 1979), in which the highly-evolved women of Gilman's feminist utopia employed eugenical doctrines to reach their present, idyllic state of socialist-motherhood. The narrator details their practice of "negative eugenics" to control and shape population (68–70).

29. Tuma argues that, in addition to being critical of Surrealism (also implicit in Loy's *Insel*, ed. Elizabeth Arnold [Santa Rosa, Calif.: Black Sparrow P., 1991]), "Anglo-Mongrels" "is critical of Freud and the various discourses of impulse then ascendant on the European intellectual scene" (207–8). Tuma asserts that the poem "resists both Freudianism and Christian dogma in favor of . . . mystical experience" (210). As I see it, the broad strokes of both Freud and Jung can be seen in "Anglo-Mongrels," even as Loy's emphasis on class division and the fear of economic determinism tempers those elements.

30. See Haller 170–71. Kevles notes that Charles Davenport "paid no attention to Freud," yet also seems to give him credit for the omission: "He acknowledged that eugenicists were far from possessing the knowledge required to advise people on what constituted fit marriages" (53).

31. In an illuminating view of Loy's "mongrel aesthetics," DuPlessis places Loy's defense of hybridity in the context of literary debates over anti-Semitism and the nature of national identity or character. Loy sought to "valorize the mongrel, to claim that subject place as fruitful and creative," and her poetics emerged from these convictions. In "Modern Poetry," for example, "mongrel language and the mongrel city are categorically praised as vital generators," and Loy asserts "that poetry itself would be reinvigorated by mongrelization, new vocabularies, the heteroglossias of immigration, and the pressure of the city" (*Genders, Races* 159, 165, 164). See also Spahr on the influence of immigration and second-language speakers on modern poetics.

32. See Haller 148–49 for a summary.

33. See Kevles: "Some eugenicists expected that, just as with vigorous hybrids, miscegenation might yield racially beneficial results. . . . The weight of eugenic opinion, however, lay with Michael Guyer, who observed that 'many students of heredity feel that there is great hazard in the mongrelizing of distinctly unrelated races no matter how superior the original strains may be'" (see 319, n. 18). In addition, Madison Grant "insisted that the intermarriage of Nordics — which Grant alleged to be the highest-order group in the white race — and the lesser Alpines or, worse, Mediterraneans inevitably led to debilitating 'mongrelization'" (75).

34. Burke's account of Julia Lowy shows the origins of Loy's rebellion against Victorian attitudes toward the body. Julia expressed disgust at her daughter's physical maturation and initial knowledge about sexuality. Julia herself was seven months pregnant when she married — a fact Burke sees as explaining in part Julia's dislike of her first-born (see *Becoming Modern* 15–16).

35. See Elsa Nettels, *Language, Race, and Social Class in Howells's America* (Lexington: U. of Kentucky P., 1988), 30. Interestingly, Burke, like Winters, faults Loy's use of heavy alliteration in "Anglo-Mongrels" (see *Becoming Modern* 353).

36. Kouidis (91–92) traces the debt to Laforgue in some of Loy's uses of neologism.

37. Ezra Pound, "Marianne Moore and Mina Loy," in *Selected Prose 1909–1965* (New York: New Directions, 1973), 424.

38. *LLB* 122. In *Becoming Modern* Burke similarly notes that Loy conflates femininity and empire (see 324). Kevles notes: "The eugenics of Karl Pearson . . . was charged . . . with his commitment to social imperialism — the ideological system where, in fact, his eugenical convictions had originated. In Pearson's view, the imperial nation required more than an economic framework designed to give its citizens a material stake in its power; it also demanded the 'high pitch of internal efficiency' won by 'insuring that its numbers are substantially recruited from the better stocks'" (32).

39. There may be an ironic echo of "Hugh Selwyn Mauberley" here: "the face / Of Brennbaum 'The Impeccable'" (*Selected Poems of Ezra Pound* [New York: New Directions, 1957], 67). In "Anglo-Mongrels" Loy plays on the fin-de-siècle aestheticism that Pound also satirized in "Mauberley." "Brennbaum," one of the portraits in "Mauberley" (probably of Max Beerbohm), represents the same bourgeois sensibility at issue in "Anglo-Mongrels." Yet he is also the "type" of

the wandering Jew. If Loy is indeed echoing Pound, the insertion of Jewishness into the "impeccable" English speech she is notating here further undercuts English respectability as based on race and class bias.

40. See Haller 148.

41. While pointing out that Galton "saw 'genius' as primarily a male attribute," Battersby nonetheless acknowledges that even Galton included four "women geniuses" in a chapter on great literary men (126). Haller and Barkan do not discuss sex differences in the process of heredity.

42. See Battersby, *Gender and Genius: Towards a Feminist Aesthetics* (Bloomington: Indiana U. P., 1989), 49–50 for the impact of "the spermatic word" on Western thinking from the Stoics through Jung.

43. Haller 147 describes stereotypical representations of "the Jewish brain" and the "tricky, underhanded business practices" attributed to Jews in various anti-Semitic theories. Kevles details Davenport's "findings" on the Jewish temperament: "The Hebrews [were] 'intermediate between the slovenly Servians and Greeks and the tidy Swedes, Germans, and Bohemians'" (Davenport, *Heredity in Relation to Eugenics* [Henry Holt, 1911] 216–19, as cited by Kevles 46–47). Also, Barkan (154ff) details Pearson's study "The Problem of Alien Immigration into Great Britain, Illustrated by an Examination of Russian and Polish Jewish Children." Kevles notes that Davenport held that "if a Jew and a Gentile mated, ninety percent of the offspring would resemble the Gentile parent: 'In general, the Jewish features are recessive to the non-Jewish'" (74–75). As another race, Jews were not equal to, or appropriate mates for, Anglo-Saxons.

44. In *Becoming Modern* Burke reveals the source for this reminiscence: Loy's reading of *Chaucer for Children*, a volume compiled by Mrs. H. R. Haweis and dedicated to her four-year-old son, Stephen. Burke contends that the young Loy "envied the young boy in the dedicatory portrait" (26). Burke also notes that the volume "retold and illustrated Chaucer's tales to make them suitable for Victorian readers" (83).

45. Battersby argues that within Romantic theory "Creativity was displaced by *male* procreativity: male sexuality made sublime" (3); she also sees Jungian "androgyny" as sex-specific, for Jung "insists that a woman's creativity reaches only as far as *inspiring* a man to productive activity" (7). I see Loy as influenced by Jungian philosophy, subscribing to the limitations of female creativity that afflict Ova in cultural as well as biological terms. Yet the role of Patricia Penfold unmistakably parodies this notion of female literal "creation" and male "figurative" creation. Homans also elaborates on the association of women and the literal in Romantic ideology.

46. In "Thieves of Language" in *Stealing the Language* (210–40), Ostriker describes "the invasion of the sanctuaries of existing language" (211) as an introduction to her treatment of feminist myth-making.

47. That "Ova Begins to Take Notice" follows "Enter Esau Penfold" in the *Contact* edition of 1923 underlines the importance of the contrast between the two child-poets and their "Opposed Aesthetics," as in the next section's title, in Loy's original conception of the poem.

48. See Suleiman's chapter "Feminist Intertextuality and the Laugh of the Mother."

49. Margaret Homans (*Bearing the Word: Language and Female Experience in Nineteenth-Century Women's Writing* [Chicago: U. of Chicago P., 1986], 13) thus provides a linguistic version of Chodorow's mother-daughter bond.

50. See David Graddol and Joan Swann, *Gender Voices* (Cambridge, Mass.: Basil Blackwell, 1986), 110, for some examples of "lexical gaps" in the diction of gender-specific terms, including many terms associated with sexuality or the sexual act.

51. Graddol and Swann provide brief accounts of linguistic determinism, both in the Whorfian theory that became popular in the 1950s and, they assert, in post-structuralist theory as well. Although they make little effort to address the range of work commonly labeled "post-structuralist," they argue convincingly that radical feminism has frequently embraced a deterministic view of language, as in Spender. Graddol and Swann detail sexism *in* language, but they argue that linguists have dismissed determinism as inaccurate. See 10 and 146ff.

52. In her unpublished memoir *The Child and the Parent*, Loy depicts a similar act of coming to consciousness as an awakening merely to adult authority and "loss of the child's sense of oneness with the world" (*Becoming Modern* 354).

53. "According to Galton, 'what Nature does blindly, slowly, and ruthlessly, man may do providently, quickly, and kindly'" (quoted in Pearson, *The Life, Letters, and Labours of Francis Galton*, vol. 1 [Cambridge University Press, 1914], 203, as cited by Kevles 12).

54. See *Becoming Modern* 354–55 concerning imagery in *The Child and Parent*. The most striking parallel is Loy's use of the phrase "brick box" to describe the state of marriage. Burke also notes parallels with an example of Loy's juvenalia called "Nat and Daisy," in which an upwardly mobile gnat woos a rose — anticipating the imagery of "Anglo-Mongrels" (31).

55. See *Becoming Modern* 234–35 for accounts of Cravan's Dadaesque adventures in New York.

56. See *Becoming Modern* 23 for an account of the childhood incident that Loy used as the basis of this episode.

57. Tillyard, *English Epic* 8. See Friedman's "Gender and Genre Anxiety" for an astute treatment of this question. Loy is perhaps responding to the kind of cultural bias about "normality" that informs Tillyard's study. The difference between the "epic genius" of morality and Battersby's Romantic feminine-male genius may point to a shifting ideology that Battersby does not address.

58. By contrast, Tuma reads this final passage as part of Loy's meditation not on her own life but on "the fate of Christianity in the modern era" (224). Among other possibilities, the "tailor" is, most likely, "a figure for a secularized Christianity or just simply . . . modernity." The poem then, "professes a Christ that had survived an English upbringing, a Christ that could look Freud in the eye without blinking" (225). Sigmund Lowy was in fact the best-paid tailor in London (*Becoming Modern* 17) and a man of artistic background.

59. Battersby notes the prevalence of the stereotype of the male Jew as effeminate (116). See Inez Hedges, *Languages of Revolt: Dada and Surrealist Literature and*

Film (Durham, N.C.: Duke U. P., 1983), chap. 1, for an account of relationships among alchemy, androgyny (and hermaphroditism), and Surrealism.

60. Hedges argues that Breton idealizes the androgyne as creative figure; many writers have attributed what is tantamount to a feminized principle of creativity to men only (see Battersby 7–8).

61. During her Paris years (1923–1936), when she wrote "Anglo-Mongrels" and a good deal of prose, Loy designed art deco-style lampshades to commercial success (though little money; see *LLB* lxxxi and *Becoming Modern*, chapter 17).

CHAPTER 3

1. "Black Art" (Dudley Randall, ed., *The Black Poets* [New York: Bantam, 1971], 223–24). Baraka plays on Apollinaire's *Le Poète assassiné* (1916).

2. Haki Madhubuti, "Sonia Sanchez: The Bringer of Memories," in *Black Women Writers (1950–1980): A Critical Evaluation*, ed. Mari Evans (New York: Anchor P./Doubleday, 1984), 426.

3. Madhubuti says that Sanchez has been neglected: "Not as well known as Toni Morrison, Ntozake Shange, Alice Walker, or Nikki Giovanni, she has out-produced them and has been active in her chosen craft longer" (Madhubuti in Evans 419). He notes that "more than any other poet, she has been responsible for legitimatizing [*sic*] the use of urban Black English in written form," and that "long before the discovery of Ntozake Shange, Sanchez set the tone and spaces of modern urban written Black poetry" (421).

4. Walker's poem appears before the table of contents in the book. Sanchez is described as "the most representative of the Black women revolutionary playwrights" who uses "the Black agit-prop method of short play forms, simplistic action, and direct language." It is noted that Sanchez is "also a well-known poet" (287–88).

5. "Our Lady: Sonia Sanchez and the Writing of a Black Renaissance," in *Black Feminist Criticism and Critical Theory*, vol. 3 of *Studies in Black American Literature*, ed. Joe Weixlmann and Houston A. Baker Jr. (Greenwood, Fla.: Penkevill, 1988), 199.

6. My citations reproduce Sanchez's slashes and indicate line breaks by a slash in brackets: [/].

7. Baker's "Our Lady" discusses the choice of this term in the context of "a hermeneutics of overthrow" that dominated black nationalism in the 1960s and 1970s: The leaders of the movement were ultimately "REINTERPRETERS OF OPPRESSION rather than informed transmitters of venerable cultural wisdom." One of the crucial missing pieces was "a distinctive Afro-American critical and creative vocabulary." Baker points to the use of "alien vocabulary": "rather than rejecting out of hand the entire discursive field surrounding a deeply class-invested word like *aesthetic*, black literary critics and artists merely readopted the field, proclaiming themselves BLACK AESTHETICIANS." These revolutionary theorists ironically reinforced the movement toward "a bourgeois orientation in black America" (Baker, "Our Lady" 177).

8. See Baker, "Generational Shifts and the Recent Criticism of Afro-American Literature," *Black American Literature Forum* 9 for a discussion of this politicized aesthetics.

9. Cleveland Sellers, *The River of No Return: The Autobiography of a Black Militant and the Life and Death of SNCC* (New York: William Morrow, 1973), 166–67, cited by William L. Van Deburg, *New Day in Babylon: The Black Power Movement and American Culture, 1965–1975* (Chicago: U. of Chicago P., 1992), 32. See his chapters 2 and 4 on the emergence of Black Power and the diverse positions it is used to describe.

10. "We Walk the Way of the New World" in Randall, *Black Poets* 309.

11. Larry Neal, "And Shine Swam On," "Afterword" in *Black Fire*, ed. Jones and Neal, 656. Amiri Baraka, "Black Art," "Black People!" in Randall, *Black Poets* 224, 226–27.

12. Claude McKay, "If We Must Die," "The White House," *The Portable Harlem Renaissance Reader*, ed. David Levering Lewis (New York: Penguin, 1994), 290, 291. Helene Johnson — like Langston Hughes, Jean Toomer, Countee Cullen, and others — provides examples of the "black is beautiful" motif, evoking the splendor of black culture; a "dark, big-eyed" boy sings in one poem like "a prince, a jazz prince" ("Poem," 277–78).

13. See Lorenzo Thomas, "'Classical Jazz' and the Black Arts Movement," *African-American Review* 29.2 (Summer 1995): 237–40.

14. "Afterword," in *Black Fire: An Anthology of Afro-American Writing*, ed. LeRoi Jones and Larry Neal (New York: William Morrow, 1968), 649.

15. Smitherman, 259; Neal, "Afterword," 649–50. Neal calls the Harlem Renaissance "a fantasy-era for most black writers and their white friends. For the people of the community, it never even existed" ("Afterword" 650). See Bibby's chapter on black liberation poetry for an excellent treatment of both the integrationist aesthetic of postwar African-American poetry and the transition to the radicalism of what he describes as the Vietnam era. Van Deburg discusses the rejection of both "art for art's sake" and "protest" writing (see 184–85).

16. Karenga cited by Neal in "The Black Arts Movement," in Gayle 278.

17. See Neal, "The Black Arts Movement," in Gayle 272–90.

18. Neal "Afterword" 653; Smitherman, 259–60; Clarence Major, "A Black Criterion," in *Black Voices: An Anthology of Afro-American Literature*, ed. Abraham Chapman (New York: Mentor/New American Library, 1968), 698–99.

19. Neal argues that the "New Breed" of black youth can benefit little from Ellison's vision: "We know who we are, and we are not invisible" ("Afterword" 652). See Baraka's "The Revolutionary Tradition in Afro-American Literature," in *Selected Plays and Prose of Amiri Baraka/LeRoi Jones* (New York: William Morrow, 1979): "Both James Baldwin and Ralph Ellison condemned . . . 'protest literature,' and the general tone put out by well-published 'spokespersons for black people' was that it was time to transcend the 'limitations' of race" (249). Baraka's view of Ellison's acceptance by the literary establishment was played out fifteen years after this essay appeared in Baraka's *Selected Plays and Prose*;

the rhetoric of "universality" was applied to *Invisible Man* upon the author's death at eighty. Ellison is lauded by the *New York Times* for writing "more than" a novel about race: *Invisible Man* is praised for its invocations of the European tradition ("Virgil, and Dante, and Dostoyevsky"), and Ellison, because of this "broader" vision, is described as "a writer of universal reach" (*New York Times*, Op Ed page, April 20, 1994, A18).

20. Johnetta Cole, "Culture: Negro, Black and Nigger," in *New Black Voices: An Anthology of Contemporary Afro-American Literature*, ed. Abraham Chapman (New York: New American Library, 1972), 494.

21. See Baker, "Generational Shifts." Baker refers to Henderson's introduction to *Understanding the New Black Poetry* (7), titled "The Forms of Things Unknown," after Richard Wright's phrase describing writing "derived from the inner life of the folk" (Stephen Henderson, *Understanding the New Black Poetry: Black Speech and Black Music as Poetic References* [New York: Morrow, 1973], 5). Von Hallberg emphasizes that the concept of performance unites the four groups he sees as postwar avant-gardes in American poetry, including Black Arts.

22. Cited by Baker, "Generational Shifts" 5. Baraka also points out the fact of the affiliation between Black Arts and Black Power in "Revolutionary Tradition" 250–51. Concerning the Umbra group as a predecessor to Black Arts, see Lorenzo Thomas's *Extraordinary Measures* and Nielsen's chapter 3, also mentioned below. Nielsen argues that "Poets like Baraka and the Umbra group are the connectors . . . by which a postmodern rebellion against the idea of the poem as icon was joined to an ideology of the social functioning of the poet posited as African-derived tradition and brought into the Black Arts movement" (*Black Chant* 152).

23. Neal says simply, "The key is in the music" ("Afterword" 653). According to Baker, Henderson "proposes . . . a theory to account for the continuity — the unity in theme, structure, and semantics — of black speech, music, and poetry (both oral and written)." He argues that "the oral tradition of the urban masses is the dominant force shaping the work of Afro-American poets" ("Generational Shifts" 8). Concerning Umbra and black identity, Nielsen points out that "the name 'Umbra' was a positive assertion of cultural blackness, but it was never totalizing" (Nielsen, *Black Chant* 125). In its inclusion of some whites (as Nielsen mentions), Umbra had a less nationalist, militant orientation than Black Arts. See also Nielsen's final two chapters on music and African-American poetics.

24. Blount describes the first of these, focusing on what he calls the "African American 'preacherly text'" (Marcellus Blount, "The Preacherly Text: African American Poetry and Vernacular Performance," *PMLA* 107 [1992]: 584): "When black writers turn to African American vernacular performance, they call into question the authority of the literary conventions and racial ideologies of the dominant society" (583). In "Dis and Dat: Dialect and the Dissent," Henry Louis Gates Jr. explores the African roots of the "coded, secret, hermetic world" (*Figures in Black: Words, Signs, and the "Racial" Self* [New York: Oxford, 1987], 167)

of the African mask (from Yoruba, among other sources) as an origin of what he calls "the masking function of dialect" (171).

25. Neal, "And Shine Swam On" ("Afterword" to *Black Fire*) 653, as cited by Baker, "Generational Shifts" 21 n. 41. See, too, *The Journey Back: Issues in Black Literature and Criticism* (Chicago: U. of Chicago P., 1980), 127–28, for Baker's account of Neal's call for a performative poetics.

26. Major, *Dictionary* 9 and 10. The *Dictionary* provides a dated but enlightening collection of what he called "Afro-American slang." See Gates's *Figures in Black* for debates about BEV and the earlier concept of "dialect" in African-American writing. Major points out the influence of this "underground" language on young, rebellious white Americans, particularly since the 1960s — a transmission of black culture into the mainstream; Mullen explores this phenomenon.

27. *Home* (New York: William Morrow, 1966, 171–72), cited by Smitherman 262.

28. See Van Deburg's conclusion on the legacy of Black Arts. Brown, for one, points to often strategic deployments of essentialist rhetoric. On the label "avant-garde," many who don't invoke the phrase describe Black Arts in precisely these terms. Defining poetic "excess," Karen Jackson Ford delineates the elements of avant-gardism in Black Arts: it staged "a literary spectacle with a style of poetry that was threatening to the oppressor, expressive of the people, and committed to artistic and political revolution" (*Gender and the Poetics of Excess: Moments of Brocade* [Jackson: U. P. of Mississippi, 1997], 176). David Lionel Smith observes that Black Arts writers and theorists argued that "they had few if any antecedents," contending they would be "unlikely to learn much from those generations of writers whom [they had] dismissed. In effect, such an attitude embraces historical ignorance as a critical premise" (96). Here lack of reference to avant-garde assertions of novelty results in banality (one who rejects past models cannot "learn" from them).

29. Neal in Gayle 272, as cited by Baker, "Generational Shifts" 5.

30. See Karenga 32–35. Negation of individualism nonetheless existed alongside "personality," a self "in relation to everyone," that remained intact in the context of a shared value system.

31. Rashidah Ismaili-Abu-Bakr, "Slightly Autobiographical: The 1960s on the Lower East Side." *African American Review* 27:4 (1993), 586, cited by Nielsen 162.

32. hooks 95 and 97. In the last passage, hooks cites an article Baraka published in *Black World* in July 1970 without further bibliographical information. She also cites E. U. Essien-Udom's *Black Nationalism: A Search for an Identity in America* (New York: Dell, 1962): "Muslim women appear to accept their men as 'first among equals,' and in theory, at least, regard the man as the breadwinner and the head of the family. The Muslim women address the men as 'sir'" (no page reference). hooks notes that while "Black women entering the Nation of Islam were treated with greater respect than they were accustomed to prior to their conversion," the reason for this treatment was that "their male leader Elijah

Muhammad decided that it would be in the movement's interest to develop a strong patriarchal base in which women were given protection and consideration in exchange for submission" (111).

33. Jones, *Home*, cited by Wallace, *Black Macho* 63.

34. Jones, *Home*, cited by Wallace, *Black Macho* 64.

35. See Calvin Hernton, "The Sexual Mountain and Black Women Writers," in *Wild Women in the Whirlwind: Afra-American Culture and the Contemporary Literary Renaissance*, ed. Joanne M. Braxton and Andrée Nicola McLaughlin (New Brunswick, N.J.: Rutgers U. P., 1990), 199–201 for a useful summary of this issue.

36. See bell hooks, *Ain't I a Woman: Black Women and Feminism* (Boston: South End P., 1981), 96; Jones, cited by hooks 97; hooks 99.

37. Critics have largely ignored this problem. Baker glosses over one of Sanchez's most homophobic poems ("To a jealous cat," in *Home Coming*) with the comment that "Male suspiciousness is archly deconstructed as latent homosexuality" ("Our Lady" 185). D. H. Melham describes this heterosexism as follows: "Like Madhubuti, she . . . views love as strictly heterosexual, ideally family-oriented, and shares his impatience with homosexuality" ("Sonia Sanchez: Will and Spirit," *MELUS: The Journal of the Study of the Multi-Ethnic Literature of the United States* 12.3 [1985]: 79).

38. Regina Jennings analyzes Afrocentric tropes in Sanchez's writing and concludes that "Sanchez's linguistic war with America comes out of the ethos of black people" (122).

39. Michael Bérubé makes this argument concerning Tolson in *Marginal Forces/Cultural Centers: Tolson, Pynchon, and the Politics of the Canon* (Ithaca, N.Y.: Cornell U. P., 1992), 189, discussed by Thomas, *Extraordinary Measures* 4.

40. *No More Masks! An Anthology of Twentieth-Century American Women Poets*, ed. Florence Howe (New York: Harper Perennial, 1993), 354–55; Toni Cade Bambara, *The Black Woman: An Anthology* (New York: Penguin, 1970), 17. Bambara's preface argues that male ignorance and (white) feminist self-absorption conspired in the profound failure of virtually all existing disciplines to study black women. Other examples of poetic resistance include Mari Evans's thoughtful political poems (see Randall 183ff); Rodgers's indictments of racism and sexism ("U Name This One," *No More Masks* 348). Giovanni's definition of "revolution" was fully realized in *The Women and the Men* (e.g., "Revolutionary Dreams," "Poem for a Lady Whose Voice I Like"). Lorde's *Sister Outsider: Essays and Speeches* (Freedom, Calif.: Crossing P., 1984), which includes "Uses of the Erotic: The Erotic as Power" (1978), remains a landmark.

41. In hooks's view, "White feminists so focused on the disparity between white male/white female economic status as an indication of the negative impact of sexism that they drew no attention to the fact that poor and lower-class men are as able to oppress and brutalize women as any other group of men in American society" (*Ain't I a Woman* 87).

42. In "Sexism: An American Disease in Blackface," in *Sister Outsider*, Lorde enters into the tumult over Shange's *for colored girls who have considered suicide/*

when the rainbow is enuf, which was attacked for its negative representation of black men.

43. Although "Sanchez promotes racial separatism . . . she also hints at sexist oppression within the Black movement" (Rosemary Curb, "Pre-Feminism in the Black Revolutionary Drama of Sonia Sanchez," in *The Many Forms of Drama: The University of Florida Department of Classics Comparative Literature Conference Papers*, vol. 5, ed. Karelisa V. Hartigan [New York: U. P. of America, 1985], 19). Curb mentions *The Bronx Is Next, Sister Son/ji*, and *Uh, Uh; But How Do It Free Us?* Her conclusion parallels my own: "Although none of the three revolutionary plays . . . asserts a conscious feminist position, their portrayals of the victimization of strong women constitute a preliminary raising of consciousness" (28).

44. Don L. Lee, "Two Poems" (from "Sketches from a Black-Nappy-Headed Poet") in *Understanding the New Black Poetry* 332.

45. This attitude toward language and revolution also led to claims for the tremendous power of the word: "Black art must expose the enemy, praise the people and support the revolution. It must be like LeRoi Jones's poems that are assassins' poems, poems that kill and shoot guns and 'wrassle cops into alleys taking their weapons, leaving them dead'" (Karenga, "Black Cultural Nationalism" 33–34). Language becomes inseparable from violent overthrow.

46. Harper notes Stokely Carmichael's call to act following Malcolm's death ("stop writing poems" [Phillip Brian Harper, "Nationalism and Social Division in Black Arts Poetry of the 1960s," *Critical Inquiry* 19 (1993): 253–54]), an anxiety he recognizes in the poetry itself, including Sanchez's.

47. Sanchez says that the revolutionary 1960s provoked institutional response: "The country systematically brought in more dope and systematically began to give us something called 'disco madness'" (Tate, *Black Women Writers at Work* 133).

48. Harper argues that Sanchez questions "what might happen after the calling [of black people] had been done" (237). He emphasizes, however, that the "identity of the 'enemy'" in the poem — the "white 'establishment'" — is not in doubt (238), thus downplaying feminism in Sanchez's poem.

49. Curb mentions "To All Sisters" and argues that this poem "succinctly presents the movement's orthodox position regarding the obligation of Black women to bolster Black male ego by reassuring Black men about their superior sexual power" (19).

50. Referring to Alan Lomax and Raoul Abdul, eds., *3000 Years of Black Poetry* (New York: Dodd, Mead and Company, 1970, xx), Jennings argues that the invocation of the "black queen" reveals an Afrocentric orientation and avers that this poem exemplifies the genre of "praise poem" that has existed in Africa since 2000 B.C. (123–24). Sanchez's Afrocentrism is apparent; whether she was deliberately invoking this genre appears more doubtful.

51. In *The Black Poets*, Randall reprints "The True Import of Present Dialogue: Black vs. Negro" (318) from Giovanni's volume *Black Feeling, Black Talk* (New York: Broadside P., 1970).

52. See Walker's essays on Hurston in *In Search of Our Mother's Gardens*: "Zora Neale Hurston: A Cautionary Tale and a Partisan View" (83–92) and "Looking for Zora" (93–116).

53. See Chandler 355 and 357–58.

54. "People kept saying to me, if you write a political poem, it will be considered propaganda — an ineffective and poor poem — but I read Neruda and saw that he didn't deny the personal. In the early Sixties I became aware that the personal was the political. Even my loneliness was never just my own but a much larger loneliness that came out of a society that did not encourage blacks to learn for the sheer joy of it" (*Parnassus* 364).

55. This process is illuminated by De Lancey in her treatment of Sanchez's haiku. De Lancey argues that Sanchez adapts the haiku form to very particularized African American experiences through the use of Afrocentric motifs.

56. Obeying the syllable patterns of traditional haiku (5-7-5), Sanchez nonetheless transforms the genre, as De Lancey argues: She alters haiku both by insisting on a personal voice and by particularizing the images to African-American experience. De Lancey's examples of Afrocentric motifs in Sanchez's haiku illuminate Sanchez's politicization of love poetry.

57. In "A Black Feminist's Search for Sisterhood" (in *All the Women Are White*, reprinted in *Invisibility Blues: From Pop to Theory* [New York: Verso, 1990]), Wallace relates a number of incidents to illuminate both of these dynamics. "A lot of brothers were doing double time — uptown with the sisters and downtown with the white woman whom they also vigorously claimed to hate," Wallace says; from black men's perspective, the "castrating" black woman stood in marked contrast to "'The white woman [who] lets me be a man'" (10). Barbara Smith was among the first to challenge this clearly heterosexual matrix by calling for writing about black lesbians ("Toward a Black Feminist Criticism").

58. "The Black Arts Movement" in *Cornerstones: An Anthology of African-American Literature*, ed. Melvin Donalson (New York: St. Martin's, 1996), 935–36. In his introduction to Neal's manifesto, Donalson notes Neal's one-time position as education director in the Black Panther Party, a fact relevant to both his nationalist rhetoric and his emphasis on violent revolution.

59. It is noteworthy that emphases on love and self-love appear as well in works by some male Black Arts poets, including Everett Hoagland and Yusef Iman (see Randall, 293–94, 226–27).

60. In "Black Sexuality: The Taboo Subject," in *Race Matters*, West explores the issue of black male and female sexuality, straight and gay, with a concern for turning away from imposed myths: "Black sexuality is a taboo subject in America principally because it is a form of black power over which whites have little control — yet its visible manifestations evoke the most visceral of white responses, be it one of seductive obsession or downright disgust" (87). West acknowledges that "the black male search for power often reinforces the myth of black male sexual prowess — a myth that tends to subordinate black and white women as objects of sexual pleasure" (89). There is "tragedy" in "the refusal of white and

black America to entertain seriously new stylistic options for black men caught in the deadly endeavor of rejecting black machismo identities" (89).

61 DuBois's famous "double consciousness" takes invisibility as its trope; in *Invisible Man*, Ellison traces a debt to his predecessor. Wallace's *Invisibility Blues* recasts the notion to apply to women of color, who are highly "visible" in media images, while they remain largely silent, excluded from acts of speech in political, academic, and other influential discourses.

CHAPTER 4

1. Lynn Keller, *Re-Making It New: Contemporary American Poetry and the Modernist Tradition* (New York: Cambridge U. P., 1987), 2. Keller's extended treatment of poets ranging aesthetically from Ashbery to Merrill aptly demonstrates how widespread is such invocation of modernist method.

2. Although not all writers with Language ties are concerned with Marxist thought, critics have focused on its Frankfurt school influences. George Hartley addresses "Language poets who have made specifically Marxist claims for their work," including Ron Silliman, Bob Perelman, Barrett Watten, Charles Bernstein, Bruce Andrews, and Steve McCaffery (*Textual Politics and the Language Poets* [Bloomington: Indiana U. P., 1989], xv). Kalaidjian, Jerome McGann, and Reinfeld emphasize Marxist origins. Howe shares with Bernstein and Silliman concerns about the politics of representation, canon formation, and the strictures of conventional language, and as Vickery thoroughly documents, Language writing from its inception included feminist poets whose concerns both overlapped with and diverged from those of their male colleagues. Howe's work appears in Language anthologies (Douglas Messerli, *Language Poetries*; Ron Silliman, *In the American Tree*; and Andrews and Bernstein, eds., *The L=A=N=G=U=A=G=E Book* [Carbondale: Southern Illinois U. P., 1984]); see Megan Williams concerning Howe's play with canonicity and her place in "the tradition."

3. See Lynn Keller, *Forms of Expansion: Recent Long Poems by Women* (Chicago: U. of Chicago P., 1997), 191. Keller quotes Beckett's interview with Howe (18).

4. Increasing awareness of feminist avant-garde writing has led to more attention to Howe independent of the Language connection: see DuPlessis, Quartermain, Simpson, Vickery, and Megan Williams. (Concerning feminist avantgardism, note Sloan's anthology, as well as Kinnahan's and Vickery's research on *HOW(ever)*). In "Articulating the Inarticulate: Singularities and the Counter-Method in Susan Howe," *Contemporary Literature* 36.3 (1995), Ming-Qian Ma presents Howe as a Language writer: "Although explicitly informed by a feminist perspective, Howe's poetry and her criticism present a broad range of significance and implications that embraces, but is not confined to, feminist critique" (470 n. 1); in "Poetry as History Revised: Susan Howe's 'Scattering as Behavior Toward Risk,'" *American Literary History* 6.4 (1994), Ma argues by contrast that "Howe's poems . . . subpoena history for an investigation of its violent crime against women" (718). Without alluding to Language writing,

Michael Davidson links Howe's representations of the processual to George Oppen, while Susan Schultz notes contradictions in Howe's feminism, writing of one passage from *The Nonconformist's Memorial*, "These are lines that no Language poet would set upon the page" ("Exaggerated History," *Postmodern Culture* 4.2 [1994]: n.p.).

5. In a similar conception of history and identity, Joan Wallach Scott argues that "It is not individuals who have experience, but subjects who are constituted through experience" ("Experience," in *Feminists Theorize the Political*, ed. Judith Butler and Joan W. Scott [New York: Routledge, 1992], 25–26).

6. *HOW(ever)* 6.4 (1992):15.

7. *An Anthology of New York Poets*, ed. Ron Padgett and David Shapiro (New York: Random House, 1970); "The Tradition of Marginality," in *Where We Stand: Women Poets on Literary Tradition*, ed. Sharon Bryan (New York: Norton, 1993), 57.

8. Hogue, "Interview" 17; "Tradition" 54–55.

9. Shari Benstock, "Beyond the Reaches of Feminist Criticism: A Letter from Paris" originally published in the 1984–1985 issue of *Tulsa Studies in Women's Literature* 1.2, 5–27.

10. Private communication with the author.

11. Kim Whitehead, *The Feminist Poetry Movement* (Jackson: U. P. of Mississippi, 1996), 27; see also 15, concerning Muriel Rukeyser's influence and these lines from "Käthe Kollwitz" (*The Collected Poems*, New York: McGraw-Hill, 1978, 482). Whitehead argues that Dickinson did come to symbolize "the classic conflict between one's creative possibilities and the expectation that women be only muses for men poets and never poets themselves" (14), yet, as Howe points out, this homage rarely extended to Dickinson's formal innovations. Interestingly, Fraser was represented in the first edition of *No More Masks!* but omitted in subsequent editions. See also Bibby, *Hearts and Minds* 78–100 concerning the biological imperative that fueled "movement" poetry.

12. Vickery, *Leaving Lines of Gender* 90. The first line of Moore's "Poetry" slyly confides, "I, too, dislike it," but the poem continues: "Reading it, however, with a perfect contempt for it one discovers in / it after all, a place for the genuine" (*The Complete Poems of Marianne Moore* [New York: Macmillan, 1981], 36).

13. DuPlessis, *HOW(ever)* 6.4 (1992): 14.

14. See Whitehead, *Feminist Poetry Movement* 17–22 for a summary of feminist publishing that began in the early 1970s, including anthologies, guides, journals, and small presses. Fraser mentions *Sinister Wisdom*, *Thirteenth Moon*, and *Conditions* as examples of feminist journals "often lesbian and separatist in ideology and almost exclusively focused on poems of content that described and reinforced the values and life-styles shared by this community" ("Tradition" 59).

15. *HOW(ever)* 2.4 (1984): n.p.; "Some Notes on Visual Intentionality in Emily Dickinson" (3.4 [1986]: 11–13) included a lecture delivered by Howe at the

Emily Dickinson/H.D. conference (no date), and passages excerpted from "Women and Their Effect in the Distance" (*Ironwood* 28 14.2 [1986]: n.p.). An excerpt from Howe's "Nether John and John Harbinger" (5.4 [1989]) appeared, and DuPlessis also wrote an appreciation of Howe's "subtle, intricate, formal" inquiry into gender relations (1.4 [1984]: 11).

16. *MED* 11. Howe also links Dickinson and Stein in "Encloser" (Bernstein, *Politics of Poetic Form* 179).

17. Male writers also serve as precursors or influences, of course. In particular, Howe avers that Dickinson is "Jonathan Edwards's enlightened successor" (54). In my focus on Howe's construction of lineage, I take the opposite approach to Vickery, who rejects such emphasis on lines of descent. See her extensive discussion of Howe in *Leaving Lines of Gender*.

18. In "The Difficulties Interview" (24), Howe cites James Clifford's *The Predicament of Culture: Twentieth-Century Ethnography, Literature, and Art*, in which he makes this statement about the writing of ethnography, and Howe extends it to poetry — for her, too often circumscribed by the publishing industry.

19. Thomas Shepard, "Autobiography," ed. Allyn Bailey Forbes, *Publications of the Colonial Society of Massachusetts*, vol. 27 (*Transactions*, 1927–1930), 391, cited in *BM* 58.

20. John Winthrop, *The History of New England from 1630 to 1649*, ed. James Savage. Boston: Phelps and Farnham, 1825, vol. 2:216–17, cited in *BM* 108.

21. Welde's statement appears in David D. Hall, ed., *The Antinomian Controversy, 1636–1638: A Documentary History* (Middletown: Wesleyan U. P., 1968), cited by Lang 56.

22. John Winthrop, *Winthrop Papers*, vol. 5, 1645–1649, ed. Allyn B. Forbes (Boston: Massachusetts Historical Society, 1941), 70, 144. Cited in *BM* 109.

23. See Rich's foreword to *The Works of Anne Bradstreet*.

24. See Nicholls's observations concerning Howe's embrace of an antinomian stance (597).

25. See Bibby, *Hearts and Minds* 89.

26. Private communication with the author.

27. See "Submarginalia" in *BM* (26ff), where Howe quotes Coleridge's description of himself.

28. "'Whowe': An Essay on Work by Susan Howe," *Sulfur* 20 [1987]: 161; reprinted in DuPlessis, *The Pink Guitar: Writing as Feminist Practice* (New York: Routledge, 1990).

29. Wittig, *Straight Mind* 76, 78, 81, 82. Wittig describes why, in *The Opoponax*, she chooses the pronoun "on": "With this pronoun, that is neither gendered nor numbered, I could locate the characters outside of the social division by sexes and annul it for the duration of the book." In *Les Guérillères*, the feminine collective "elles" is universalized, "not to feminize the world but to make the categories of sex obsolete in language" ("The Mark of Gender," 83, 85). On Howe's "anti-foundationalist" stance, see Simpson, who asserts that "Howe's is an antiessentialist view of gender: whoever is outside the bounds of the law, order,

and codes of behavior is equally subject to historical invisibility" (*Poetic Epistemologies* 170). Further, "Howe's poetic-historical project involves a deconstruction of the opposition textuality-reality on which most conventional historiography depends, and . . . in turn, this deconstruction is a defining feature of the language-oriented feminist epistemology on which her project rests" (195). Simpson's excellent readings address several texts by Howe, including *Articulation*.

30. See Scott, *Gender and the Politics of History* (New York: Columbia U. P., 1988), 18, 40–41. Howe's decreation is thus not exactly revisionist, as Peter Quartermain claims (*Disjunctive Poetics: From Gertrude Stein and Louis Zukofsky to Susan Howe* [New York: Cambridge U. P., 1992], 182), for "revision" implies a retelling that would impose a new narrative. Compare with Schultz: Howe "disrupts old narratives not because she has no faith in narratives, but because she means for the reader to see in her gaps and verbal impasses the opening for new narratives" ["Exaggerated History" n.p.]. Howe's claims for women's affinity with the symbolic do not preclude her critique of a tyranny of the symbolic over other more disruptive modes. Howe finds a prominent example in the editing of Dickinson, whose work was effectively rewritten, appropriated into acceptable usages of symbolic language. Howe wishes to undermine the pervasive gendering of both convention and transgression — a perhaps utopian goal; it nonetheless does not imply that she is uncritical of the historic practice of bowdlerizing texts, particularly female-authored ones, into forms palatable to patriarchal authorities.

31. Miller explains that the equation between nature and text is crucial to Puritan thought: "If traces of the image of God are still to be found in the soul, they should even more clearly be manifested in the material universe, where all can decipher them at will" (*Errand into the Wilderness* [Cambridge, Mass.: Harvard U. P., 1956], 77); citing John Preston, Miller illustrates the Puritan conviction that the world is a text on which God's words are written.

32. Howe describes the assaults of King Philip's War as "the most serious threat to English interests to date" (*BM* 91). Miller describes the literature of the declension (after 1660) — whose themes are the failure of the city on the hill and the dreadful judgment that will arrive — as tied to "the slaughter of King Philip's War." Increase Mather's *A Brief History of the Warr with the Indians in New-England . . . Together with a Serious Exhortation to the Inhabitants of that Land*, reprinted in *So Dreadfull a Judgment: Puritan Responses to King Philip's War, 1676–1677*, ed. Richard Slotkin and James K. Folsom (Middletown, Conn.: Wesleyan U. P., 1978) saw "the decimating conflict with Philip . . . as a revenge upon the people for their transgressions" (7). The declension is crucial to understanding the historical point at which Hope's wanderings took place; his "loss" is also that of the Puritan errand.

33. In this unusual use of the word "pacification," Howe may be indebted to Cixous, who uses a remarkably similar set of terms, invoking the same history of exploration and colonization in terms of gender: "As soon as they [women]

begin to speak, at the same time they're taught their name, they can be taught that their territory is black. . . . Your continent is dark. . . . You can't see anything in the dark, you're afraid. Don't move, you might fall. Most of all, don't go into the forest" ("Laugh of the Medusa" 247–48). The constellation of name, forest, and darkness suggests Hope Atherton. Even more striking is Cixous's use of the word "pacify": men have failed to speak their own sexuality because they are invested in "a fantasized obligatory virility meant to invade, to colonize, and the consequential phantasm of woman as a 'dark continent' to penetrate and to 'pacify'" (247 n.1). Cixous's piece was translated and published in *Signs* in 1976.

34. Plumstead, *Wall and the Garden* 50, referring to Samuel Danforth's sermon "Errand into the Wilderness," also the source for Miller's book.

35. Nicholls shows Howe's use of George Sheldon's *A History of Deerfield, Massachusetts* in the words "grandmother," "revived," "Gone and signal," "deep water," and others (Peter Nicholls, "Difference Spreading: From Gertrude Stein to L=A=N=G=U=A=G=E Poetry," in *Contemporary Poetry Meets Modern Theory*, ed. Antony Easthope and John O. Thompson [New York: Harvester, 1991], 595–96).

36. McCorkle argues for Howe's "formation as well as retrieval of a prophetic poetics. By shifting the attention from writer to reader there is a similar shift from prophet to prophecy." Thus Hope is "a mirror for ourselves as readers," struggling to maintain identity and avoid "being reduced to someone's (Mr. Atherton's) story."

37. Perloff describes the writing in this passage as "a syntax that all but breaks down into babble" (*Poetic License* 304). Compare to Peter Middleton's assertion that contrary to "Kristeva's account of the radicalism of avant-garde literary practice," Howe shows that experiment is not necessarily "destructivism" ("On Ice: Julia Kristeva, Susan Howe, and Avant Garde Poetics," in *Contemporary Poetry Meets Modern Theory*, ed. Antony Easthope and John O. Thompson [New York: Harvester, 1991], 92–93). Concerning the visible signs of grace, Puritans believed that "social facts are signs of spiritual facts," whereas for the antinomian, "Outward sign and inner conviction have no bearing on one another" (Lang, *Prophetic Woman* 31, 34).

38. As DuPlessis points out, Howe is as suspicious of "the paradigm of the semiconscious, mad woman artist" as she is of "pacifying" the feminine. DuPlessis summarizes Howe's discomfort with Gilbert and Gubar's portrait of Dickinson in *Madwoman*: "The apparent insanity of other women artists blocked her from her own declarations; to struggle against such received interpretations of other women artists by analyses of their intellectual breadth was to struggle for one's own ambition and achievement, at once an act of cultural criticism and of personal necessity" ("Whowe" 160).

39. Howe criticizes Gilbert and Gubar's mention of a feminine "Magical Stitchery of Art" in Dickinson's poetry (Sandra M. Gilbert and Susan Gubar, *The Madwoman in the Attic: The Woman Writer and the Nineteenth-Century Literary Imagination* [New Haven, Conn.: Yale U. P., 1984], 639), cited in *MED* 14.

40. See also McCorkle's linking of this passage to Hope's wanderings as an instrument of prophecy and a challenge to singular origins; the play on the "eve" figure evokes the awareness of "multiple sources, hence multiple identities."

41. See Bruce Campbell's reading of this and other passages from *Articulation*: of this line, Campbell says, "perception must be returned to the body" ("'Ring of Bodies'/'Sphere of Sound': An Essay on Susan Howe's *Articulation of Sound Forms in Time, The Difficulties* 3.2 [1989]: 91).

42. "The shifting and overlapping of terms from various disciplines" corresponds to "one means Howe uses to prevent her discourse from solidifying" (Campbell 93).

43. Plumstead describes the Puritan mission as follows: "a flight away from courtly pomp and an overly sensuous and worldly court" (A. W. Plumstead, ed., *The Wall and the Garden: Selected Massachusetts Election Sermons, 1670–1775* [Minneapolis: U. of Minnesota P., 1968], 51).

44. Concerning the strategy through which New England's theologians created the notion of the covenant of grace to encourage the "saints" to believe in the efficacy of work and also to dread God's judgment, see Miller, *Errand into the Wilderness* 60–63. Through covenant theology, Puritan leaders "secur[ed] a basis for moral obligation and for assurance of salvation while yet not subtracting from God's absolute power or imposing upon Him any limitations prescribed by merely human requirements" (63).

45. See Hogue, "Infectious Ecstasy" 58.

46. According to Kristeva or Cixous, by contrast, poetry unleashes language's "other" possibilities; its associative and sonic resonances disrupt the syntax and logic we might associate with the concept "history." Hence the privileging of poetry in accounts of disruptive language: for Cixous, "the poet slips something by, for a brief span, of woman," "when every structure is for a moment thrown off balance and an ephemeral wildness sweeps order away" ("Laugh of the Medusa" 249). Stanton argues that such emphasis on a *metaphorical* feminine devalues "'the real' or the historical" ("Difference on Trial" 160) by likening one present thing to an absent one, thus presupposing an ontological function: "That Cixous upholds metaphor as desirable and efficacious . . . presupposes faith in its capacity to transform existing meanings, ultimately, the system of significance."

47. Shepard's *Autobiography* depends on the trope of crossing geographically as well as spiritually: the conversion experience is figured in the removal to the New World, which itself becomes a figure for the ultimate crossing into the afterworld.

48. See *Forms of Expansion* 191–92. As Keller points out, "Howe is committed to fragmentation, not as a mirror of modern life, but as a politically necessary disruption of the forms of knowledge that confine us" (192). In my formulation, this political intent undergirds Howe's feminist avant-gardism, particularly as it reflects the rejection of gender types.

49. See Leverenz, *Language of Puritan Feeling* 4–5 for an account of this trope in St. John of the Cross.

50. Michael Colacurcio, "'The Woman's Own Choice': Sex, Metaphor, and the Puritan 'Sources' of *The Scarlet Letter*," in *New Essays on The Scarlet Letter*, ed. Michael J. Colacurcio (New York: Cambridge U. P., 1985), 117.

51. According to Leverenz, "To receive grace, the sinner has to take the feminine posture for Christ the bridegroom" (*Language of Puritan Feeling* 130). By contrast, Scott points out the extent to which "the abstract rights-bearing individual who came into being as the focus of liberal political debate in the seventeenth and eighteenth centuries somehow became embodied in male form and it is his-story that historians have largely told" (*Gender* 25).

52. Hooker, *The Soules Union with Christ* (1638), cited by Robert Daly in *God's Altar: The World and The Flesh in Puritan Poetry* (Los Angeles: U. of California P., 1978), 26. See Colacurcio, "The Woman's Own Choice" 117 for the "relevant historical context" in which such images evolved.

53. Daly was among the first to refute the notion that "the Puritans were hostile to art and consequently produced none whatever" (*God's Altar* 4). He discusses sensuality and eroticism in Puritan poetry in "The World's Body" (6–39).

54. Miller, *Errand into the Wilderness* 14–15 describes declension jeremiads. The notion of decline is the tragic subtext of Bradford's *Of Plymouth Plantation*, in which the sins of the sons (including murder and bestiality) spawn meditations on the failure of the first generation's errand.

55. "Collusion" is a powerful word in Howe's vocabulary, especially in her writing about history: "I know records are compiled by winners, and scholarship is in collusion with Civil Government. I know this and go on searching for some trace of love's unfolding through all the paper in all the libraries I come to" (*BM* 4). The "trace of love's unfolding" is linked to the mysteries archives yield — such arduous (and often random) searching subverts the "collusion" of silence in historical narratives. For a superb explication of Howe's phrase "Collision or collusion with history" as central to a reading of *Articulation*, see Perloff's *Poetic License*.

56. See the opening of "The Captivity and Restoration," *BM* 89. Howe argues, "All testimonies are bereft, brief, hungry, pious, *authorized*"; she ironically observes, "Shock of God's voice speaking English" (*BM* 50). See also Derounian-Stodola's introduction concerning the editing of Rowlandson's text.

57. *Articulation* is one of the least visual of Howe's sequences. Her recent writing, particularly *Eikon Basilike*, uses crossed lines, blank spaces, and overlapping type in the manner of Marinetti, Apollinaire, Cage, and others. These sequences raise issues in terms of criticism: Printing and reproducing them is difficult, raising issues about the politics of publication and reproduction. See Keller's interview for discussion of this issue and Vickery's chapter for an account of Howe's undermining of printing conventions.

58. The words are Hugh Peter's, quoted by David D. Hall, ed., *The Antinomian Controversy, 1636–1638: A Documentary History* (Middletown, Conn.: Wesleyan University Press, 1968), 382–83, as cited by Howe, *BM* 52.

59. Lang illustrates this gendering of Hutchinson's story. She points out that the "disproportionate numbers of women, children, and young men among the

newly converted" proved the misguided nature of this enthusiasm, for "women who acted like men, boys who spoke like ministers, blacks who preached like whites" clearly upset the divine scheme (see *Prophetic Woman* 75 and 103).

CHAPTER 5

1. Concerning the primacy of Stein (and *Tender Buttons*) to contemporary avant-garde writing, see among other assertions Linda Reinfeld, *Language Poetry: Writing as Rescue* (Baton Rouge: Louisiana State U. P., 1992), 31; Charles Bernstein, *A Poetics* 55–56 (concerning the extent to which recent "anti-absorptive" techniques are frequently traceable to *Tender Buttons*); and Bob Perelman, *The Marginalization of Poetry: Language Writing and Literary History* (Princeton, N.J.: Princeton U. P., 1996), 15.

2. Like Mackey, Mullen seeks to diversify the canon beyond the aesthetic of "accessibility" that dominates publication of contemporary African American poetry: "My view is that there has been far too much emphasis on accessibility when it comes to writers from socially marginalized groups. This has resulted in shallow, simplistic readings that belabor the most obvious aspects of the writer's work and situation" (17–18). Nielsen offers a similar critique.

3. See my article "'Ruses of the Lunatic Muse': Harryette Mullen and Lyric Hybridity," *Women's Studies* 27 (1998) for the first elaboration of this idea; compare with Juliana Spahr's "connective reading" and questions of community concerning *Muse & Drudge*. Of Mullen's "challenge to readerly conventions," Spahr argues that readers "are invited to be constantly shifting locations, constantly struggling with a sampled and punned language, to talk back and to talk with" (*Everybody's Autonomy* 117).

4. Andrews and Bernstein, *L=A=N=G=U=A=G=E Book* 195–207. The writers in the section on Stein were Michael Davidson, Larry Eigner, Bob Perelman, Steve McCaffery, Peter Seaton, Jackson Mac Low, and Robert Grenier (see also Ron Silliman, ed., *In the American Tree*, for what is perhaps the most comprehensive collection of Language writings, both poetry and theory).

5. Since the early 1980s, Kruger's work has made use of the various traditions of advertising, agit-prop, and feminist (and psychoanalytic) theory to raise questions about gender and consumerism; Kruger recycles advertising images (often from the 1950s), with aggressive use of irreverent red slogans superimposed over the originals. Anna Deveare Smith's performance art merges parody, documentary, and political critique to address topical issues, as in her multitude of characters and scenarios concerning the 1992 Los Angeles uprising in her "Twilight Los Angeles."

6. See Fifer, as well as Gass and Stimpson's "Somagrams," mentioned in Chapter 1.

7. Davidson makes a similar point. For him the breakdown is between the idea that "her writing is all play" and the view that "Stein is a kind of hermetic Symbolist who encodes sexual and biographical information in complex verbal machines." For Davidson, the commonality between these two is not that they are both fundamentally "private" but that they both "operate on either side of a ref-

erential paradigm," and we need to "learn to read *writing*, not read *meanings*." In this, he reinstates the formal, closed, nature of *Tender Buttons* itself (Andrews and Bernstein, *L=A=N=G=U=A=G=E Book* 196–98). By contrast, DeKoven (*A Different Language*) is influenced by Kristeva, as is Ruddick.

8. Frost, interview with Mullen (unpublished, 1993, n.p.).

9. Frost, interview with Mullen (unpublished, 1993, n.p.).

10. Mullen discusses this conjunction of Armstrong references in her interview with Farah Griffin, Michael Magee, and Kristen Gallagher, "A Conversation with Harryette Mullen," http://wings.buffalo.edu/epc/authors/mullen/interview.html (January 26, 1999).

11. Frost, "An Interview with Harryette Mullen," 416.

12. See Ruddick's "A Rosy Charm," discussed in chapter 1.

13. See DuBois's famous passage from *The Souls of Black Folk* (New York: Penguin, 1989): "It is a peculiar sensation, this double-consciousness, this sense of looking at one's self through the eyes of others. [. . .] One ever feels his two-ness — an American, a Negro; two souls, two thoughts, two unreconciled strivings, two warring ideals in one dark body" (5). Addison Gayle Jr., ed., *The Black Aesthetic* (New York: Doubleday, 1971), among a number of anthologies from the early 1970s mentioned in Chapter 3, provide some of the most important theoretical writings of the Black Arts movement and the revolutionary impulse to change both the political and psychic realities of African Americans.

14. Barbara Smith, Gayatri Chakravorty Spivak, Trinh Minh-ha, hooks, Hazel Carby, and Gloria Anzaldúa are just a few of the critics who reshaped feminist thinking with attention to postcoloniality and racial difference. See Smith's classic "Toward a Black Feminist Criticism" (in *All the Women Are White*), Spivak's *In Other Worlds: Essays in Cultural Politics* (New York: Routledge, 1989), Minh-ha's *Woman, Native, Other: Writing Postcoloniality and Feminism* (Bloomington: Indiana U. P., 1989), and hooks's *Feminist Theory: From Margin to Center* (Boston: South End P., 1984) for influential explorations of feminism and race in the United States and internationally. Anthologies from the 1980s have been crucial in collecting revisionist feminist work by women of color, especially *This Bridge Called My Back*, *All the Women Are White*, and *Coming to Terms*.

15. Saldívar-Hull argues that racism in "Melanctha" has been either excused or ignored by feminist and other critics who champion Stein. See also Cohen and Bernstein's chapter "Professing Stein/Stein Professing," in *Poetics* (142–49).

16. See in particular Ruddick's article, "A Rosy Charm," for a reading of this passage.

17. Marianna Torgovnick, *Gone Primitive: Savage Intellects, Modern Lives* (Chicago: U. of Chicago P., 1990), 99. See Torgovnick 99–102 for an account of Manet's painting and numerous other examples of the "primitive" in modern art. She discusses Picasso's *Parody of Manet's "Olympia,"* in which the painter places himself at the edge of the bed as admirer, and the white woman is replaced by a black woman — the "role" of the maid is eliminated altogether. Torgovnick suggests that, with the more explicitly sexual representation of the black

woman's body, the maid was rendered unnecessary. A second version is Larry Rivers's *I Like Olympia in Black Face*, in which a reverse image of the "colors" of all the players appears in front: a black woman is reclining, with a bleached-white maid and cat in the same relative positions.

18. In this respect, on the "hidden" or "shadow" nature of black female sexuality, Mullen's critique of the politics of erotic dress is consonant with West's discussion of the extent to which black sexuality in general remains a taboo subject in American culture; her work also benefits from Sanchez's earlier exploration of this subject in her poetry.

19. Private communication with the author.

20. Mullen's third book, *S*PeRM**K*T* (Philadelphia: Singing Horse P., 1992), is a companion piece to *Trimmings*. These Steinian prose poems take aim at marketing, consumption, and erotics in the "supermarket" that in altered form supplies Mullen's title. The volume corresponds to the "Food" section of *Tender Buttons*, as *Trimmings* corresponded to "Objects."

21. "Optic White: Blackness and the Production of Whiteness," *Diacritics* 24.2–3 (1994): 87. Mullen refers to Ralph Ellison's *Invisible Man* (in the Liberty Paint Factory episode), as well as James Weldon Johnson's *The Autobiography of an Ex-Coloured Man* (New York: Hill and Wang, 1960), but the statement suggests a broader application as well.

22. Mullen points out that the mix of influences and regions in her family background created a "disruption in the notion of a black identity or a black subject. [*Muse & Drudge*] is partly trying to enlarge what the black culture or the black tradition might be" (Calvin Bedient, "The Solo Mysterioso Blues: An Interview with Harryette Mullen," *Callaloo* 19.3 [1996], 655–56).

23. I use the term "hybrid," as in Chapter 2, to describe this inescapably mixed state because it suggests not fusing or cultural forgetting (as in Mullen's critique) but a grafting of distinct forces. Linguistically, hybridity is found in what M. M. Bakhtin identifies as "an utterance that . . . contains mixed within it two utterances, two speech manners, two styles, two 'languages,' two semantic and axiological belief systems" (*Dialogic Imagination* 304); thus "two different linguistic consciousnesses, separated from one another by epoch, by social differentiation or by some other factor" come into focus (358). Hybridity as linguistic practice and cultural metaphor suggests the interlocking elements that comprise both individuals and the cultures that shape them.

24. See Margaret Homans and Christine Battersby for accounts of the association between woman and materiality and the invocation of a feminine agent in the service of models of androgynous creativity for the male artist. In a recent exploration of woman poet and muse, DuPlessis asks what happens when a woman poet "wander[s] in the . . . mausoleums of poetry" ("Manifests" 35–36). The answer, DuPlessis speculates, is that she gains an awareness that the muses who symbolically inspire lyric poetry mask the material conditions of its production, "the labor of females and others" (36–37). DuPlessis refers to Adorno's "Lyric Poetry and Society." See also Jonathan Arac and Jed Rasula for critiques of aspects of subjectivity in the lyric mode.

25. See Barbara Henning, "An Interview with Harryette Mullen," *Poetry Project Newsletter* 162 (1996), 7, for Mullen's description of her use of the "minor" form of the prose poem in *Trimmings* and *S*PeRM**K*T*.

26. Mullen notes the hybrid nature of her book-length poems, describing each as "a kind of long poem composed of discreet [*sic*] units" (Henning, "Interview" 10).

27. Mullen distances herself from conventions of the Sapphic stanza, which tends to be serious in tone: "Because of its inevitable association with the poems of Sappho, the Sapphic stanza . . . seems to imply a certain passion and seriousness: frivolity and comedy and wit are not among its conventions" (Fussell, *Poetic Meter* 138). Mullen does allude both to the ballad stanza and to classical modes as a means to circumvent the recent prevalence of individual subjectivity as the sole matter of lyric. David Lindley, among others, points out that the association between lyric and subjective experience did not become predominant until the Romantics; see also Theodor Adorno ("Lyric Poetry and Society," in *Critical Theory and Society: A Reader*, ed. Stephen Eric Bronner and Douglas MacKay Kellner [New York: Routledge, 1989], 158) and Jonathan Arac ("Afterword: Lyric Poetry and the Bounds of New Criticism," in *Lyric Poetry: Beyond New Criticism*, ed. Chaviva Hošek and Patricia Parker [Ithaca, N. Y.: Cornell U. P., 1985], 352–53). Furthermore, Mullen asserts that there is indeed a link "between the quatrain form and the blues form" (Bedient, "Solo Mysterioso Blues" 660); see Murray's *Stomping the Blues* (170) for a discussion of the Kansas City Four/Four beat that resembles Mullen's four quatrains per page.

28. Mullen notes, "There's the blues on the one hand and lyric poetry on the other hand, and where they intersect or overlap. Thinking of this poem as the place where Sappho meets the blues at the crossroads, I imagined Sappho becoming Sapphire and singing the blues" (Bedient 654). See "Sapphire's" recent novel, *Push* (New York: Knopf, 1996). The name "Sapphire" has also been used for a compact disc compilation of women blues artists.

29. Mullen points out that "the female vocal singer has been more important than the female instrumentalist"; thus in "styles / plucked eyebrows," Sapphire embodies "an association of the woman's body with her instrument. . . . So there's a reflection on these traditions in which women's voices are important but their musical expression is also limited in certain respects, where men are given instruments that women are not supposed to play" (Bedient 658–59).

30. See Homans, *Bearing the Word*, for an extended discussion of this question.

31. See Nancy I. Vickers, "Diana Described: Scattered Woman and Scattered Rhymes," in *Writing and Sexual Difference*, ed. Elizabeth Abel (Chicago: U. of Chicago P., 1982), 95–109, for a detailed account of Petrarchan conceits and the female body.

32. I am grateful to Melissa Jones for first bringing these two references to my attention; see the Rosetta Records recording, among others. This argument originally appeared in my "'Ruses of the Lunatic Muse'"; subsequently, Spahr has provided an even more extensive genealogy of the peaches/tree trope in songs by artists ranging from Ma Rainey through Steve Miller and the Beatles, among

others (in her chapter on Mullen, see 112–13). As Mackey points out, Bessie Smith and other jazz and blues musicians have long served as aesthetic sources (whether directly acknowledged or not) for any number of poets, from William Carlos Williams to Amiri Baraka (see *Discrepant Engagement* 243 and 248).

33. See Lorenzo Thomas, "Neon Griot: The Functional Role of Poetry Readings in the Black Arts Movement," in *Close Listening: Poetry and the Performed Word*, ed. Charles Bernstein (New York: Oxford U. P., 1998), 316; the author cites Ugo Rubeo, "Voice as Lifesaver: Defining the Function of Orality in Etheridge Knight's Poetry," in *The Black Columbiad: Defining Moments in African American Literature and Culture*, ed. Werner Sollers and Maria Diedrich (Cambridge, Mass.: Harvard U. P., 1994), 278.

34. Nielsen, *Black Chant* 159, 35–36. The author further points out that although publications devoted to black experimental writing in the 1950s and 1960s did feature writing by women, few of those poets published books, and, like "anthologies published by Beat and Black Mountain groups," these collections were run by avant-garde "coteries" that "operated as male enclaves. . . . Black women were for the most part offered little incentive to pursue poetic experimentation in America" during the Umbra period, and "things did not improve markedly with the advent of the Black Arts movement" (*Black Chant* 161–62).

35. Mullen notes that this quatrain was partly inspired by a black woman with a bleached yellow Afro selling African masks and sculptures on the street outside a New York museum that was exhibiting Brancusi's sculpture "Blonde Negress" (private communication with the author).

36. Private communication with the author.

37. Baker calls rap a "nonauthoritative collaging or archiving of sound and styles" (*Black Studies* 89). Mullen discusses rap in Henning, "Interview" 6. See Keyes, who argues that female rappers "make use of the pronoun *you*, which strategically serves to distract from gender or sex" (Cheryl Keyes, "'We're More Than a Novelty, Boys': Strategies of Female Rappers in the Rap Music Tradition," in *Feminist Messages: Coding in Women's Folk Culture*, ed. Joan Newlon Radner [Chicago: U. of Chicago P., 1993], 210); she holds that "female rappers have recognized they will gain an audience for their raps only by adopting the male aesthetic" (208), however subtly altered. Mullen rejects that degree of accommodation, offering instead ways to adapt conventions to specifically feminist ends.

38. See "Optic White" 87. I am indebted to Murray's *Omni-Americans*: "*American culture, even in its most rigidly segregated precincts, is patently and irrevocably composite. It is . . . incontestably mulatto*" (22; Murray's italics). By comparison, Mackey theorizes, by way of accounts by Steven Feld and Victor Zuckerkandl, that "Poetic language is language owning up to being an orphan," just as black music is "a critique of social arrangements in which, because of racism, one finds oneself deprived of community and kinship" (*Discrepant Engagement* 234).

39. See Mullen's explanation (Bedient, "Solo Mysterioso Blues" 667).

40. Amiri Baraka, *Blues People* (New York: Morrow, 1963, p. 181), cited by Mackey 275.

41. Rayor, *Sappho's Lyre* 80. Mullen notes, among others, the following sources for treatments of cross-cultural appropriation: bell hooks, *Black Looks: Race and Representation* (Boston: South End Press, 1992), and Lucy Lippard, *Mixed Blessings: New Art in a Multicultural America* (New York: Pantheon Books, 1990) (private communication with the author).

42. See Frost, "An Interview," 403ff. Mullen points out that Shine is a folklore hero, a black worker aboard the *Titanic* who, through ingenuity, was said to have survived the disaster. Among other versions, the story also appears in Etheridge Knight's "I Sing of Shine" (Randall, *Black Poets* 209–10) and at the start of Neal's "And Shine Swam On" ("Afterword" to *Black Fire*).

EPILOGUE

1. See Mary Margaret Sloan, ed., *Moving Borders: Three Decades of Innovative Writing by Women* (Jersey City, N.J.: Talisman, 1998) and Maggie O'Sullivan, ed., *Out of Everywhere: Linguistically Innovative Poetry by Women in North America and the U.K.* (London: Reality Street Editions, 1996). A number of conferences (including "Poetry and the Public Sphere" at Rutgers in 1997; "Page Mothers" in San Diego in 1999; and "Where Lyric Tradition Meets Language Poetry" at Barnard in 1999) represent marked scholarly interest in experimental women's writing, as do such recent studies as Simpson, Spahr, and Vickery, and the collections *American Women Poets in the Twenty-First Century* (ed. Claudia Rankine and Juliana Spahr) and *We Who Love to Be Astonished* (ed. Hinton and Hogue). See also Hank Lazer, *Opposing Poetries*, vol. 1, *Issues and Institutions* and vol. 2, *Readings* (Evanston, Ill.: Northwestern U. P., 1996); Quartermain (*Disjunctive Poetics*); Perelman (*Marginalization of Poetry*); Perloff (*Radical Artifice: Writing Poetry in the Age of Media* [Chicago: U. of Chicago P., 1991]); and Bernstein (*Poetics*) for treatments of experimental women poets in various contexts; Kinnahan (*Poetics of the Feminine*) and Keller (*Forms of Expansion*) both address women poets who favor a range of aesthetics and formal strategies. Among the poets I have addressed, Howe has received particular attention.

2. Perelman's chapter on Stein is only one example of recent scholarly treatments. Canonical sources like the New American Library edition of Stein also bear witness to explorations of twentieth-century women avant-gardists. In addition to the excellent studies by Susan Edmunds, *Out of Line: History, Psychoanalysis, and Montage in H.D.'s Long Poems* (Stanford, Calif.: Stanford U. P., 1994) and Cassandra Laity, *H.D. and the Victorian Fin de Siècle: Gender, Modernism, Decadence* (New York: Cambridge U. P., 1996), H.D. scholarship has been forwarded by such newly available work as H.D.'s correspondence with Norman Holmes Pearson (*Between History and Poetry: The Letters of H.D. and Norman Holmes Pearson*, ed. Donna Krolik Hollenberg [Iowa City: U. of Iowa P., 1997]); *The Gift: The Complete Text* by H.D., ed. and annotated, with an intro-

duction by Jane Augustine (Gainesville: U. P. of Florida, 1998); and Cassandra Laity's edition of *Paint It Today* (New York: New York U. P., 1992), among others. Publication of Lorine Niedecker's *Collected Works*, ed. Jenny Penberthy (Berkeley: U. of Calif. P., 2002) is another such welcome source.

3. It is notable that both academic and commercial presses are participating in this trend. A few examples: Wesleyan has published Fraser, Scalapino, and Brenda Hillman; Grove/Atlantic has released Rankine's *The End of the Alphabet* (New York: Grove P., 1998) and *Plot* (New York: Grove P., 2001); Ecco publishes Jorie Graham; the new series at U. of California P., edited by Calvin Bedient, Robert Hass, and Brenda Hillman includes Mullen's (*Sleeping with the Dictionary*), new work by Carol Snow (*For* 2000), and Fanny Howe's *Selected Poems* (2000); and Penguin publishes Ann Lauterbach and Alice Notley.

WORKS CITED

Abel, Elizabeth. "Race, Class, and Psychoanalysis? Opening Questions." In *Conflicts in Feminism*, ed. Marianne Hirsch and Evelyn Fox Keller, 184–204. New York: Routledge, 1990.

Adorno, Theodor W. "Lyric Poetry and Society." In *Critical Theory and Society: A Reader*, ed. Stephen Eric Bronner and Douglas MacKay Kellner, 155–71. New York: Routledge, 1989.

Andrews, Bruce, and Charles Bernstein, eds. *The L=A=N=G=U=A=G=E Book*. Carbondale: Southern Illinois U. P., 1984.

Anzaldúa, Gloria, and Cherríe Moraga, eds. *This Bridge Called My Back: Writings by Radical Women of Color*. New York: Kitchen Table, Women of Color P., 1983.

Apter, Emily. *Feminizing the Fetish: Psychoanalysis and Narrative Obsession in Turn-of-the-Century France*. Ithaca, N.Y.: Cornell U. P., 1991.

Apter, Emily, and William Pietz, eds. *Fetishism as Cultural Discourse*. Ithaca, N.Y.: Cornell U. P., 1993.

Arac, Jonathan. "Afterword: Lyric Poetry and the Bounds of New Criticism." In *Lyric Poetry: Beyond New Criticism*, ed. Chaviva Hošek and Patricia Parker, 345–55. Ithaca, N.Y.: Cornell U. P., 1985.

Arnold, Elizabeth. "Mina Loy and the Futurists." *Sagetrieb: A Journal Devoted to Poets in the Imagist/Objectivist Tradition* 8.1–2 (1989): 83–117.

Baker, Houston A., Jr. *Afro-American Poetics: Revisions of Harlem and the Black Aesthetic*. Madison: U. of Wisconsin P., 1988.

———. *Black Studies, Rap, and the Academy*. Chicago: U. of Chicago P., 1993.

———. *Blues, Ideology, and Afro-American Literature*. Chicago: U. of Chicago P., 1985.

———. "Generational Shifts and the Recent Criticism of Afro-American Literature." *Black American Literature Forum*. Reprinted in *Blues, Ideology, and Afro-American Literature*. 64–112.

———. *The Journey Back: Issues in Black Literature and Criticism*. Chicago: U. of Chicago P., 1980.

———. *Modernism and the Harlem Renaissance*. Chicago: U. of Chicago P., 1987.

———. "Our Lady: Sonia Sanchez and the Writing of a Black Renaissance." In *Black Feminist Criticism and Critical Theory*, vol. 3 of *Studies in Black American Literature*, ed. Joe Weixlmann and Houston A. Baker Jr., 170–202. Greenwood, Fla.: Penkevill, 1988.

Bakhtin, M. M. *The Dialogic Imagination: Four Essays*. Ed. Michael Holquist and trans. Caryl Emerson and Michael Holquist. Austin: U. of Texas P., 1981.

Bambara, Toni Cade. *The Black Woman: An Anthology*. New York: Penguin, 1970.

Baraka, Amiri. "Afro-American Literature and Class Struggle." *Black American Literature Forum* (spring 1980): 5–14.

———. "The Revolutionary Tradition in Afro-American Literature." In *Selected Plays and Prose of Amiri Baraka/LeRoi Jones*, 242–51. New York: William Morrow, 1979.

Barkan, Elazar. *The Retreat of Scientific Racism: Changing Concepts of Race in Britain and the United States between the World Wars*. New York: Cambridge U. P., 1992.

Barthes, Roland. *The Pleasure of the Text*. Trans. Richard Miller. New York: Farrar, Straus and Giroux, 1973.

———. "Whose Theater? Whose *Avant-Garde*?" In *Critical Essays*, trans. Richard Howard, 67–70. Evanston, Ill.: Northwestern U. P., 1972.

———. *Writing Degree Zero*. Trans. Annette Lavers and Colin Smith. New York: Farrar, Straus and Giroux, 1968.

Battersby, Christine. *Gender and Genius: Towards a Feminist Aesthetics*. Bloomington: Indiana U. P., 1989.

Beckett, Tom. "The Difficulties Interview." *The Difficulties* 3.2 (1989): 17–27.

Bedient, Calvin. "The Solo Mysterioso Blues: An Interview with Harryette Mullen." *Callaloo* 19.3 (1996): 651–69.

Benstock, Shari. "Beyond the Reaches of Feminist Criticism: A Letter from Paris." In *Feminist Issues in Literary Scholarship*, ed. Shari Benstock, 7–29. Bloomington: Indiana U. P., 1987.

———. *Textualizing the Feminine: On the Limits of Genre*. Norman: U. of Oklahoma P., 1991.

———. *Women of the Left Bank: Paris, 1900–1940*. Austin: U. of Texas P., 1986.

Bernstein, Charles. *A Poetics*. Cambridge, Mass.: Harvard U. P., 1992.

———, ed. *The Politics of Poetic Form*. New York: Roof, 1990.

Berry, Ellen E. *Curved Thought and Textual Wandering: Gertrude Stein's Postmodernism*. Ann Arbor: U. of Michigan P., 1992.

Bibby, Michael. *Hearts and Minds: Bodies, Poetry, and Resistance in the Vietnam Era*. New Brunswick, N.J.: Rutgers U. P., 1996.

BLAST 1 (Santa Barbara, Calif.: Black Sparrow P., 1981).

Blount, Marcellus. "The Preacherly Text: African American Poetry and Vernacular Performance." *PMLA* 107 (1992): 582–93.

Blues Masters: The Essential Blues Collection. Rhino Records. Vol. 5, 1992.

Boland, Eavan, and Kathleen Fraser. "A Conversation." *Parnassus: Poetry in Review* 23 (1998): 387–403.

Bradford, William. *Of Plymouth Plantation*. New York: The Modern Library, 1981.

Bradstreet, Anne. *The Works of Anne Bradstreet*. Ed. Jeannine Hensley. Cambridge, Mass.: Harvard U. P., 1967.

Breton, André. *Manifestoes of Surrealism*. Trans. Richard Seaver and Helen R. Lane. Ann Arbor: U. of Michigan P., 1969.

Bridgman, Richard. *Gertrude Stein in Pieces*. New York: Oxford U. P., 1970.

Brogan, Jacqueline Vaught. *Part of the Climate: American Cubist Poetry*. Los Angeles: U. of California P., 1991.

Brown, Kimberly N. "Of Poststructuralist Fallout, Scarification, and Blood Poems: The Revolutionary Ideology behind the Poetry of Jayne Cortez." In *Other Sisterhoods: Literary Theory and U.S. Women of Color*, ed. Sandra Kumamoto Stanley, 63–85. Chicago: U. of Chicago P., 1998.

Bürger, Peter. *Theory of the Avant-Garde*. Trans. Michael Shaw. Minneapolis: U. of Minnesota P., 1984.

Burke, Carolyn. *Becoming Modern: The Life of Mina Loy*. New York: Farrar, Straus and Giroux, 1996.

———. "Getting Spliced: Modernism and Sexual Difference." *American Quarterly* 39 (1987): 98–121.

———. "The New Poetry and the New Woman: Mina Loy." In *Coming to Light: American Women Poets in the Twentieth Century*, ed. Diane Wood Middlebrook and Marilyn Yalom, 37–57. Ann Arbor: U. of Michigan P., 1985.

———. "Supposed Persons: Modernist Poetry and the Female Subject." *Feminist Studies* 11.1 (1985): 131–47.

Butler, Judith. *Gender Trouble: Feminism and the Subversion of Identity*. New York: Routledge, 1990.

Butterick, George F. "The Mysterious Vision of Susan Howe." *North Dakota Quarterly* 55 (1987): 312–21.

Calinescu, Matei. *Five Faces of Modernity: Modernism, Avant-Garde, Decadence, Kitsch, Postmodernism*. Durham, N.C.: Duke U. P., 1987.

Cameron, Deborah. *Feminism and Linguistic Theory*. New York: St. Martin's, 1985.

———. *The Feminist Critique of Language: A Reader*. New York: Routledge, 1990.

Campbell, Bruce. "'Ring of Bodies'/'Sphere of Sound': An Essay on Susan Howe's *Articulation of Sound Forms in Time*." *The Difficulties* 3.2 (1989): 89–96.

Carby, Hazel. *Reconstructing Womanhood: The Emergence of the Afro-American Woman Novelist*. New York: Oxford U. P., 1987.

Caws, Mary Ann, Rudolf Kuenzli, and Gwen Raaberg, eds. *Surrealism and Women*. Cambridge, Mass.: MIT P., 1991.

Cha, Theresa Hak Kyung. *Dictée*. New York: Tanam P., 1982.

Chandler, Zala. "Voices Beyond the Veil: An Interview of Toni Cade Bambara and Sonia Sanchez." In *Wild Women in the Whirlwind: Afra-American Culture and the Contemporary Literary Renaissance*, ed. Joanne M. Braxton and Andrée Nicola McLaughlin, 342–62. New Brunswick, N.J.: Rutgers U. P., 1990.

Chapman, Abraham, ed. *New Black Voices: An Anthology of Contemporary Afro-American Literature*. New York: New American Library, 1972.

Chessman, Harriet Scott. *The Public Is Invited to Dance: Representation, the Body, and Dialogue in Gertrude Stein*. Stanford, Calif.: Stanford U. P., 1989.

Chodorow, Nancy. *The Reproduction of Mothering: Psychoanalysis and the Sociology of Gender*. Los Angeles: U. of California P., 1978.

Cixous, Hélène. "The Laugh of the Medusa." In *New French Feminisms: An Anthology*, trans. Keith Cohen and Paula Cohen and ed. Elaine Marks and Isabelle de Courtivron, 245–64. New York: Schocken Books, 1981.

Clausen, Jan. "A Movement of Poets: Thoughts on Poetry and Feminism." In *Books and Life*, 3–44. Columbus, Ohio: Ohio State U. P., 1989.

Cleaver, Eldridge. *Soul on Ice*. New York: McGraw-Hill, 1968.

Cohen, Milton. "Black Brutes and Mulatto Saints: The Racial Hierarchy of Stein's 'Melanctha.'" *Black American Literature Forum* 18 (1984): 119–21.

Colacurcio, Michael J. "'The Woman's Own Choice': Sex, Metaphor, and the Puritan 'Sources' of *The Scarlet Letter*." In *New Essays on The Scarlet Letter*, ed. Michael J. Colacurcio, 101–35. New York: Cambridge U. P., 1985.

Cole, Johnetta B. "Culture: Negro, Black and Nigger." In *New Black Voices: An Anthology of Contemporary Afro-American Literature*, ed. Abraham Chapman, 491–98. New York: New American Library, 1972.

Conte, Joseph. *Unending Design: The Forms of Postmodern Poetry*. Ithaca, N.Y.: Cornell U. P., 1991.

Curb, Rosemary K. "Pre-Feminism in the Black Revolutionary Drama of Sonia Sanchez." In *The Many Forms of Drama: The University of Florida Department of Classics Comparative Literature Conference Papers*. Vol. 5, ed. Karelisa V. Hartigan, 19–29. New York: U. P. of America, 1985.

Daly, Robert. *God's Altar: The World and the Flesh in Puritan Poetry*. Los Angeles: U. of California P., 1978.

Davidson, Michael. *Ghostlier Demarcations: Modern Poetry and the Material Word*. Berkeley: U. of California P., 1997.

DeKoven, Marianne. *A Different Language: Gertrude Stein's Experimental Writing*. Madison: U. of Wisconsin P., 1983.

———. "Male Signature, Female Aesthetic: The Gender Politics of Experimental Writing." In *Breaking the Sequence: Women's Experimental Fiction*, ed. Ellen G. Friedman and Miriam Fuchs, 72–81. Princeton, N.J.: Princeton U. P., 1989.

De Lancey, Frenzella Elaine. "Refusing to Be Boxed In: Sonia Sanchez's Transformation of the Haiku Form." In *Language and Literature in the African American Imagination*, ed. Carol Aisha Blackshire-Belay, 21–36. Westport, Conn.: Greenwood P., 1992.

Doane, Mary Ann. "Film and the Masquerade: Theorising the Female Spectator." *Screen* 23.3–4 (1982): 74–87.

———. "Masquerade Reconsidered: Further Thoughts on the Female Spectator." *Discourse* 11.1 (1988–1989): 42–54.

Donalson, Melvin, ed. *Cornerstones: An Anthology of African-American Literature*. New York: St. Martin's, 1996.

Donne, John. *The Complete Poetry of John Donne*. Ed. John T. Shawcross. New York: Doubleday, 1967.

H.D. *Collected Poems 1912–1944*. New York: New Directions, 1983. Abbreviated *CP* within the text.

Dubnick, Randa. *The Structure of Obscurity: Gertrude Stein, Language, and Cubism*. Chicago: U. of Illinois P., 1984.

DuBois, Ellen Carol, and Linda Gordon. "Seeking Ecstasy on the Battlefield: Danger and Pleasure in Nineteenth-Century Feminist Sexual Thought." *Feminist Studies* 9.1 (1983): 7–25.

DuBois, W. E. B. *The Souls of Black Folk*. New York: Penguin, 1989.

DuPlessis, Rachel Blau. *Genders, Races and Religious Cultures in Modern American Poetries, 1908–1934*. New York: Cambridge U. P., 2001.

———. "Manifests." *Diacritics* 26.3–4 (1996): 31–53.

———. *The Pink Guitar: Writing as Feminist Practice*. New York: Routledge, 1990.

———. "'Seismic Orgasm': Sexual Intercourse, Gender Narratives, and Lyric Ideology in Mina Loy." In *Studies in Historical Change*, ed. Ralph Cohen, 264–91. Charlottesville: U. of Virginia P., 1992.

———. "'Whowe': An Essay on Work by Susan Howe." *Sulfur* 20 (1987): 157–65. Reprinted in DuPlessis, *The Pink Guitar: Writing as Feminist Practice*, 123–39. New York: Routledge, 1990.

Easthope, Antony, and John O. Thompson, eds. *Contemporary Poetry Meets Modern Theory*. New York: Harvester, 1991.

Echols, Alice. *Daring to Be Bad: Radical Feminism in America 1967–1975*. Minneapolis: U. of Minnesota P., 1989.

Ellison, Ralph. *Invisible Man*. New York: Vintage Books, 1972.

Erkkila, Betsy. *The Wicked Sisters: Women Poets, Literary History, and Discord*. New York: Oxford U. P., 1992.

Evans, Mari, ed. *Black Women Writers: A Critical Evaluation*. New York: Anchor P. / Doubleday, 1984.

Faderman, Lillian. *Odd Girls and Twilight Lovers: A History of Lesbian Life in Twentieth-Century America*. New York: Penguin, 1991.

Falon, Janet Ruth. "Speaking with Susan Howe." *The Difficulties* 3.2 (1989): 28–42.

Felski, Rita. *Beyond Feminist Aesthetics: Feminist Literature and Social Change*. Cambridge, Mass.: Harvard U. P., 1989.

Fiedler, Leslie. "The Death of *Avant-Garde* Literature." In *The Collected Essays of Leslie Fiedler*. Vol. 2, 454–61. New York: Stein and Day, 1971.

Fifer, Elizabeth. "Is Flesh Advisable? The Interior Theater of Gertrude Stein." *Signs: Journal of Women in Culture and Society* 4.3 (1979): 472–83.

Ford, Karen Jackson. *Gender and the Poetics of Excess: Moments of Brocade*. Jackson: U. P. of Mississippi, 1997.

Foster, Edward. "Interview with Susan Howe." *Talisman: A Journal of Contemporary Poetry and Poetics* 4 (1990): 14–38. Reprinted in Howe, *The Birth-Mark: Unsettling the Wilderness in American Literary History*, 155–81. Hanover, N.H.: Wesleyan U. P., 1991. Abbreviated *Tal* within the text.

Foster, Hal. "What's Neo about the Neo-Avant-Garde?" *October* 70 (1994): 5–32.

Foucault, Michel. *Language, Counter-Memory, Practice: Selected Essays and Interviews*. Trans. and ed. Donald F. Bouchard and Sherry Simon. Ithaca, N.Y.: Cornell U. P., 1977.

Fraser, Kathleen. "The Tradition of Marginality." In *Where We Stand: Women Poets on Literary Tradition*, ed. Sharon Bryan, 52–65. New York: Norton, 1993. Reprinted in Fraser, *Translating the Unspeakable: Poetry and the Innovative Necessity*, 25–38. Tuscaloosa: U. of Alabama P., 2000.

———. *Translating the Unspeakable: Poetry and the Innovative Necessity*. Tuscaloosa: U. of Alabama P., 2000.

Freud, Sigmund. "Fetishism." In *The Standard Edition of the Complete Psychological Works of Sigmund Freud*, trans. and ed. James Strachey. Vol. 21, 149–57. London: Hogarth P., 1961.

———. "Humour." In *The Standard Edition of the Complete Psychological Works of Sigmund Freud*, trans. and ed. James Strachey. Vol. 21, 160–66. London: Hogarth P., 1961.

———. "Leonardo da Vinci and a Memory of His Childhood." In *The Standard Edition of the Complete Psychological Works of Sigmund Freud*, trans. and ed. James Strachey. Vol. 11, 59–139. London: Hogarth P., 1961.

———. "Splitting of the Ego in the Process of Defence." In *The Standard Edition of the Complete Psychological Works of Sigmund Freud*, trans. and ed. James Strachey. Vol. 23, 273–78. London: Hogarth P., 1961.

Friedman, Susan Stanford. "Gender and Genre Anxiety: Elizabeth Barrett Browning and H.D. as Epic Poets." *Tulsa Studies in Women's Literature* 5.2 (1986): 203–28.

Frost, Elisabeth A. "Fetishism and Parody in Stein's *Tender Buttons*." In *Sexual Artifice: Persons, Images, Politics* (*Genders* 19), ed. Ann Kibbey, Kayann Short, and Abouali Farmanfarmaian, 64–93. New York: New York U. P., 1994.

———. Interview with Harryette Mullen (unpublished), March 26, 1993.

———. "An Interview with Harryette Mullen." *Contemporary Literature* 41.3 (Fall 2000): 397–421.

———. Interview with Susan Howe (unpublished), August 25,1993.

———. "'Ruses of the Lunatic Muse': Harryette Mullen and Lyric Hybridity." *Women Studies* 27 (1998): 465–81.

———. "Signifyin(g) on Stein: The Revisionist Poetics of Harryette Mullen and Leslie Scalapino." In *Postmodern Culture: An Electronic Journal of Interdisciplinary Criticism* 5.3 (1995): n.p. http://jefferson.village.virginia .edu/pmc/contents.all.html.

Fuller, Hoyt W. "Towards a Black Aesthetic." In *The Black Aesthetic*, ed. Addison Gayle Jr., 3–11. New York: Doubleday, 1971.

Fuss, Diana. *Essentially Speaking: Feminism, Nature and Difference*. New York: Routledge, 1989.

Fussell, Paul. *Poetic Meter and Poetic Form*. New York: Random House, 1979.

Garber, Marjorie. "Fetish Envy." *October* 54 (1990): 45–56.

Gass, William. *The World Within the Word*. New York: Knopf, 1978.

Gates, Henry Louis, Jr. *Figures in Black: Words, Signs, and the "Racial" Self*. New York: Oxford U. P., 1987.

———. *The Signifying Monkey: A Theory of African American Literary Criticism*. New York: Oxford U. P., 1988.

Gayle, Addison, Jr., ed. *The Black Aesthetic*. New York: Doubleday, 1971.

Gilbert, Derrick I. M., ed. *Catch the Fire!!! A Cross-Generational Anthology of Contemporary African-American Poetry*. New York: Riverhead Books, 1998.

Gilbert, Sandra, and Susan Gubar. *Letters from the Front*. Vol. 3 of *No Man's Land: The Place of the Woman Writer in the Twentieth Century*. New Haven, Conn.: Yale U. P., 1994.

———. *The War of the Words.* Vol. 1 of *No Man's Land: The Place of the Woman Writer in the Twentieth Century.* New Haven: Yale U. P., 1988.

Gilman, Charlotte Perkins. *Herland.* New York: Pantheon Books, 1979.

Giovanni, Nikki. *The Women and the Men.* New York: William Morrow, 1975.

Golding, Alan. "Avant-Gardes and American Poetry." *Contemporary Literature* 35.1 (1994): 156–70.

Gordon, Linda. *Woman's Body, Woman's Right: A Social History of Birth Control in America.* New York: Penguin, 1986.

Graddol, David, and Joan Swann. *Gender Voices.* Cambridge, Mass.: Basil Blackwell, 1986.

Gray, Nancy. *Language Unbound: On Experimental Writing by Women.* Chicago: U. of Illinois P., 1992.

Griffin, Farah, Michael Magee, and Kristen Gallagher. "A Conversation with Harryette Mullen." http://wings.buffalo.edu/epc/authors/mullen/interview.html. January 26, 1999.

Grosz, Elizabeth. *Jacques Lacan: A Feminist Introduction.* New York: Routledge, 1990.

———. "Lesbian Fetishism?" In *Fetishism as Cultural Discourse*, ed. Emily Apter and William Pietz, Ithaca, N.Y.: Cornell U. P., 1993. 101–115.

Haller, Mark H. *Eugenics: Hereditarian Attitudes in American Thought.* New Brunswick, N.J.: Rutgers U. P., 1984.

Harper, Phillip Brian. "Nationalism and Social Division in Black Arts Poetry of the 1960s." *Critical Inquiry* 19 (1993): 234–55.

Hartley, George. *Textual Politics and the Language Poets.* Bloomington: Indiana U. P., 1989.

Hassan, Ihab. "The Culture of Postmodernism." In *Modernism: Challenges and Perspectives*, ed. Monique Chefdor, Ricardo Quinones, and Albert Wachtel, 304–24. Urbana: U. of Illinois P., 1986.

Hedges, Inez. *Languages of Revolt: Dada and Surrealist Literature and Film.* Durham, N.C.: Duke U. P., 1983.

Henderson, Stephen. *Understanding the New Black Poetry: Black Speech and Black Music as Poetic References.* New York: William Morrow, 1973.

Henning, Barbara. "An Interview with Harryette Mullen." *Poetry Project Newsletter* 162 (1996): 5–10.

Hernton, Calvin. "The Sexual Mountain and Black Women Writers." In *Wild Women in the Whirlwind: Afra-American Culture and the Contemporary Literary Renaissance*, ed. Joanne M. Braxton and Andrée Nicola McLaughlin, 195–202. New Brunswick, N.J.: Rutgers U. P., 1990.

Hinton, Laura, and Cynthia Hogue, eds. *We Who Love to Be Astonished: Experimental Women's Writing and Performance Poetics.* Tuscaloosa: U. of Alabama P., 2001.

Hoffman, Michael J., ed. *Critical Essays on Gertrude Stein.* Boston: G. K. Hall, 1986.

———. *Gertrude Stein.* Boston: Twayne, 1976.

Hogue, Cynthia. "Infectious Ecstasy: Toward a Poetics of Performative Transformation." In *Women Poets of the Americas: Toward a Pan-American*

Gathering, ed. Jacqueline Vaught Brogan and Cordelia Chávez Candelaria, 51–67. Notre Dame, Ind.: U. of Notre Dame P., 1999.

———. "Interview with Harryette Mullen." *Postmodern Culture: An Electronic Journal of Interdisciplinary Criticism* 9.2 (1999): n.p. http://jefferson.village.virginia.edu/pmc.

———. "An Interview with Kathleen Fraser." *Contemporary Literature* 39.1 (1998): 1–26.

Homans, Margaret. *Bearing the Word: Language and Female Experience in Nineteenth-Century Women's Writing*. Chicago: U. of Chicago P., 1986.

Homer. *The Odyssey*. Trans. Robert Fitzgerald. New York: Doubleday, 1963.

hooks, bell. *Ain't I a Woman: Black Women and Feminism*. Boston: South End P., 1981.

Howe, Florence, ed. *No More Masks! An Anthology of Twentieth-Century American Women Poets*. New York: HarperPerennial, 1993.

Howe, Susan. *The Birth-Mark: Unsettling the Wilderness in American Literary History*. Hanover, N.H.: Wesleyan U. P., 1991. Abbreviated *BM* within the text.

———. *Defenestration of Prague*. New York: Kulchur Foundation, 1983. Abbreviated *Def* within the text.

———. *The Europe of Trusts*. Los Angeles: Sun and Moon, 1990.

———. *Frame Structures: Early Poems 1974–1979*. New York: New Directions, 1996.

———. *My Emily Dickinson*. Berkeley: North Atlantic Books, 1985. Abbreviated *MED* within the text.

———. *The Nonconformist's Memorial*. New York: New Directions, 1993. Abbreviated *NCM* within the text.

———. *Pierce-Arrow*. New York: New Directions, 1999.

———. *Singularities*. Hanover, N. H.: Wesleyan U. P., 1990.

———. "Sorting Facts: Or, Nineteen Ways of Looking at Marker." In *Beyond Document: Essays on Nonfiction Film*, ed. Charles Warren, 295–343. Hanover, N. H.: U. P. of New England, 1996.

———. "Statement for the New Poetics Colloquium, Vancouver, 1985." *Jimmy and Lucy's House of K* 5 (1985): 13–17.

———. "Where Should the Commander Be." *Writing* 19 (1987): 3–20.

Hull, Gloria, Patricia Bell Scott, and Barbara Smith, eds. *All the Women Are White, All the Blacks Are Men, But Some of Us Are Brave*. New York: Feminist P., 1982.

Hulme, T. E. *Speculations: Essays on Humanism and the Philosophy of Art*. Ed. Herbert Read. New York: Humanities P., 1924.

Hurston, Zora Neale. *Mules and Men*. New York: HarperCollins, 1990.

Huyssen, Andreas. *After the Great Divide: Modernism, Mass Culture, Postmodernism*. Bloomington: Indiana U. P., 1986.

Irigaray, Luce. *Speculum of the Other Woman*. Trans. Gillian C. Gill. Ithaca, N.Y.: Cornell U. P., 1985.

———. *This Sex Which Is Not One*. Trans. Catherine Porter. Ithaca, N.Y.: Cornell U. P., 1985.

James, William. "The Moral Equivalent of War." In *William James: The Essential Writings*, ed. Bruce W. Wilshire, 349–61. Albany: SUNY P., 1984.

Jameson, Fredric. "Postmodernism and Consumer Society." In *The Anti-Aesthetic: Essays on Postmodern Culture*, ed. Hal Foster, 111–25. Seattle: Bay P., 1983.

Jennings, Regina B. "The Blue/Black Poetics of Sonia Sanchez." In *Language and Literature in the African American Imagination*, ed. Carol Aisha Blackshire-Belay, 119–32. Westport, Conn.: Greenwood P., 1992.

Johnson, James Weldon. *The Autobiography of an Ex-Coloured Man*. New York: Hill and Wang, 1960.

Jones, LeRoi, and Larry Neal, eds. *Black Fire: An Anthology of Afro-American Writing*. New York: William Morrow, 1968.

Kalaidjian, Walter. "Transpersonal Poetics: Language Writing and the Historical Avant-Gardes in Postmodern Culture." *American Literary History* 3 (1991): 319–36.

Kaplan, Louise J. *Female Perversions: The Temptations of Emma Bovary*. New York: Doubleday, 1991.

Karenga, Ron. "Black Cultural Nationalism." In *The Black Aesthetic*, ed. Addison Gayle Jr., 32–38. New York: Doubleday, 1971.

Keller, Lynn. *Forms of Expansion: Recent Long Poems by Women*. Chicago: U. of Chicago P., 1997.

———. "An Interview with Susan Howe." *Contemporary Literature* 36.1 (1995): 1–34.

———. *Re-Making It New: Contemporary American Poetry and the Modernist Tradition*. New York: Cambridge U. P., 1987.

Keller, Lynn, and Cristanne Miller, eds. *Feminist Measures: Soundings in Poetry and Theory*. Ann Arbor: U. of Michigan P., 1994.

Kevles, Daniel J. *In the Name of Eugenics: Genetics and the Uses of Human Heredity*. New York: Knopf, 1985.

Keyes, Cheryl L. "'We're More than a Novelty, Boys': Strategies of Female Rappers in the Rap Music Tradition." In *Feminist Messages: Coding in Women's Folk Culture*, ed. Joan Newlon Radner, 203–20. Chicago: U. of Illinois P., 1993.

Kinnahan, Linda. "'A Peculiar Hybrid': The Feminist Project of *HOW(ever)*." *HOW2* 1.5 (March 2001). http://www.scc.rutgers.edu/however/vi_5_2001/current/index.html.

———. *Poetics of the Feminine: Authority and Literary Tradition in William Carlos Williams, Mina Loy, Denise Levertov, and Kathleen Fraser*. New York: Cambridge U. P., 1994.

Kofman, Sarah. "Ca Cloche." In *Les Fins de l'homme: A partir de Jacques Derrida*, ed. Philippe Lacoue-Labarthe and Jean-Luc Nancy, 83–116. Paris: Gallilée, 1981.

Korg, Jacob. *Ritual and Experiment in Modern Poetry*. New York: St. Martin's, 1995.

Kouidis, Virginia. *Mina Loy: American Modernist Poet*. Baton Rouge: Louisiana State U. P., 1980.

Krauss, Rosalind. *The Originality of the Avant-Garde and other Modernist Myths*. Cambridge, Mass.: MIT P., 1985.

Kristeva, Julia. "About Chinese Women." In *The Kristeva Reader*, ed. Toril Moi, 138–59. New York: Columbia U. P., 1986.

———. *The Kristeva Reader*. Ed. Toril Moi. New York: Columbia U. P., 1986.

————. *Revolution in Poetic Language*. Trans. Margaret Walker. New York: Columbia U. P., 1984.

————. "Stabat Mater." In *Tales of Love*, trans. Leon S. Roudiez, 234–63. New York: Columbia U. P., 1983.

Kuhn, Annette. *The Power of the Image: Essays on Representation and Sexuality*. Boston: Routledge, 1985.

Lacan, Jacques. "The Agency of the Letter in the Unconscious or Reason since Freud." In *Ecrits*, trans. Alan Sheridan, 146–78. New York: W. W. Norton, 1977.

————. "The Signification of the Phallus." In *Ecrits*, trans. Alan Sheridan, 281–91. New York: W. W. Norton, 1977.

Lacan, Jacques, and Wladimir Granoff. "Fetishism: The Symbolic, the Imaginary and the Real." In *Perversions: Psychodynamics and Therapy*, ed. Sandor Lorand, 265–76. New York: Random House, 1956.

Lang, Amy Schrager. *Prophetic Woman: Anne Hutchinson and the Problem of Dissent in the Literature of New England*. Los Angeles: U. of California P., 1987.

Lauretis, Teresa de . *Technologies of Gender: Essays on Theory, Film, and Fiction*. Bloomington: Indiana U. P., 1987.

Leibowitz, Herbert. "Exploding Myths: An Interview with Sonia Sanchez." *Parnassus* (1985): 357–68.

Lehman, David. *The Last Avant-Garde: The Making of the New York School of Poets*. New York: Doubleday, 1998.

Leverenz, David. *The Language of Puritan Feeling: An Exploration in Literature, Psychology, and Social History*. New Brunswick, N.J.: Rutgers U. P., 1980.

Lewis, Wyndham, ed. *BLAST 1*. Santa Rosa, Calif.: Black Sparrow P., 1989.

Lindley, David. *Lyric*. New York: Methuen, 1985.

Longenbach, James. *Wallace Stevens: The Plain Sense of Things*. New York: Oxford U. P., 1991.

Lorde, Audre. *Sister Outsider: Essays and Speeches*. Freedom, Calif.: Crossing P., 1984.

Loy, Mina. *The Last Lunar Baedeker*. Highlands, N.C.: Jargon Society, 1982. Abbreviated *LLB* within the text.

————. *The Lost Lunar Baedeker*. New York: Farrar, Straus and Giroux, 1996. Abbreviated *Lost* within the text.

————. "Psycho-Democracy." *Little Review* 8.1 (1921): 14–19.

Lyotard, Jean-Francois. *The Postmodern Condition: A Report on Knowledge*. Trans. Geoff Bennington and Brian Massumi. Minneapolis: U. of Minnesota P., 1984.

Ma, Ming-Qian. "Articulating the Inarticulate: Singularities and the Counter-Method in Susan Howe." *Contemporary Literature* 36.3 (1995): 466–89.

————. "Poetry as History Revised: Susan Howe's 'Scattering as Behavior Toward Risk.'" *American Literary History* 6, no. 4 (1994): 716–37.

Mackey, Nathaniel. *Discrepant Engagement: Dissonance, Cross-Culturality, and Experimental Writing*. New York: Cambridge U. P., 1993.

Major, Clarence. "A Black Criterion." In *Black Voices: An Anthology of Afro-American Literature*, ed. Abraham Chapman, 698–99. New York: Mentor/New American Library, 1968.

————. *The Dictionary of Afro-American Slang*. New York: International Publishers, 1970.

Mann, Paul. *Theory-Death of the Avant-Garde*. Bloomington: Indiana U. P., 1991.

Marinetti, F. T. *Let's Murder the Moonshine: Selected Writings*. Trans. R. W. Flint. Los Angeles: Sun and Moon, 1991.

Matlock, John. "Masquerading Women, Pathologized Men: Cross-Dressing, Fetishism, and the Theory of Perversion, 1882–1935." In *Fetishism as Cultural Discourse*, ed. Emily Apter and William Pietz, 31–61. Ithaca, N.Y.: Cornell U. P., 1993.

McCorkle, James. "Prophecy and the Figure of the Reader in Susan Howe's *Articulation of Sound Forms in Time*." *Postmodern Culture: An Electronic Journal of Interdisciplinary Criticism* 9.3 (1999): n.p. http://jefferson.village.virginia.edu/pmc.

McGann, Jerome. "Contemporary Poetry, Alternate Routes." *Critical Inquiry* 13 (1987): 624–47. Reprinted in *Politics and Poetic Value*, ed. Robert von Hallberg, 253–76. Chicago: U. of Chicago P., 1987.

————. "Language Writing." In *London Review of Books*, 6–8, October 15, 1987.

Melham, D. H. "Sonia Sanchez: Will and Spirit." *MELUS: The Journal of the Study of the Multi-Ethnic Literature of the United States* 12.3 (1985): 73–98.

Messerli, Douglas, ed. *Language Poetries: An Anthology*. New York: New Directions, 1987.

Middleton, Peter. "On Ice: Julia Kristeva, Susan Howe and Avant Garde Poetics." In *Contemporary Poetry Meets Modern Theory*, ed. Antony Easthope and John O. Thompson, 81–95. New York: Harvester, 1991.

Mihn-ha, Trinh. *Woman, Native, Other: Writing Postcoloniality and Feminism*. Bloomington: Indiana U. P., 1989.

Miller, Perry. *Errand into the Wilderness*. Cambridge, Mass.: Harvard U. P., 1956.

Moi, Toril. *Sexual/Textual Politics: Feminist Literary Theory*. New York: Routledge, 1985.

Montefiore, Jan. *Feminism and Poetry: Language, Experience, Identity in Women's Writing*. San Francisco: HarperCollins, 1994.

Moore, Marianne. *The Complete Poems of Marianne Moore*. New York: Macmillan, 1981.

Morrison, Toni. *Playing in the Dark*. New York: Random House, 1992.

Mort, Frank. *Dangerous Sexualities: Medico-Moral Politics in England since 1830*. New York: Routledge, 1987.

Mullen, Harryette. *Muse & Drudge*. Philadelphia: Singing Horse P., 1995. Abbreviated *M&D* within the text.

————. "Optic White: Blackness and the Production of Whiteness." *Diacritics* 24.2–3 (1994): 71–89.

————. "Runaway Tongue: Resistant Orality in *Uncle Tom's Cabin, Our Nig, Incidents in the Life of a Slave Girl*, and *Beloved*." In *The Culture of Sentiment: Race, Gender, and Sentimentality in Nineteenth-Century America*, ed. Shirley Samuels, 244–64. New York: Oxford U. P., 1992.

————. *Sleeping with the Dictionary*. Los Angeles: U. of Calif. P., 2002.

———. *S*PeRM**K*T*. Philadelphia: Singing Horse P., 1992.

———. *Tree Tall Woman*. Austin, Tex.: Energy Earth, 1981.

———. *Trimmings*. New York: Tender Buttons P., 1991. Abbreviated *Tr* within the text.

Murphy, Margueritte S. "'Familiar Strangers': The Household Words of Gertrude Stein's *Tender Buttons*." *Contemporary Literature* 32 (1991): 383–402.

Murray, Albert. *The Omni-Americans: New Perspectives on Black Experience and American Culture*. New York: Outerbridge and Dienstfrey, 1970.

———. *Stomping the Blues*. New York: McGraw Hill, 1976.

Murray, Pauli. "The Liberation of Black Women." In *Voices of the New Feminism*, ed. Mary Lou Thompson, 87–102. Boston: Beacon P., 1970.

Neal, Larry. "The Black Arts Movement." In *The Black Aesthetic*, ed. Addison Gayle Jr., 272–90. New York: Doubleday, 1971.

———. "Some Reflections on the Black Aesthetic." In *The Black Aesthetic*, ed. Addison Gayle Jr., 13–16. New York: Doubleday, 1971.

Nelson, Cary. *Repression and Recovery: Modern American Poetry and the Politics of Cultural Memory, 1910–1945*. Madison: U. of Wisconsin P., 1989.

Nettels, Elsa. *Language, Race, and Social Class in Howells's America*. Lexington: U. of Kentucky P., 1988.

Nicholls, Peter. "Difference Spreading: From Gertrude Stein to L=A=N=G=U=A=G=E Poetry." In *Contemporary Poetry Meets Modern Theory*, ed. Antony Easthope and John O. Thompson, 116–27. New York: Harvester, 1991.

———. "Unsettling the Wilderness: Susan Howe and American History." *Contemporary Literature* 37.4 (1996): 586–601.

Nielsen, Aldon Lynn. *Black Chant: Languages of African-American Postmodernism*. New York: Cambridge U. P., 1997.

Ostriker, Alicia. *Stealing the Language: The Emergence of Women's Poetry in America*. Boston: Beacon P., 1986.

O'Sullivan, Maggie, ed. *Out of Everywhere: Linguistically Innovative Poetry by Women in North America and the U.K.* London: Reality Street Editions, 1996.

Owens, Craig. "The Discourse of Others: Feminists and Postmodernism." In *The Anti-Aesthetic: Essays on Postmodern Culture*, ed. Hal Foster, 57–82. Port Townsend, Wash.: Bay P., 1983.

Perelman, Bob. *The Marginalization of Poetry: Language Writing and Literary History*. Princeton, N.J.: Princeton U. P., 1996.

Perloff, Marjorie. "The Coming of Age of Language Poetry." *Contemporary Literature* 38.3 (1997): 558–68.

———. *The Dance of the Intellect: Studies in the Poetry of the Pound Tradition*. New York: Cambridge U. P., 1985.

———. *The Futurist Moment: Avant-Garde, Avant Guerre, and the Language of Rupture*. Chicago: U. of Chicago P., 1986.

———. "New Nouns for Old: 'Language' Poetry, Language Game, and the Pleasure of the Text." In *Exploring Postmodernism: Selected Papers Presented at a Workshop on Postmodernism at the XIth International Comparative Literature*

Congress, Paris, 20–24 August 1985, ed. Matei Calinescu and Douwe Fokkema, 95–108. Philadelphia: John Benjamines Publishing, 1987.

———. *Poetic License: Essays on Modernist and Postmodernist Lyric.* Evanston, Ill.: Northwestern U. P., 1990.

———. *Radical Artifice: Writing Poetry in the Age of Media.* Chicago: U. of Chicago P., 1991.

———. *Wittgenstein's Ladder: Poetic Language and the Strangeness of the Ordinary.* Chicago: U. of Chicago P., 1996.

———. "The Word as Such: L=A=N=G=U=A=G=E Poetry in the Eighties." *American Poetry Review* May/June 1984: 15–22.

Plumstead, A. W., ed. *The Wall and the Garden: Selected Massachusetts Election Sermons, 1670–1775.* Minneapolis: U. of Minnesota P., 1968.

Poggioli, Renato. *The Theory of the Avant-Garde.* Trans. Gerald Fitzgerald. Cambridge, Mass.: Harvard U. P., 1968.

Pound, Ezra. *The Cantos of Ezra Pound.* New York: New Directions, 1986.

———. *Gaudier-Brzeska.* New York: New Directions, 1970.

———. *Literary Essays of Ezra Pound.* Ed. T. S. Eliot. New York: New Directions, 1935.

———. *Selected Poems of Ezra Pound.* New York: New Directions, 1957.

———. *Selected Prose 1909–1965.* New York: New Directions, 1973.

Quartermain, Peter. *Disjunctive Poetics: From Gertrude Stein and Louis Zukofsky to Susan Howe.* New York: Cambridge U. P., 1992.

Rainey, Gertrude ("Ma"). *Ma Rainey's Black Bottom.* Yazoo Records, 1990.

Randall, Dudley, ed. *The Black Poets.* New York: Bantam, 1971.

Rankine, Claudia, and Juliana Spahr, eds. *American Women Poets in the Twenty-First Century.* Hanover, N. H.: Wesleyan U. P., 2002.

Rasula, Jed. "Gendering the Muse." *Sulfur* 35 (1994): 159–75.

Rayor, Diane J., trans. *Sappho's Lyre: Archaic Lyric and Women Poets of Ancient Greece.* Berkeley: U. of California P., 1991.

Rayor, Diane J., and William W. Batstone, eds. *Latin Lyric and Elegiac Poetry: An Anthology of New Translations.* New York: Garland Publishing, 1995.

Re, Lucia. "Futurism and Feminism." *Annali d'Italianistica* 7 (1989): 253–72.

Re/Search: Angry Women. San Francisco: Re/Search Publications, 1991.

Redmond, Eugene B. *Drumvoices: The Mission of Afro-American Poetry: A Critical History.* New York: Doubleday, 1976.

Reinfeld, Linda. *Language Poetry: Writing as Rescue.* Baton Rouge: Louisiana State U. P., 1992.

Rich, Adrienne. *Blood, Bread, and Poetry: Selected Prose 1979–1985.* New York: Norton, 1986.

———. *The Dream of a Common Language: Poems 1974–1977.* New York: Norton, 1978.

———. *On Lies, Secrets, and Silence: Selected Prose 1966–1978.* New York: Norton, 1979.

Robinson, Lou, and Camille Norton, eds. *Resurgent: New Writing by Women.* Chicago: U. of Illinois P., 1992.

Rosetta Records. *Mean Mothers: Independent Women's Blues.* Vol. 1, 1990.

Rowlandson, Mary. "A True History of the Captivity and Restoration of Mrs. Mary Rowlandson (1682)." In *Women's Indian Captivity Narratives*, ed. Kathryn Zabelle Derounian-Stodola, 1–51. New York: Penguin, 1998.

Ruddick, Lisa. *Reading Gertrude Stein: Body, Text, Gnosis.* Ithaca, N.Y.: Cornell U. P., 1990.

———. "A Rosy Charm: Gertrude Stein and the Repressed Feminine." In *Critical Essays on Gertrude Stein*, ed. Michael J. Hoffman, 225–40. Boston: G. K. Hall, 1986.

Russell, Charles. *Poets, Prophets, and Revolutionaries: The Literary Avant-Garde from Rimbaud through Postmodernism.* New York: Oxford U. P., 1985.

Saldívar-Hull, Sonia. "Wrestling Your Ally: Stein, Racism, and Feminist Critical Practice." In *Women's Writing in Exile*, ed. Mary Lynn Broe and Angela Ingram, 181–98. Chapel Hill: U. of North Carolina P., 1989.

Sanchez, Sonia. *A Blues Book for Blue-Black Magical Women.* Detroit: Broadside P., 1974.

———. *Does Your House Have Lions?* Boston: Beacon P., 1997.

———. *Home Coming.* Detroit: Broadside P., 1969. Abbreviated *Home* within the text.

———. *Homegirls and Handgrenades.* New York: Thunder's Mouth P., 1984.

———. *I've Been a Woman: New and Selected Poems.* Chicago: Third World P., 1985.

———. *Like the Singing Coming off the Drums: Love Poems.* Boston: Beacon P., 1998.

———. *Love Poems.* New York: Third P., 1973. Abbreviated *Love* within the text.

———. "Ruminations/Reflections." In *Black Women Writers (1950–1980): A Critical Evaluation*, ed. Mari Evans, 415–50. New York: Anchor P./Doubleday, 1984.

———. *We a BaddDDD People.* Detroit: Broadside P., 1970. Abbreviated *Bad* within the text.

———. *Wounded in the House of a Friend.* Boston: Beacon P., 1995. Abbreviated *Wounded* within the text.

Sappho. *A New Translation.* Trans. Mary Barnard. Los Angeles: U. of California.P., 1966.

———. *Poems and Fragments.* Trans. Guy Davenport. Ann Arbor: U. of Michigan P., 1965.

Schaum, Melita. "'Moon-Flowers Out of Muck': Mina Loy and the Female Autobiographical Epic." *Massachusetts Studies in English* 10.4 (1986): 254–76.

Schmitz, Neil. "Gertrude Stein as Post-Modernist: The Rhetoric of *Tender Buttons.*" In *Critical Essays on Gertrude Stein*, ed. Michael J. Hoffman, 117–30. Boston: G. K. Hall, 1986.

Schneir, Miriam, ed. *Feminism: The Essential Historical Writings.* New York: Random House, 1992.

Schor, Naomi. "Female Fetishism: The Case of George Sand." In *The Female Body in Western Culture: Contemporary Perspectives*, ed. Susan Rubin Suleiman, 363–72. Cambridge, Mass.: Harvard U. P., 1985.

———. "Fetishism and Its Ironies." In *Fetishism as Cultural Discourse*, ed. Emily Apter and William Pietz, 92–100. Ithaca, N.Y.: Cornell U. P., 1991.

Schultz, Susan. "Exaggerated History." *Postmodern Culture* 4.2 (1994): n.p. http://jefferson.village.virginia.edu/pmc/.

Scobie, Stephen. "The Allure of Multiplicity: Metaphor and Metonymy in Cubism and Gertrude Stein." In *Gertrude Stein and the Making of Literature*, ed. Shirley Neuman and Ira B. Nadel, 98–118. Boston: Northeastern U. P., 1988.

Scott, Joan Wallach. "Experience." In *Feminists Theorize the Political*, ed. Judith Butler and Joan W. Scott, 22–40. New York: Routledge, 1992.

———. *Gender and the Politics of History*. New York: Columbia U. P., 1988.

Segal, Naomi. "Sexual Politics and the Avant-Garde: From Apollinaire to Woolf." In *Visions and Blueprints: Avant-Garde Culture and Radical Politics in Early Twentieth-Century Europe*, ed. Edward Timms and Peter Collier, 235–49. New York: Manchester U. P., 1988.

Shepard, Thomas. *God's Plot: The Paradoxes of Puritan Piety Being the Autobiography and Journal of Thomas Shepard*. Ed. Michael McGiffert. Amherst: U. of Massachusetts P., 1972.

Showalter, Elaine. "Feminist Criticism in the Wilderness." In *The New Feminist Criticism: Essays on Women, Literature, and Theory*, ed. Elaine Showalter, 243–70. New York: Pantheon Books, 1985.

———. "Toward a Feminist Poetics." In *The New Feminist Criticism: Essays on Women, Literature, and Theory*, ed. Elaine Showalter, 125–43. New York: Pantheon Books, 1985.

Silliman, Ron, ed. *In the American Tree*. Orono, Maine: National Poetry Foundation, 1986.

Silverman, Kaja. *The Acoustic Mirror: The Female Voice in Psychoanalysis and Cinema*. Bloomington: Indiana U. P., 1988.

Simon, Linda. *Gertrude Stein Remembered*. Lincoln: U. of Nebraska P., 1994.

Simpson, Megan. *Poetic Epistemologies: Gender and Knowing in Women's Language-Oriented Writing*. Albany, N.Y.: SUNY P., 2000.

Sloan, Mary Margaret, ed. *Moving Borders: Three Decades of Innovative Writing by Women*. Jersey City, N.J.: Talisman, 1998.

Smith, Barbara. "Toward a Black Feminist Criticism." In *All the Women Are White, All the Blacks Are Men, But Some of Us Are Brave*, ed. Gloria Hull, Patricia Bell Scott, and Barbara Smith, 157–75. New York: Feminist P., 1982.

Smith, David Lionel. "The Black Arts Movement and Its Critics." *American Literary History* 3.1 (spring 1991): 93–111.

Smitherman, Geneva. "The Power of the Rap: The Black Idiom and the New Black Poetry." *Twentieth Century Literature* 19.4 (1973): 259–71.

Spahr, Juliana. *Everybody's Autonomy: Connective Reading and Collective Identity*. Tuscaloosa: U. of Alabama P., 2000.

Spender, Dale. *Man-Made Language*. New York: Routledge, 1985.

Spivak, Gayatri Chakravorty. *In Other Worlds: Essays in Cultural Politics*. New York: Routledge, 1988.

————. "Who Claims Alterity?" In *Remaking History*, ed. Barbara Kruger and Phil Mariani. Seattle: Bay P., 1988.

Stanton, Domna C. "Difference on Trial: A Critique of the Maternal Metaphor in Cixous, Irigaray, and Kristeva." In *The Poetics of Gender*, ed. Nancy K. Miller, 157–82. New York: Columbia U. P., 1986.

Stein, Gertrude. *The Autobiography of Alice B. Toklas*. In *Selected Writings of Gertrude Stein*, ed. Carl Van Vechten, 1–237. New York: Random House, 1962.

————. "Composition as Explanation." In *Selected Writings of Gertrude Stein*, ed. Carl Van Vechten, 511–23. New York: Random House, 1962.

————. *Lectures in America*. New York: Random House, 1985. Abbreviated *LIA* within the text.

————. *Selected Writings of Gertrude Stein*. Ed. Carl Van Vechten. New York: Random House, 1962.

————. *Gertrude Stein Reader*. Ed. Ulla E. Dydo. Evanston, Ill.: Northwestern U. P., 1993. Abbreviated *GSR* in text.

————. *Tender Buttons*. In *Selected Writings of Gertrude Stein*, ed. Carl Van Vechten, 459–509. New York: Random House, 1962. Abbreviated *TB* within the text.

Steiner, Wendy. "The Steinian Portrait." In *Critical Essays on Gertrude Stein*, ed. Michael J. Hoffman, 130–39. Boston: G. K. Hall, 1986.

Stendhal, Renate, ed. *Gertrude Stein in Words and Pictures*. Chapel Hill, N.C.: Algonquin Books, 1994.

Stimpson, Catharine R. "Gertrice/Altrude: Stein, Toklas, and the Paradox of the Happy Marriage." In *Mothering the Mind: Twelve Studies of Writers and Their Silent Partners*, ed. Ruth Perry and Martine Watson Brownley, 122–39. New York: Holmes and Meier, 1984.

————. "Gertrude Stein and the Transposition of Gender." In *The Poetics of Gender*, ed. Nancy K. Miller, 1–18. New York: Columbia U. P., 1986.

————. "The Somagrams of Gertrude Stein." In *Critical Essays on Gertrude Stein*, ed. Michael J. Hoffman, 183–96. Boston: G. K. Hall, 1986.

Suleiman, Susan Rubin. *Subversive Intent: Gender, Politics, and the Avant-Garde*. Cambridge, Mass.: Harvard U. P., 1990.

Tate, Claudia, ed. *Black Women Writers at Work*. New York: Continuum, 1990.

Thomas, Lorenzo. "'Classical Jazz' and the Black Arts Movement." *African-American Review* 29.2 (summer 1995): 237–40.

————. *Extraordinary Measures: Afrocentric Modernism and Twentieth-Century American Poetry*. Tuscaloosa: U. of Alabama P., 2000.

————. "Neon Griot: The Functional Role of Poetry Readings in the Black Arts Movement." In *Close Listening: Poetry and the Performed Word*, ed. Charles Bernstein, 300–323. New York: Oxford U. P., 1998. Reprinted in Thomas, *Extraordinary Measures: Afrocentric Modernism and Twentieth-Century American Poetry*, 189–218. Tuscaloosa: U. of Alabama P., 2000.

Tillyard, E. M. W. *The English Epic and Its Background*. London: Chatto and Windus, 1954.

Tolson, Melvin B. *The Harlem Gallery, Book I: The Curator*. New York: Twayne, 1965.

Torgovnick, Marianna. *Gone Primitive: Savage Intellects, Modern Lives*. Chicago: U. of Chicago P., 1990.

Tuma, Keith. "Anglo-Mongrels and the Rose." *Sagetrieb* 11.1–2 (1992): 207–25.

Van Deburg, William L. *New Day in Babylon: The Black Power Movement and American Culture, 1965–1975*. Chicago: U. of Chicago P., 1992.

Vickers, Nancy J. "Diana Described: Scattered Woman and Scattered Rhyme." In *Writing and Sexual Difference*, ed. Elizabeth Abel, 95–109. Chicago: U. of Chicago P., 1982.

Vickery, Ann. *Leaving Lines of Gender: A Feminist Genealogy of Language Writing*. Hanover, N.H.: Wesleyan U. P., 2000.

von Hallberg, Robert. "Avant-Gardes." In *The Cambridge History of American Literature*, ed. Sacvan Bercovitch. Vol. 8, 83–122. New York: Cambridge U. P., 1996.

Walker, Alice. *In Search of Our Mothers' Gardens: Womanist Prose*. New York: Harcourt Brace Jovanovich, 1983.

Walker, Jayne L. *The Making of a Modernist: Gertrude Stein from Three Lives to Tender Buttons*. Amherst: U. of Mass. P., 1984.

Wallace, Michele. *Black Macho and the Myth of the Superwoman*. New York: Verso, 1990.

———. *Invisibility Blues: From Pop to Theory*. New York: Verso, 1990.

Weed, Elizabeth, ed. *Coming to Terms: Feminism, Theory, Politics*. New York: Routledge, 1989.

West, Cornel. *Race Matters*. Boston: Beacon P., 1993.

Whitehead, Kim. *The Feminist Poetry Movement*. Jackson: U. P. of Mississippi, 1996.

Williams, Megan. "Howe Not to Erase(her): A Poetics of Posterity in Susan Howe's *Melville's Marginalia*." *Contemporary Literature* 38.1 (1997): 106–32.

Winters, Yvor. "Mina Loy." *Dial* 80 (1926): 496–99.

Wittig, Monique. *The Lesbian Body*. Trans. David Le Vay. Boston: Beacon P., 1975.

———. *The Straight Mind and Other Essays*. Boston: Beacon P., 1992.

Woodhull, Victoria, and Tennessee Claflin. "Virtue: What It Is, and What It Is Not"; "Which Is to Blame"; and "The Elixir of Life." In *Feminism: The Essential Historical Writings*, ed. Miriam Schneir, 145–54. New York: Random House, 1992.

Woolf, Virginia. "Professions for Women." In *Collected Essays*, vol. 2. New York: Harcourt, Brace, Jovanovich, 1953.

———. *A Room of One's Own*. New York: Harcourt, Brace, Jovanovich, 1929.

Yaeger, Patricia. *Honey-Mad Women: Emancipatory Strategies in Women's Writing*. New York: Columbia U. P., 1988.

PERMISSIONS

Fragment #8 from *Sappho: A New Translation*, translated by Mary Barnard © 1958 by the Regents of the University of California; © renewed 1986 Mary Barnard. Reprinted by permission of the University of California Press.

Excerpts from *Sappho's Lyre: Archaic Lyric and Women Poets of Ancient Greece*, translated by Diane J. Rayor © 1991 by Diane Rayor. Reprinted by permission of the University of California Press.

Excerpt from Sappho, *Poems and Fragments*, translated by Guy Davenport ©1965 by the University of Michigan. Reprinted by permission of the University of Michigan Press.

Excerpts from works by Sonia Sanchez reprinted by permission of the author: *We a BaddDDD People* (Broadside Press ©1970 by Sonia Sanchez Knight); *Love Poems* (The Third Press ©1973 by Sonia Sanchez); *Home Coming* (Broadside Press ©1969 by Sonia Sanchez).

I am grateful to Kathleen Fraser and Harryette Mullen for permission to quote from unpublished interviews and correspondence.

INDEX

aesthetics: and accessibility, 202n2; aestheticism, 30, 57; Anglo-European tradition, 70, 80; feminist forms of, 46; "mongrel" aesthetics, 185n31. *See also* Black Aesthetics; Black Arts movement

Afrocentrism, in Sanchez, 192n38, 193n43, 193n50, 194n55, 194n56

allegory, 31, 51, 61, 120–21

alliteration, 44–45, 185n35

Alta, 118

alterity, 132–33, 153, 200n46

American culture: feminist poetics, xvii–xxi, xxviii, 105–108, 170n7; gender divisions, xiv, xvii–xviii, xx–xxii, xxiv, xxvi, xxviii; hybridity of, 155, 160–63; language and heritage, 141; mongrel nature of, xiii, 155, 164

"Amos 'n Andy," 157–58

anatomical puns (Mullen), 157–58, 160–61

Andrews, Bruce, 106

androgyny, 60–62, 186n45, 188n59, 188n60, 204n24

Anglocentrism, 82, 94–95, 97, 192n40, 192n41

"Anglo-Mongrels and the Rose" (Loy), 29–62; as allegory, 31, 51, 61; alliteration, 44–45, 185n35; as autobiography, 31, 32, 37; biblical parallels in, 38–39; class hierarchy, 39–42, 49, 57; and epic form, 33, 37–38, 60; and Futurism, xxvi; gender typing, 38, 44–47, 58–62, 100; irony in, 54–56; language acquisition, 52–55; national symbolism, 36–38, 43–47;

organization, 182n17, 186n47; origins of, 36–40, 50–57, 60–61; race concepts in, 33, 42–43, 50, 153. *See also* eugenics; Loy, Mina

antinomianism, 130, 133, 199n37; in American culture, 107–108; and feminist avant-garde writing, xxvii, 114–17, 122, 127, 135, 179n6; and gender typing, 115–17, 127

anti-Semitism, 185n31, 186n39, 186n43

apocalyptic narrative, 125

Apollinaire, Guillaume, 6, 65, 83, 201n57

Apter, Emily, 180n45

Armstrong, Louis, 149

Arnold, Elizabeth, 30, 180n2

Artaud, Antonin, xix

Articulation of Sound Forms in Time (Howe), 108–35; as allegory, 119–20; gender coding in, 119, 122–23, 127–35; Language writing in, 195–96n4; sections cited: "Alfather's Path," 134–35; "The Falls Fight," 119, 125; "Hope Atherton's Wanderings," 120–22, 124–27, 198n32, 198n33; "Taking the Forest," 127–35. *See also* Howe, Susan; *Singularities*

assimilation, 154, 163

avant-garde: and aestheticism, 30, 57; alienation, 169–70n6; attitudes toward human body, 28, 175n10; defined, xiv–xvii, xxi, 166, 169n6, 170n8, 171n11; emphasis on verbs, xxv, 4; gender typing, 43–47, 176n17; "historical" avant-gardes, xii, xiv; interest in technology, 3, 4,

Cortez, Jayne, 66, 69
Cotton, John, 129
Crane, Hart, 107, 128
Cravan, Arthur, 57
Cubism, 3, 15, 173n1, 175n12
Cullen, Countee, 71, 187n12
cultural inheritance: Black Cultural Heritage, 71–72; and determinism, 31, 37–40, 71, 72; gendering of genius, 50–62, 186n41, 186n42, 186n45, 188n60, 204n24; hybridity of, 149, 155, 157, 160–63, 204n22, 204n23; and language, 31, 39, 54, 55, 74–75, 148; mongrel nature of, 32–33, 37–40, 164; racial attitudes, 79–82, 148–49, 153–54, 161; standards of beauty, 147–49, 160–61, 163. *See also* gender norms as cultural heritage; race; woman, notion(s) of
cummings, e. e., 78–80
Curb, Rosemary K., 193n49

Dadaism, 3–4, 7, 11, 175n12, 178n33, 182n10
Dahlen, Beverly, 111
Darwinism/social Darwinism, 32, 40, 56, 182n20
Davenport, Charles, 184n30, 186n43
Davidson, Michael, 196n4, 202–203n7
De Lancey, Frenzella Elaine, 194n55, 194n56
DeKoven, Marianne, xvii, xviii, xix, 171n13, 175n10, 176n17, 176n19
determinism, 31, 37–40, 71, 72, 180n3, 187n51
Dickinson, Emily: antinomianism, xxvii, 122–23; in avant-garde tradition, xiii, xx, xxvii, 107–109, 111–14, 118, 196n11; editing of, 107, 112–13, 198n30; interpretations of, 199n38; *My Emily Dickinson* (Howe), 112, 113, 118, 122–23, 131–32, 135; and patriarchal control, 112–13, 118, 122
domestic motifs: in Cubism, 175n12; in

Mullen, 137, 144–47, 149–51, 154; in Stein, 3–4, 9–10, 15–16, 22, 28, 177–78n28, 179n38
Donne, John, 93
dualism, 38, 107
DuBois, Ellen Carol, 5, 174n6, 203n13
DuBois, W. E. B., 99, 150
Duchamp, Marcel, 7, 175n12, 178n33, 181–82n10
Dudley, Thomas, 117
Duncan, Robert, 107, 112, 128
DuPlessis, Rachel Blau: on avant-garde tradition, xix, 109, 118; on Howe, 120, 199n38; on language acquisition, 52–54; on Loy, 185n31; on lyric poetry, 154, 204n24; on Romantic poetry, 43
Dyer, Mary, 116–17

écriture féminine, xvii, xix
Edwards, Jonathan, 134
Egoist, The, 169n5
Eliot, T. S., xx, 169n5
Ellis, Havelock, 174n5, 183n25, 184n28
Ellison, Ralph, 73, 99, 149, 189–90n19, 195n61, 204n21
epic genre, 33, 36–38, 60, 158, 181n6, 182n13, 182n14, 182n15
Erkkila, Betsy, 171–72n14
eroticism: coding in *Tender Buttons* (Stein), 17, 19, 21–28; coding in *Trimmings* (Mullen), 145–46, 154; language as objects of, 26–27, 141; in Puritan poetry, 201n53
essentialism, xxii–xxiii, 5, 87, 99, 117–18, 173n19, 173n20, 179n41. *See also* woman, notion(s) of
eugenics: Darwinism, 56, 182n20; and identity, xxvi, 33; ideology of, 39–43, 50, 183n27, 185n33, 185n38; in Progressive Era, 183n25, 184n28; racism, 183n23
Evans, Mari, 66, 192n40

evolution, 40, 41, 60–62
experimental writing, xv, xxii, 165–67, 169n3, 172n17, 173n19

Fabian Socialism, 41, 184n28
Faderman, Lillian, 174n5, 178n29
Fanon, Frantz, 80–81, 93–94, 142
female avant-garde tradition: in American literary history, xiv, 105–108, 118, 130, 170n7, 173–74n2; and black culture, 164, 166–67; DuPlessis on, xix, 109, 118; Fraser on, xiii, xvii–xviii, 108–12, 113, 136, 154, 169n3; marginality of, xii–xiii, xviii–xxi, xxvii–xxviii, 108–12, 120–21, 165, 169n2, 169n3, 171n13; radicalism, 199n37; recognition of, 107, 117, 195–96n4, 196n11, 196n12, 196n14, 206n34. *See also individual poets*
female experience, xix, 157, 196n5
feminism: Anglocentrism of, 82, 94–95, 97, 192n40, 192n41; assumptions of, xiii, 118, 152–53, 186n46; linguistic-based, xi–xiii, 165; Loy's views on, 36; origin, 175n7; radical feminism, 41, 58, 82, 117–18, 166, 173n19, 187n51, 199n37. *See also* black feminism; politics; Suffrage movement; "woman movement"
feminist poetics: assumptions of, xix, xx, 107–108, 166; avant-garde aesthetics, 46, 57, 60; bilingualism, 53–54, 161; birth of, xiv; confessional mode, 110–11, 172n14; cult of personality, 113; epic genre, 33, 37–38, 60, 182n14; experimental writing, xv, xxii, 165–67, 169n3, 172n17, 173n19; Howe on, 111–12; hybrid ("mongrel") nature of, xiii, 50–57, 60–61, 108–109, 135–38; individualism of, xv; language-oriented, xiv, xviii, 106, 138–41, 166, 169n3, 172n18, 195n2, 195n4, 198n29; online innovations, 166; and politics,

xvii–xviii, 5–6, 36, 56, 58, 71–73, 99, 117–18, 135, 166, 195–96n4; theoretical models, xiv, xix–xx, xxiii–xxvi. *See also* antinomianism; female avant-garde tradition; masculine writing
fetishism: Barthes's view of, 176–77n20; Freudian model of, 14, 18–20, 23–24, 25, 178n30, 178n31, 180n43; Kaplan on, 179n39, 179n40; lesbian fetishism, 4, 19–24, 178n31, 180n43, 180n45; in *Tender Buttons* (Stein), xxv–xxvi, 13–18, 21, 23–24; of words, 6, 13–17, 21, 26–27, 140–41
Fifer, Elizabeth, 20, 27
Finley, Karen, 139
Fitzgerald, Ella, 101, 158
fragmentation, of language, 140–41, 199n37, 200n42, 200n48
Frankfurt School, 195n2
Fraser, Kathleen: on avant-garde tradition, 154; on gendered cultural expression, 107, 135, 196n14; *HOW2*, 166; *HOW(ever)*, xi, 105, 108, 118, 165, 167; on place of feminist poetics, xiii, xvii–xviii, 108–13, 136, 154, 169n3; on radical feminism, 117; on revolutionary language, xix; "tradition of marginality," xiii
free love, 5, 10, 181n10
free verse, 91
Freewoman Discussion Circle, 169n5
French feminist theory, xix, 169n2. *See also écriture féminine*
Freud, Sigmund: castration anxiety, xxvi, 19, 22, 23, 178n30, 179n41; fetishism, 13, 14, 18–20, 23–25, 178n30, 178n31; on humor, 25; on impulses, 184n29; on women, 174n5, 174n6
Freudian theory: in Loy, 184n29; and masculine writing, 27–28; in Stein, 18–20, 25, 27–28

ideology, literature as tool of, 37–38, 47–50, 95, 152, 189n19, 190n22, 190n24
Imagism, xv, 11, 169n5
Iman, Yusef, 194n59
Irigaray, Luce, xxiii, 20, 139–40, 171n14, 173n22, 181n5
irony, 32, 54–56

Jackson, Laura Riding, 37
Jaffer, Frances, xi, xii, 111
James, William, 4, 8, 18, 40, 183n22
jazz, 74, 143–44, 163
Jennings, Regina, 192n38, 193n50
Jewishness, 186n39, 186n43, 187n59. *See also* anti-Semitism
Johnson, Helene, 187n12
Johnson, James Weldon, 204n21
Johnson, Thomas, 112
Jones, LeRoi. *See* Baraka, Amiri
Jones, Melissa, 205–206n32
Jordan, David Starr, 183n20
Jordan, June, 69, 153
Joyce, James, xix, 38, 60
Jungian theory, 40, 46, 186n45

Kalaidjian, Walter, 172n18
Kaplan, Louise J., 179n39, 179n40
Karenga, Ron, 72, 73, 75, 83, 91, 92, 163
Keayne, Sarah Dudley, 117
Keith, Arthur, 182n20
Keller, Lynn, 106, 107, 128, 195n1
Kenner, Hugh, 113
Kevles, Daniel, 41, 183n20, 183n25, 184n27, 184n28, 186n43
King, Martin Luther, Jr., 76
King Philip's War, 119, 198n32
Kinnahan, Linda, 105, 113
kinship, 155, 163
Knight, Etheridge, 159
Koffman, Sarah, 28
Koudis, Virginia, 181n8
Krauss, Rosalind, 170n8
Kristeva, Julia: language styles, xix, 140, 199n37, 200n46; patriarchal

authority, 172n17; semiotics, 14, 175n10, 176n17, 177n26
Kruger, Barbara, xvi–xvii, 139, 202n5

labeling, 14
Lacan, Jacques, 177n26
Lang, Amy Schrager, 115–16, 201–202n59
language: acquisition of, 52–55; as clothing (Mullen), 154; consciousness, 30, 34, 52–53; as cultural inheritance, 31, 39, 54–55, 74–75, 137–38; expressions of beauty, 160–61, 163; gender constructions, xxiv, xxv, 47, 105, 107–108, 114, 118–27, 138–35; hybridity in, 155, 158, 160–61, 166–67, 204n23; and identity, xxvi, 31, 39, 110, 153–54, 160–61; linguistic determinism, 180n3, 187n51; male domination of, 58; materiality of, 11, 177n26; as musical composition, 66, 74; object status of, 10–11, 140; "of the Future" (Loy), 49; privacy of, 139, 141; and race/racism, xxiv–xxv, 75, 152–54; rhetoric of revolution, 83–92, 193n45; social implications of, xiii, 30, 39–40, 139, 141–42; transformation of, 58–62; use of mathematical symbols, 6, 11. *See also* signification; word(s)
Language writing: Howe associated with, 106, 195–96n4; and *HOW(ever)*, 172n18; *The L=A=N=G=U=A=G=E Book*, 138–41; the Language group, xviii, 106; language-oriented writing, xiv, 166, 169n3, 195n4, 198n29; and Marxism, 195n2, 198n29
Lauretis, Teresa de, xxiii
Lawrence, D. H., 112
Lee, Don L. *See* Madhubuti, Haki
lesbianism: black feminism, 82, 194n57; feminist writing, 174n5, 178n29, 196n14; fetishism, 4, 19–24, 178n31, 180n43, 180n45; and sexual-

marginality of female avant-garde poets, xii–xiii, xvi–xvii, xxvii–xxviii, 108–12, 120–21, 165, 171n13, 172n14

Marinetti, F. T.: on avant-garde writing, 170n8; hypersymbolism, 11; and Loy, 29–36; on marriage, 10; mathematical symbols, 6, 11; militarism of, xii, 8–10, 74; on nouns, 13; poetic style and themes, xxv, 3, 4, 6–8, 11, 201n57; and Pound, 178n14; on Romantic love, 29–30; as Steinian target, 8–10, 12–13, 28, 176n15, 176n16; on women, 35; works cited: "Against *Amore* and Parliamentarianism," 10, 12–13; "Founding and Manifesto of Futurism," xv, 176n16; *Mafarka*, 35; "Technical Manifesto of Futurist Literature," 11. *See also* Futurism

marriage: and eugenics, 184n30; Loy's views on, 47–50, 56; Marinetti's views on, 10, 29; states of, 8–10, 41, 187n54

"Marry Nettie" (Stein), 8–10

Marsden, Dora, 5, 169n5

Marxism, 106, 172–73n18, 195n2, 198n29

masculine writing: avant-gardism, xi, xii, xix, xxi–xxiii, 30, 105–106, 109, 169n5, 181n5, 206n34; Black Arts movement, xxvii, 66, 68, 75–77, 82–84, 101, 206n34; and Freudian theory, 27–28; gender division, 44–47; gendering of genius, 50–62, 186n41, 186n42, 186n45, 188n60; Loy critique of, 35–36; militarism of, 8–10, 31, 36, 40, 60, 66, 68, 91–92; and Symbolic language structure, xx, xxv; traditional poetic genres, 34, 36–38, 182n13; views on women, 47, 58–59; and Vorticism, 6–7. *See also* avant-garde; feminist poetics; fetishism

masquerade, 20, 179n34, 180n45, 181n5

mass media, 147–48, 162–63, 202n5

Massachusetts Bay Colony, 115, 133

materialism, 33, 84–85, 87

materiality: as avant-garde theme, 4, 11; and creativity, 204n24; of language, 11, 177n26

mathematical symbols, 6, 11

Mather, Cotton, 115

Mather, Increase, 198n32

Matlock, John, 178n31

Medusa, 25

Melham, D. H., 192n37

Melville, Herman, 114, 119

militarism, 8–10, 31, 36, 40, 60, 66, 68, 91–92

Miller, Perry, 119, 125, 198n31, 198n32

mimicry, 181n5

miscegenation, 37, 155, 185n33

misogyny, 171n11

modernism, 44, 47, 169–70n6, 195n1. *See also* avant-garde

Moi, Toril, xxv, 169n2

mongrel(s): cultural hybridity, xiii, 32–33, 37–40, 155, 164; cyborg, 162; female poets as, 50–57, 60–61; "mongrel" aesthetics, 185n31; mongrel nature of race, 185n33

"monsters," birth of, 116–17

Montefiore, Jan, 171n14

Moore, Marianne, 109, 111, 112, 165, 196n12

Morgan, Robin, 118

Morris, Tracie, 167

Morrison, Toni, 100–101, 188n3

Mort, Frank, 174n6, 175n7, 175n9

"movement" poetry, 111, 118, 196n11

Muhammad, Elijah, 76, 100, 191–92n32

Mullen, Harryette, 136–64; allusion in, 137; and black feminism, 141–42, 147–48; "black tradition" in, 142–44; black vernacular, 137, 148, 160; on black writers, 159, 202n2, 202n3; "collective reading," 138; domestic motifs in, 137, 144–51, 154; on gen-

181n4; and Marinetti, 8–10, 12–13, 176n15,16; and Mullen, 78, 136–41, 144–54, 162; new focus on, xii, 166, 202–203n7; and patriarchal authority, xx; poetic content, xxv–xxvi; privacy of language, 139, 141; punning in, 17, 19, 21, 22, 26, 179n37, 179n38; racism in, 203n15; radical non-meaning, 140–41; signification in, 10–13, 15–18, 177n25, 177n26; and Victorian values, 20–21, 22; views on poetry, 3; works cited: "As a Wife Has a Cow: A Love Story," 16; *Lectures in America*, 4, 12, 14, 16, 22, 23, 26; "Lifting Belly," 13–14; *The Making of Americans*, 18; "Marry Nettie," 8–10; "Poetry and Grammar," 3, 4, 11–13, 14; "A Substance in a Cushion," 15–16; "Susie Asado," 16; *Three Lives*, 151. *See also Tender Buttons* (Stein)

Stein, Leo, 18

stereotypes, 148–49, 153–54, 163, 187–88n59

Stevens, Wallace, 107, 128

Stimpson, Catharine R., 5

Stoller, Robert, 179n39

stuttering, 119

Suffrage movement, 5, 30, 36, 175n7, 182n12

Suleiman, Susan, xviii, 171n11, 178n32, 178n33

Surrealism, xv, 61, 71, 170n6, 171n11, 178n33, 184n29, 188n59

Swann, Joan, 187n51

Sweet Honey in the Rock, 101

Swift, Jonathan, 107

symbolic, as masculine language structure, xx, xxv, 118, 122, 198n30

symbolism: hypersymbolism, 11; and nationalism, 36–38, 43–50; phallic symbolism, 14–15, 19, 25, 177n26, 179n34, 180n43, 180n45; in Pound, 11, 44–47; the rose as, 36–38, 43–50, 93; of stuttering, 119; symbolic

language structure, xx, xxv. *See also* signification

syntax: and feminine writing, 173n22; language fragmentation, 140–41, 199n37, 200n42, 200n48; sensuality of, 132

tanka, 101

Tate, Claudia, 66

technology, 3–4, 6–8, 31, 176n14, 176n16

Tender Buttons (Stein): domestic motifs in, 3, 15–16, 22, 28, 139, 179n38; erotic encoding, 17, 19, 21–23, 24–27, 28; and gender typing, 20–22, 175n12; interpretations of, 138–41, 202–203n7; language systems, 16, 122; lesbian themes in, 4, 17, 19, 22–24; and male dominated avant-gardes, xxv–xxvi; and Mullen poetry, 139–41, 144–54, 204n20; organization of, 14–15, 162, 177n21, 177n24, 177n25; puns in, 17, 19, 21–22, 26, 179n37, 179n38; role of nouns, 12, 26, 27; romantic love, 13–14, 20; sections cited: "Food," 9, 20–21, 204n20; "A Little Called Pauline," 26–27; "Objects," 15, 24–26, 177n22, 204n20; "A Petticoat," 24–25, 27, 152; "Rooms," 23; "Shawl," 27; "Shoes," 25–26; "This Is This Dress, Aider," 21–23, 149–50, 179n36; "A Waist," 16–17. *See also* Stein, Gertrude

Thom, Rene, 127

Thomas, Clarence, 100–101

Thomas, Lorenzo, 72, 73, 141, 159, 160

Tillyard, E. M. W., 37, 60, 187n57

"To CHucK" (Sanchez), 78–80

Toklas, Alice B., 5, 8, 13, 17, 22, 26, 150, 175n9

Tolson, Melvin B., 141, 161, 162, 173n23

Toomer, Jean, 141, 187n12

Torgovnick, Marianna, 152, 203–204n17

Woodhull, Victoria, 5
Woolf, Virginia, 61, 109, 113, 172n17
word(s): fetishizing of, 6, 13–17, 21,
    25–27, 140–41, 176n19, 176n20;
    physical qualities of, 55; subversive
    nature of, 18, 60. *See also* language
World War I, 8–10, 36–37

Wright, Richard, 92, 190n21

xenophobia, 41

Yaeger, Patricia, 178n32